365
Bible Stories
and Verses

Retold by Muriel Grainger

Hamlyn
London New York Sydney Toronto

Illustrations by
David Bryant, Richard Hook, Reg Gray,
Tony and Roger Hutchings, Porter G.,
Ron Hanna, Alan Jessett,
Liz and Gerry Embleton, Chris Skilton,
Michael Whittlesea, Kenneth Petts,
Bernard Brett, Sara Silcock and
Neville Mardell

First published 1971
Sixth impression 1978
Published by The Hamlyn Publishing Group Limited
London · New York · Sydney · Toronto
Astronaut House, Feltham, Middlesex, England
© Copyright The Hamlyn Publishing Group Limited 1971
ISBN 0 601 08760 7
Printed in Czechoslovakia by Severografia, Liberec
51084/6

The
Old
Testament

In the Beginning

Long, long ago people looked up at the moon and the stars at night-time, just as you do, and they asked, 'Who made them and set them in the sky?' And they looked at the green hills and the birds and the flowers and they asked, 'How did this, our beautiful world, begin? Who created it?'

Many years later it was revealed to them, and the best writers among them wrote down the story of God's creation of the universe for all to read.

In the beginning, God made the heaven and the earth. It had not really got a shape, and it was quite empty – there were no birds and animals on it, and no people. All round the earth was darkness. But then God said: 'Let there be light!' And God saw the light, that it was good; and he divided the light from the darkness. And God called the light DAY, and the darkness he called NIGHT.

Next, God made the starry sky that looked so like a dome arched over the earth, and this he called THE HEAVEN. And God saw that it was good.

Then he let dry land appear and God called the dry land EARTH and the water he called SEAS. And God saw that it was good.

Then he said, 'Let the earth be covered with grass and green plants and beautiful fruit trees.' And it was so. The grass scattered seed, and the trees grew fruit, and there were green plants and grass and fruit trees for evermore. And God saw that it was good.

Next God said, 'Let there be lights in the heaven, to divide the day from the night. And let them mark the seasons, and the days and the years. Let them give light on the earth.' And it was so. God made two great lights: the greater light, the SUN, to rule by day; and the lesser light, the MOON, to rule the night; and he also made the stars.

And God saw that it was good.

shone down on it, the trees and the flowers spread over it, the animals brought up their babies; but there was no one to enjoy all these lovely things – no one to pick the fruit and flowers, or to look after the animals. Then God said the most wonderful thing of all:

'I will make MAN, who will be like me, and he shall have charge of all the birds and animals, and he shall care for the fruit and vegetables, which will provide food.'

So God made man, and breathed the breath of life into him, and he became a living soul.

And God saw everything that he had made, and behold, it was very good. Then God rested.

Psalm 107
A Psalm about the Sea

The men who go to work in ships
And on the waters be,
Know well the great deeds of the Lord,
His wonders in the sea.

They see the stormy winds that blow,
The waves that rear up high;
How ships sink down into the depths,
Or seem to touch the sky.

Then sailors cry unto the Lord,
To save them all from ill;
To make the sea grow calm again
And bid the storm be still.

Then they are glad, because they come
In safety to the port.
O that men would praise the Lord,
And thank him as they ought!

Birds and Beasts – and Man

Now, God had made the earth and the sky, the seas, and the sun, moon and stars. He made the trees, the grass and the flowers – but it was a very lonely world, for there were no living creatures in it. So next, God created great whales, and animals that could climb out of the water and move and breathe and birds that could fly. And God saw that it was good.

He said to the creatures that he had made, 'There shall be more and more birds and fish and animals like you.' He made cattle, and every kind of beast that could live on dry land. And God saw that it was good.

The beautiful world was made; the sun

9

The Garden of Eden

After God had made a man, he made a most beautiful garden in Eden, and into it he put the man he had created, who was named Adam.

Adam was to look after the garden. A river ran through it, and in it there were two special trees. One was called 'The Tree of Life', and the other was called 'The Tree of the Knowledge of Good and Evil'.

'You may eat the fruit of any tree in the garden,' God told Adam, 'except The Tree of the Knowledge of Good and Evil.' That tree Adam was not to touch.

All the animals came up to Adam, as he worked in the garden, and he gave them all names. The birds flew round him, too, and perched on the branches. Adam named them, also.

The birds and the animals all had creatures like themselves for company, but Adam was alone.

'It isn't good for him to be alone,' God thought. 'I will make someone to live in the garden with him.'

So, while Adam was asleep, God made a woman to share his life. She was his wife, and Adam gave her a name. He called her Eve.

They were so happy, living and working in the beautiful garden. The animals came to them, unafraid, and they picked the fruit that grew on the trees. There was just one tree that Adam would not let Eve touch, because God had told him not to go near it. Do you remember its name? It was called 'The Tree of the Knowledge of Good and Evil'.

From Psalm 8
About the marvellous World God created

When I look up at the heavens,
At the wonderful work of God's hand,
The moon and the stars that he fashioned,
I think I can just understand
That man is a little below the angels,
And God has set him to be
In charge of the birds and creatures,
And the fish that live in the sea.

A Song of Praise

Praise the Lord, ye sun and moon.
Praise him, every star —
Praise him in the highest heaven,
And where the waters are.
Let them all in their own ways
Praise the Lord, as we would praise.

The Tree

Now, in the Garden of Eden there was a serpent, and in those days, serpents were quite different creatures: they could talk.

The serpent was very cunning, and one day it came up to Eve and whispered, 'Did God tell you that you can eat the fruit of every tree in the garden?'

'Yes,' said Eve, 'we may eat the fruit of all the trees in the garden, except one – and that is the tree in the middle. God told us that we must not eat the fruit of it, or even touch it.'

'Ah,' hissed the serpent in her ear, 'that's because he knows that, if you eat that fruit, it will give you a very special power. You will know all about good things and wicked things. You will be like gods yourselves.'

Eve looked at the tree, and the lovely fruit growing on it. It did look so tempting. And to know so much, and become so very wise – that would be wonderful.

Timidly she stretched out her hand, and picked a fruit from the tree. She bit into it. It was juicy and ripe. When would the wonderful thing happen, as the serpent had said?

She turned, with the fruit in her hand, and saw Adam watching her. She held it out to him, and told him what the serpent had promised.

Adam, too, disobeyed the command of God, and took a bite of the fruit.

Then they heard God's voice, as he walked in the garden, in the cool of the evening, and they were afraid because they had disobeyed him. They ran quickly, and hid among the trees. They heard God calling, 'Where are you, Adam?'

Adam and Eve came out of their hiding-place, looking ashamed of themselves, and Adam said, 'I heard your voice in the garden, and I was afraid. I hid myself.'

'Have you eaten the fruit of the tree I told you not to touch?' God asked, and Adam hung his head.

'Eve gave it to me,' he said, 'and I ate it.'
God turned to Eve.

'What have you done?' he asked sadly.

'The serpent tempted me,' said Eve, hanging her head, too, 'and I ate it.'

Because they had been so disobedient, and they might next eat the fruit of the other special tree, the Tree of Life, there was only one thing to be done.

God told them they must leave the garden, and work in the world outside. Adam must dig the ground and sow seed for their food; they would not find life at all easy.

Sadly, they left the Garden of Eden. When Adam and Eve looked back, they saw angels with a flaming sword, guarding the way that led to the Tree of Life.

11

Cain and Abel

Adam and Eve had two sons. Their names were Cain and Abel. Abel was a shepherd; he would take the sheep out on to the hillside and guide them home again in the evening, and if the lambs were very small, Abel would carry them till their legs grew strong.

Cain was a farmer; he dug the ground and planted crops, so that he and his family would have food to eat.

There came a day when Cain brought some of the crops he had grown as an offering to God. Abel, too, brought his first lambs, and God accepted them. But he would not take Cain's gift. This angered Cain, and his face fell when he understood that his offering did not please God. He could not understand why his offering of the fruits of his harvest had not been acceptable to God, who had accepted Abel's gift of lambs. God saw that Cain was not happy, and he questioned him about it.

'Why are you angry?' the Lord God asked him. 'Why did your face fall when you heard that your present would not please me?'

Cain was very annoyed and very jealous, because Abel's present had been accepted, and his had not.

He quarrelled with his brother, as they stood talking in the fields. Cain grew more and more angry and at last Cain killed his brother.

Then he heard God's voice, just as Adam had heard it in the garden, but this time God asked, 'Where is your brother Abel?'

Cain was frightened, and instead of telling the truth, he said, 'I don't know where he is. Am I my brother's keeper?'

Then God knew what had happened, and he said, 'Oh Cain, what have you done? Now you must leave here and wander about the world for the rest of your life.'

Cain was very sad. He knew he had done wrong, but his punishment was more than he could bear.

So God put a special mark on him to protect him from his enemies, as he wandered.

In time, Cain had a son, whom he called Enoch. Cain must have learned to work hard, too, because he built a city, and named it after his son.

Eve, also, had another baby boy, called Seth. He made her happy, because he took the place of Abel, the son she had lost.

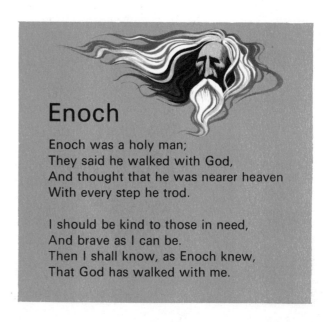

Enoch

Enoch was a holy man;
They said he walked with God,
And thought that he was nearer heaven
With every step he trod.

I should be kind to those in need,
And brave as I can be.
Then I shall know, as Enoch knew,
That God has walked with me.

The Three Brothers

In these days there lived three brothers —
Jabal, Jubal and Tubal-cain.
Jabal was a good tent-maker,
And he worked with might and main.

Also Jabal tended cattle —
Fed them; led them home at night.
Jubal was a fine musician,
Playing for his friends' delight.

Tubal-cain took brass and iron,
Making many splendid things —
Pots for cooking, knives for cutting,
Weapons, ornaments and rings.

Noah's Ark

There came a time when men began to forget God, and thought only about pleasing themselves. It grieved God very much.

But there was one man who loved him and tried to serve him: his name was Noah, and he had three sons, Shem, Ham and Japheth.

One day, God spoke to Noah. He told him to make an ark, with a door and windows — a big wooden house that would float like a ship. A great flood was coming; but if Noah and his family were safe inside the ark, the water could not touch them. The animals, too, would have to be cared for, so Noah was told to take two of every kind into the ark with him, not forgetting the birds, and to see that there was enough food for them all.

How busy they were: Noah and his wife, and Ham, Shem and Japheth — and their wives, too! Bang, bang went the hammers, as the nails were driven in and the planks were fitted together, to make the ark waterproof.

The wives were busy getting food ready, and packing up clothes. There was so much to do, and everyone had some special task. At last the ark was ready, and the animals were rounded up and taken on board.

What a sight it must have been, as they went in, two by two! The lions and the lambs, the mice and the mountain goats, the donkeys and the camels. When the last pair were safely inside, God shut the door, and knew that all would be well.

Seven days went by, and then it began to rain. It rained and it rained, for forty days

13

and forty nights, without stopping. The water crept above the houses and over the trees, and when Noah and his family looked out, they could see no land at all.

At last the rain stopped, but the flood had hidden even the mountains from sight. When the water seemed to be going down a little, Noah sent out a raven, to see if the bird could find even one green leaf anywhere; but the raven never came back. Presently, Noah let a dove fly out, and everyone watched and waited. How happy they all were when the dove came back to them, and they could see that the bird had an olive leaf in her beak. It meant that the tops of the trees were appearing.

A week later, Noah sent the dove out again, and she did not come back. It meant that the water had sunk still further, and the bird had found a new home.

At last, very slowly, the water sank until they were able to climb out on to dry land, and set all the animals free.

How glad they were, and how grateful to God for taking care of them!

Noah collected big stones and built an altar, where he could praise God and say 'Thank you'.

Then God made Noah a wonderful promise. 'While the earth remains,' he said, 'seed-time and harvest, and cold and heat,

and summer and winter, and day and night shall not cease.'

There would never be another flood like that one, and as a token of his promise, God set a rainbow in the sky. We can see it, when the sun shines while it is still raining or has just rained. Its lovely, coloured arch stretching across the sky reminds us that God loves and cares for all his children everywhere.

Noah's Name

Noah's name means 'Comfort',
Another meaning is 'Rest',
And when he took the animals
From north, south, east and west,
And kept them safely in his ark,
He well deserved his name.
Within the ark was shelter
For every beast who came.
The lion was well looked after;
The bears and sheep were fed,
And Noah's wife and children
All had their daily bread.

After the Flood

They opened the ark, and out they came —
Ham, Shem, Japheth and Noah.
The world looked even more beautiful
Than it had ever looked before.

'What shall we do?' Noah asked his sons,
And then made up his mind.
'We must plough and sow and reap,' he said,
'Till all the land we find.

'We must grow good crops for us all to eat,
Humans and animals, too.
We must tend the vines of sweet young grapes —
Yes, that is what we must do.'

So Noah was a farmer, in those days,
And a grower of vines as well,
And when he thought of the Ark and Flood,
What stories he had to tell!

The Tower of Babel

In those days, long, long ago, everyone spoke the same language. If, today, we go across the sea to France or Italy, we cannot understand what people are saying, and they can't understand us. We must learn their language. But when the world was young, everyone used the same language.

Then, one day, a group of people were wandering across a stretch of wide, flat land, and there they pitched their tents. Someone said, 'Let's build a city here,' and they all thought it was a splendid idea.

They made bricks and mortar to hold the bricks together, and they all worked with a will until the city was built.

Then someone said, 'Now let's build a tall tower, so high that its top reaches heaven. And let us all keep together; we don't want to be spread out, far apart.'

So they kept on putting bricks one on top of the other, until they had built the highest tower that anyone had ever seen. The builders were quite sure that they were going to reach heaven, where God was, for they thought that he lived above the sky.

God saw what they were doing, and he knew that these people were trying to show how great and clever they were. He knew, too, that they would have to learn not to be so proud of themselves. In order to teach the people a lesson, God decided to make life more difficult for them. He took away their power to speak the same language!

No longer could they talk together and understand one another. Suddenly, people began to use different words, and one group did not know what the next group was saying.

Of course, they could not go on building the tower in the city, which was now named Babel, for they could not tell each other what to do.

So the people broke up into little groups and parted from each other. Each group went its own way and used its own words, which no other group understood.

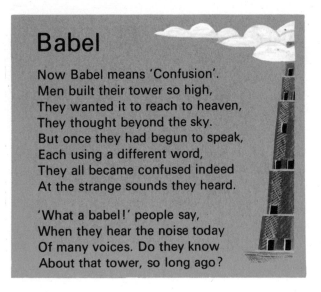

Babel

Now Babel means 'Confusion'.
Men built their tower so high,
They wanted it to reach to heaven,
They thought beyond the sky.
But once they had begun to speak,
Each using a different word,
They all became confused indeed
At the strange sounds they heard.

'What a babel!' people say,
When they hear the noise today
Of many voices. Do they know
About that tower, so long ago?

The Call of Abram

In a city named Ur, there lived a good man whose name was Abram. One day, it seemed to Abram that God was speaking to him.

'I want you to leave your country, and your father's house, say good-bye to your friends and relations, and go to another land that I will show you. I will bless you, and you shall be a blessing to others. I will make your name great, and a great nation shall come after you.'

Could it really be that God was asking this of him? It would be such a big step to take – to leave his home, where he knew everyone and everyone knew him, and to go a long journey to an unknown land. But Abram loved God, and he had enough faith to trust him, and to do what he asked.

So he talked to his wife Sarai, and his nephew Lot, and they said they would go with him. Others joined them, and they packed up their clothes and cooking pots, brought out their camels, sheep and asses, and started out.

They did not know where they were going, but they wandered on under the hot sun, camping at night, and journeying by day. Every now and then, Abram stopped and gathered big stones to build an altar to God, where he could worship him. He built one at Bethel, and another one at Moreh, and there God cheered him with another promise that he would be blessed.

As they journeyed through the land of Canaan, there was a famine. As there was little food they went down into Egypt.

At last the time came to go on, and by now the procession had grown longer, for in Egypt both Abram and Lot had collected new tents, and big herds of cattle.

They travelled on and on, until at last they were back at Bethel, the place where Abram had built his altar to God. There they stopped and pitched their tents, and Abram gave thanks to the Lord for all his goodness to them. They had not reached the end of their journey, but God was with them.

Abram in Egypt

This is a story of something that happened in Egypt, while Abram and his followers were on their long journey to the Promised Land.

As we heard in the last story, they had gone there because they hoped to find food. There had not been enough for everyone in the country through which they had been wandering, but they hoped that in Egypt they would find plenty; perhaps grain would grow beside the River Nile, and there would be some to spare for them.

When they were close to Egypt, Abram said to Sarai, 'You are so beautiful, Sarai. When the Egyptians see you, they may want to kill me, because I am your husband and they would like you to be free. So let us pretend that you are my sister; then they will not harm me.'

They rode into Egypt with their camels, their goats and sheep, their tents and bundles. As the procession passed, everyone stopped to look at Sarai, because she was so beautiful.

The ruler of Egypt, Pharaoh, heard how lovely she was, and sent for her.

Sarai knew that he was somebody who must be obeyed, so she went to his court; and, for her sake, Pharaoh was good to Abram, giving him sheep and oxen, asses, camels, men-servants and maid-servants.

Somehow Pharaoh found out that Sarai was only pretending to be Abram's sister, and that really she was his wife. He sent for Abram.

'What have you done to me?' he asked sternly. 'Why did you not tell me that Sarai was your wife? Why did you say she was your sister? I might have wanted to make her my wife. Anyway, she is yours, so take her, and go on your way.'

Pharaoh told his men to see that Abram left Egypt, and they started off once more on their long journey.

Abram probably felt sorry that he had told Pharaoh something that was not true, but he must have been very thankful that his life and that of his wife had been spared. He and Sarai were still together, in spite of his fears.

Abram gathered all his flocks and cattle and men about him, and Lot did the same thing.

Lot moved off into the pleasant-looking land, and pitched his tent there. Abram stayed in the land of Canaan. Lot seemed to have chosen the better place, but Abram trusted in God who was his leader.

He heard God speaking to him: 'Lift up your eyes, and look north and south, east and west. I will give you all the land you can see, and to your children, and your children's children, for ever and ever. Arise, walk through the land, from one end to the other, for I give it all to you.'

So Abram folded up his tent and set off for the last time. In front of him lay the Promised Land; his journey was ended.

Abram and Lot

For many days, Abram and Lot journeyed on after leaving Bethel. It was hot and dusty, and of course they did not know where their final resting place would be, or when the journey would end. Some of the men who were looking after the sheep and cattle began to get tired and cross, and they started quarrelling. Abram's men wanted to go one way, and Lot's men wanted to go another.

At last Abram said to Lot, 'Don't let there be any quarrels between you and me, or between your herdsmen and mine. We are like brothers, and we should be friends. Here is the whole land spread out before us, so let us go different ways. If you will take the road to the left, I will go to the right – or, if you go to the right, I will go to the left.'

So Lot shaded his eyes against the sun and looked about him. He saw the wide, open land which was called Jordan. It was well watered, and looked like a garden; everything was fresh and growing well.

'I will take the plain of Jordan,' said Lot, so they said good-bye to one another.

Psalm 23
The Shepherd's Psalm

The Lord's my shepherd. He will see
That in green fields I lie,
And by quiet waters he will lead
His sheep. We shall go by
The path called 'Righteousness', and if
We reach a shadowed place,
I will not be afraid of harm,
For still I see his face.
His shepherd's staff will comfort me,
And he will surely spread
A meal for me. He fills my cup;
He will anoint my head.
Goodness and mercy follow me,
And I shall always rest
In God's own house my whole life long,
And may his name be blest!

18

Abram looks at the Stars

Four kings came from eastern lands and fought the kings in the region where Lot had chosen to live. Lot and his people were captured and taken away by the eastern kings, together with their sheep and cattle.

One prisoner escaped, however, and managed to find Abram.

When Abram heard what had happened, he gathered together all his men who could fight, and they set off to rescue Lot. They won their battle and brought Lot back, with all the people who had been taken prisoner – and all the sheep and cattle, too.

The king of Sodom, which was the place where Lot lived, met them, and the king of Salem, priest of the most high God, brought them bread and wine. He blessed Abram, and thanked God for their victory.

The king of Sodom said to Abram, 'Give me these people, and you can have all that they have brought back with them.'

But Abram said, 'I have promised God that I will take nothing – not even a thread or a shoe-lace, and so I will not take anything lest you should say: "I have made Abram rich." I will take only the food that the young men have eaten; and they may take their share of the spoil.'

After that, Abram heard God speaking to him again, 'Do not be afraid, Abram. I am your shield and your great reward.'

'Lord God,' Abram answered, 'what will you give me? I have no child to be my heir.'

But God told him that he would have a son to be his heir. Then it seemed to Abram that God led him out, to stand under the starry sky.

'Look towards heaven,' God told him, 'and count the stars, if you can. So large shall your family be – one generation after another – in the years that are to come.'

Abram believed him, and his heart was full of joy and thankfulness. Then God said, 'I am the Lord, who brought you out of Ur, to give you this land, and it shall be yours.'

'Lord,' Abram asked, 'how shall I know that it shall be mine?' He wanted to believe, but sometimes a doubt crept into his heart.

When the sun was going down, Abram fell asleep. In his sleep he heard God telling him many things that were going to happen to him and his family. The land was indeed theirs, now and in the years ahead.

Hagar runs away

Sarai, Abram's wife, was very sad that she had no baby of her own, and when her maid, Hagar, knew that a baby was coming to her, the news made Sarai very jealous.

Sarai became so unkind to Hagar that the maid felt she could not stay with her mistress any longer, and so she ran away.

Hagar walked a long, long way through a hot and dusty land. She was tired and thirsty, and when at last she came to a fountain of cool water, Hagar sank down beside it, too tired to go on walking.

An angel of the Lord found her there, and asked, 'Hagar, where have you come from, and where are you going?'

Hagar hung her head. 'I ran away from my mistress, Sarai,' she said.

'Go back to her,' said the angel, 'and be her good and faithful servant. You are going to have a little son, and you must call him Ishmael.'

'God sees me,' thought Hagar, and she knew that he would take care of her and her baby boy.

Hagar turned back, and went along the way by which she had come. She would do what the angel had told her to do – she would go back to Sarai.

Abram has Visitors

One day, God reminded Abram of the promise he had made him. Abram was an old man now, and Sarai was growing old, but they were indeed going to have a baby son. They were to call him Isaac, and Abram and Sarai were to have new names: they would be called Abraham and Sarah.

Later, when Abraham was sitting at the door of his tent, trying to find a little shade on a very hot day, he looked up and saw three men standing near him.

It was a great surprise to Abraham, for travellers did not often pass that way, and somehow he felt that these men were messengers from God. He jumped up and ran towards them, bowing humbly before them.

'My Lords,' he said, 'if you will, do not go away. Someone shall fetch water to wash your feet, and you can rest under that tree. I will bring some bread, for you are welcome guests, and when you have eaten and rested, you can go on. You have come to your servant, and he will look after you.'

'Very well,' said Abraham's visitors. 'We will do as you say.'

Abraham hurried into the tent and said to Sarah, 'Quickly – measure out the flour, make three cakes, and bake them on the hearth.'

Then he ran outside again and told a young man to get some meat ready, and to make sure that it was tender and good. Nothing but the very best would do for these special visitors!

He himself fetched butter and milk, and when the cakes and the meat were ready, they were set before the young men – a splendid meal indeed.

When they had eaten, one of the men asked Abraham, 'Where is Sarah, your wife?'

'She is in the tent,' Abraham said.

'Sarah shall have a son,' said the man.

Sarah was standing in the doorway of the tent, and was able to hear what he said.

She was going to have a baby of her own, after all this time? Sarah could not believe it; indeed, the very idea made her laugh!

God knew what Sarah was thinking, although she pretended not to doubt his word; but nothing was impossible when planned by God, and Sarah would have her son.

The young men rose to go, and Abraham went with them a little way. He knew that they were no ordinary travellers; he had indeed entertained God's messengers.

Joel 3, 13
Picking Olives

Pick ripe olives from the trees,
Or they will shrink and spoil.
Olives are such useful fruit,
Full of good, pure oil.
Tread them now beneath your feet,
Or beat them on the ground.
Thus they knew, in Bible days,
How precious oil was found.

The Ten Good Men

At this time, there were cities where the people did not love and serve God. Everyone was selfish, and did just as he pleased. Some people were unkind to their neighbours; and some quarrelled with anyone they met. One of these towns was Sodom, where Lot was living with his family.

God was angered with the people, and chose to punish them by destroying their cities.

But Abraham was troubled about the few good people who might be living there. He plucked up courage and spoke to God.

'Ought the good people to suffer with the bad ones?' he asked. 'Suppose there were fifty men in the city who were trying to do right – would you save the town, for their sakes? You are the judge of all the earth; surely you will do what is right?'

And the Lord said, 'Yes, if I find fifty good men in Sodom, I will spare the city for their sakes.'

Abraham was still worried.

'I know that I have no right to ask these things,' he said, 'for you are the Lord, and I am only your humble servant. But supposing there were five good men less than that – supposing there were only forty-five – would you spare the city for their sakes?'

'If I could find forty-five good men, I would spare the city,' God answered.

Still Abraham was worried.

'Suppose there were only forty good men!' he said. 'What would you do then?'

God said, 'I would save the city for forty.'

Still Abraham was troubled, and he felt he must go on.

'Don't be angry with me, Lord,' he said, 'but I must speak. Suppose there were thirty?'

'I will save the city, if there are thirty good men,' God promised.

Still Abraham went on with his questioning.

'I've taken it upon myself to speak to you, Lord,' he said. 'Supposing there were twenty?'

God said, 'I will not destroy it, for the sake of twenty.'

Abraham felt he must be brave enough to go even a little further. He plucked up his courage once more, and he said, 'Lord, don't be angry with me; this is the last time that I am going to ask you. Suppose there were only ten?'

And God said, 'If there were only ten good men, the city would be saved.'

Then Abraham went back to his own home, glad to know that he could talk to God as a man would talk to his friend.

Hagar's Son

God's promise to Abraham and Sarah came true: they had a baby son, and they called him Isaac. How pleased and proud they were, after waiting such a very long time, to have a little child of their own.

They gave a party, with good things to eat, and all their friends came to admire the baby, and wish them happiness.

But Sarah, from where she was sitting, looked up and saw Ishmael, the son of her servant, Hagar, laughing and making fun of baby Isaac and his parents.

Sarah was very cross with him, and she said to Abraham, 'Send Hagar and her son away – I don't want them here.'

Abraham did not want to do this, but somehow he felt that God had a plan for the boy, Ishmael, as well as for Isaac, and that thus it would all turn out right in the end.

The next morning Abraham got up early, and took bread, and water in a skin bottle, and put it on Hagar's shoulder. Then he told her that she and Ishmael must leave their tent home, and go away.

Hagar took her son's hand, and sadly they left their home, walking through wild, lonely country, with the sun beating down.

'I'm thirsty,' said Ishmael, and his mother gave him a drink from the bottle. Soon there was none left.

Then Ishmael grew very tired, for they had come a long way. 'I can't go any farther, mother,' he said.

So Hagar found a little place for him to lie down under a bush, in the shade.

She herself went a little way away, and sat where she could not see him, because Hagar felt that the hot sun had made him really ill, and she could not bear to watch. If he could not have some water to drink, Ishmael might not get better.

Poor Hagar began to cry. God knew how sad she was, and how ill Ishmael felt, so an angel carried a message to his mother,

'What is the matter, Hagar? Don't be afraid – God has heard your boy's cries. Get up, and put your arms round him and lift him up. God will make a great man of him.'

Hagar rubbed the tears from her eyes, and looked round her. Suddenly she saw a well quite close to her. It would be filled with lovely, cool water – it would save her boy's life!

She picked up the bottle, ran to the well and filled it. Then Hagar hurried to Ishmael and, just as the angel had told her, she put her arm round him and raised his head. She lifted the bottle to his lips, and he drank thirstily.

The water saved Ishmael's life. He was able to stand up and smile at his mother, and carry on with their journey.

Hagar and Ishmael made their home in the wilderness; and when Ishmael grew up, he became an archer. God was with him always, just as he was with Abraham.

23

The Song of Solomon 2, 11–13

Spring is Here!

The winter's past,
And gone the rain;
The flowers appear,
On earth again.
The sweet dove coos,
The birds all sing;
The young vines bloom –
Because it's spring!

Abraham's Well

Abraham made a journey to the south country, and there he met King Abimelech.

One day the king came to him.

'God is with you, I know,' he said. 'Will you give me your promise that you will treat me well, and my son and grandson? I have looked after you, since you have been in my land; will you do the same for me?'

Abraham promised the king that he would.

There was a well which Abraham's servants used, to get water for their cattle. It was very precious, because water was so hard to find in that hot country. Now the king's servants came along and drove Abraham's men away; they said the well was theirs, and that nobody else could use it.

Abraham went to see the king about this. He hoped that Abimelech would say, 'Of course the well is yours, and your servants can draw water from it.'

But the king said that he did not know anything about it; nobody had told him about the well till that moment.

Abraham went away, and he came back with some of his sheep and oxen, and gave them to Abimelech as a present. Then he took seven lambs from his flock, and put them in a special place by themselves.

'Why have you done that?' asked the king.

'Take these seven lambs,' said Abraham, 'as a sign that I did indeed dig this well myself.'

So Abraham and his servants were left alone, and the king went to another place. Abraham planted trees round his well, he called it Beer-sheba.

Abraham is Tested

Abraham heard the voice of God calling his name: 'Abraham! Abraham!'

'Here I am,' he answered.

'Abraham! Take your son – your only son, Isaac, whom you love – and go up into the mountains. I want you to give him to me as an offering.'

An offering? Could he have understood? Abraham sometimes made a fire, and laid on it a lamb that he had killed as an offering; it was a kind of present to God, from his faithful servant. But God surely could not ask him to offer his son?

Yet Abraham had such trust in God that, even if he wanted him to give up Isaac, whom he loved so dearly, he would obey.

So he rose early in the morning and told Isaac, and two of his young servants, that they were going on a journey up the mountainside. Abraham cut wood to make the fire, and saddled his ass, and they all set off.

Isaac did not know what was going to happen, and he looked about him, laughing and talking; but Abraham's heart was heavy.

They had to go a long way. It was three days before Abraham, shading his eyes with his hand and looking up, could see the spot which they had come to find.

'You stay here with the ass,' Abraham said to the young men. 'Isaac and I will go on to worship God, and then return.'

The young men were glad to sit down and rest, and Abraham took the bundle of wood they had brought with them and gave it to Isaac to carry. He himself took what they needed to prepare the fire and the sacrifice.

Together they began to climb the mountain.

Presently, Isaac said, 'Father!'

'Here I am, my son,' Abraham answered.

'We have the fire and the wood,' Isaac said, puzzled, 'but where is the lamb we are going to offer to God?'

Abraham's heart was heavy indeed.

'My son,' he said, 'God himself will provide a lamb for an offering.'

And they went on together.

They came to the place of which God had spoken, and sadly Abraham found stones and built an altar. He put the wood on the altar, and laid Isaac on it.

But, at that moment, an angel called to him: 'Abraham! Abraham!'

'Here I am,' he said.

'Let Isaac go,' said the angel, 'for you have proved how much you love God, and how obedient you are. You would even give up your only son, if God asked you.'

Abraham looked up, full of joy, and saw a ram caught in the bushes. He would offer the ram, instead of his beloved son!

God would not have taken Isaac from him, but he wanted to find out how obedient Abraham was. Abraham passed the test.

25

'Please listen to me. If you will let me have the field, I will give you money for it. You must let me pay you.'

Ephron answered, 'My lord, listen to me. The land is worth four hundred silver pieces. What is that, between you and me? Take it!'

But Abraham had his way in the end. He weighed out four hundred pieces of silver and gave them to Ephron. Then the field and the cave, and all the trees planted in the field and round it, rightfully became Abraham's.

Sarah was laid to rest in the cave, and it comforted Abraham to know that he had bought this quiet place for himself and Sarah and their family.

Abraham buys a Cave

The years passed and Sarah became a very old lady, but at last her life came to an end.

Abraham was very sad. He had done so many things with Sarah at his side to help him; he would miss her very much.

Now Abraham wanted to find a special place where Sarah might be buried, so he went to a group of men in the city where he was, and said, 'I am a stranger here – please help me to find a place where my family can rest when their life's work is done.'

The men said, 'You are a great man among us, Abraham. Choose the place you would like. We shall be glad to help you.'

Abraham stood up and bowed to the people. Then he said, 'Will you ask Ephron if I may have the cave at the end of his field? I will pay him whatever he asks.'

Ephron heard what Abraham said, and he answered at once, 'Hear me, my lord! I will not take money. I will give you the cave, and the field too. In the presence of the sons of my people, I give it to you.' Abraham bowed low once more. Then he said to Ephron, in front of all the people,

A Wife for Isaac

Isaac grew to be a young man, and the time came when Abraham wanted to find him a good wife. He did not want Isaac to marry a girl who lived in the land to which they had come; he felt that his son's wife should belong to the land where he himself had been born – the place he had left behind when God sent him out to find a new country.

He called one of his servants and told him what he wanted.

'You must go to my country,' he said, 'and to my people, and bring back a wife for my son Isaac.'

'Suppose the woman does not want to come?' asked the man. 'Would I then have to take Isaac to her?'

'No, you must not do that,' Abraham said. 'The Lord God of Heaven, who brought us out of that land, and said he would give the Promised Land to my son, will send an angel before you, and you will find a wife for Isaac. If she will not come with you, what I ask cannot be carried out; but, whatever happens, do not take Isaac back.'

The servant said he would do his best. He took ten of Abraham's camels and travelled to a city named Nahor. When he reached a well outside the city, the servant made his camels kneel down, and then he waited.

It was evening, and soon the women would come from the city to draw water. 'O Lord God of my master Abraham,' the man prayed, 'send me good fortune today, and be kind to my master. See, I am standing here by the well, and the girls from the city will soon come to draw water.

'Grant, Lord, that the girl to whom I shall say: "Let down your pitcher into the well and give me a drink", shall answer, "Drink, and I will give your camels drink also." Let her be the woman who is the right wife for Isaac, and then I shall know that you are indeed kind to my master.'

And the servant waited patiently.

Rebekah at the Well

Before the servant had finished speaking, Rebekah came walking towards the well, with her pitcher on her shoulder.

She was very beautiful, and the servant watched her as she stepped down to the well and filled her water-pot.

As Rebekah stood up, he ran towards her.

'Let me, I pray thee, drink a little water from your pitcher,' he pleaded.

'Drink, my lord,' she said at once; and Rebekah took the pitcher in her hand, and tipped it so that he could drink.

When he had finished, she said, 'I will draw some water for your camels, too — as much as they want.'

As she did this, the servant wondered if she was indeed the woman he had come to find, and if God had blessed his journey.

He took a golden ear-ring and two gold bracelets from his pack. When the camels had finished drinking, he held them out.

'Whose daughter are you?' he asked. 'Is there room in your father's house for me to stay?'

'I am Bethuel's daughter,' Rebekah told him. 'We have straw and food enough, and room to lodge in.'

The servant's heart was full of joy. He bowed his head and worshipped God.

'Blessed be the Lord God of my master Abraham,' he said, 'who has shown him mercy. He has led me to Abraham's own relations.'

As for Rebekah, she was already hurrying home to tell her mother what had happened.

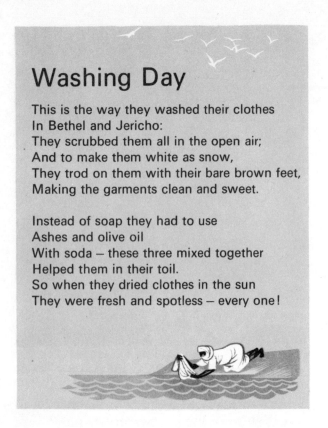

Washing Day

This is the way they washed their clothes
In Bethel and Jericho:
They scrubbed them all in the open air;
And to make them white as snow,
They trod on them with their bare brown feet,
Making the garments clean and sweet.

Instead of soap they had to use
Ashes and olive oil
With soda — these three mixed together
Helped them in their toil.
So when they dried clothes in the sun
They were fresh and spotless — every one!

Rebekah sets out

Rebekah had a brother, Laban, and when he saw the new gold ear-ring and bracelets his sister was wearing, of course he wanted to know where she had got them.

'A man spoke to me by the well,' said Rebekah, 'and he gave them to me.'

So Laban ran to the well, where the man was still waiting beside his camels.

'Follow me to our house,' he said. 'We know you come with God's blessing; why are you standing here outside? We are ready to receive and welcome you, and your camels too.'

So Abraham's servant went with him gladly. He unsaddled the camels, and there was straw for them, and food and water. There was water to wash his own dusty feet, and the feet of the men he had brought with him.

They gave him meat, but he said, 'I won't eat until you know why I am here.'

Then Abraham's servant told Rebekah and her family the whole story – how Abraham had sent him to find a wife for his son, Isaac, and all about his own plan for finding out exactly who was the right bride for Isaac.

'And now,' he said, when the story was told, 'tell me whether you will let Rebekah come back with me or not. I feel that God has led me in the right way, for she is Isaac's cousin.'

Bethuel, Rebekah's father, and Laban, her brother, both answered.

'This must have been planned by God. Here is Rebekah; take her with you and go, and let her be your master's son's wife, as God wishes her to be.'

The servant bowed low, giving thanks to God. Then he brought out gifts – jewels of silver and gold, and beautiful clothes – which he gave to Rebekah. He gave precious gifts to her mother and brother, too.

They had a meal, and the travellers were

given beds for the night. Next morning, when they got up, Abraham's servant said, 'Let us be off now, back to my master.'

But Rebekah's mother and brother could not bear to let her go.

'Let Rebekah stay with us for another ten days,' they begged.

Abraham's servant felt that they ought to return at once to Isaac and his father.

'Don't hold me back,' he said. 'Since the Lord has been with me so far, let me return to my master.'

'We will send for Rebekah,' said Laban and his mother, 'and see what she says.'

So they called Rebekah.

'Will you go with this man?' they asked.

'I will go,' Rebekah said obediently.

So they sent Rebekah, and her nurse and maids, with Abraham's servant. They were sad to see her go, but it was plain that this was what God wanted.

Isaac meets Rebekah

All this time, Isaac had been waiting, wondering what was happening. When the sun went down, on the day that Abraham's servant was nearing home once more, Isaac went out into the cool evening. He walked up and down in a field, deep in thought.

Presently, far in the distance, he saw them coming – the camels, and the people who were leading or riding them.

As they drew nearer, Isaac recognised his father's servant. Then he saw that a girl rode on one of the camels. He wondered if she was his bride.

He saw her climb down from the camel's back. He did not know that Rebekah had said to Abraham's servant, 'Who is that man, walking in the field and coming to meet us?'

On that the servant had said, 'It is my master.'

But Isaac saw Rebekah cover herself with a veil, and walk shyly towards him.

The servant hurried forward and told Isaac all that had happened.

Isaac could not see how beautiful Rebekah was, because of her veil, but he welcomed his bride, and led her into the tent that had been his mother's.

Soon Isaac found that he loved Rebekah very dearly. He made Rebekah his wife, and found great happiness with her.

Baking Bread

Outside a tent of goats'-hair cloth
The women bake their bread.
The oven, made of clay, is hot,
And on it there are spread
Thin rounds of dough; to make these crisp,
They sprinkle them with water.
In this way they supply the food
For husband, son and daughter!

Jacob and Esau

Isaac and Rebekah waited a long time for a baby of their own, but at last they had two — twin boys. They called them Esau and Jacob.

Now, Isaac loved Esau best, but Rebekah's favourite was Jacob. As they grew up, Esau became a very clever hunter, but Jacob was more of a stay-at-home.

One day Esau came in from his hunting, feeling quite faint with hunger. Jacob was busy making a lentil stew, and it smelt very good.

'Do give me some of that,' Esau begged. 'I'm very, very hungry!'

Esau was just a little older than Jacob, because he had been born first; that meant that he was looked upon as the elder son, and had special privileges. Jacob had always envied him.

'I'll give you some of my food,' he said, 'if you will give up your birthright to me.' He meant that he wanted to be treated as the elder, instead of Esau.

'Well, I'm dying of hunger,' Esau said, 'and if I died, my birthright would not be much use to me!'

'Swear that you give it to me,' said Jacob.

'I swear!' replied Esau.

So Jacob gave his brother a bowl of lentil stew and some bread, and he ate it eagerly. Esau had been so hungry that he had not cared about being the elder.

Isaac digs the Wells

There was not enough food for the people to eat, because the harvest had not given them all the grain they needed; but Isaac did not go to Egypt, as Abraham had once done.

God spoke to Isaac and told him to go to Gerar. 'I will be with you,' he said, 'and I will bless you; because your father Abraham obeyed me, I will do for you what I promised him. All these lands shall belong to you and your children, forever.'

So Isaac lived in Gerar with his family, but when people asked him who Rebekah was, he said she was his sister. He was afraid, just as Abraham had been about Sarah, that when they saw how beautiful she was, they would want to take her away from him and kill him.

Then, one day, when they had been at Gerar for a long time, King Abimelech looked out of his window and saw Isaac laughing and playing with Rebekah, and he guessed that she must be his wife.

The king sent for Isaac.

'I'm sure that Rebekah is your wife,' he said. 'Why do you call her your sister?'

Just as Abraham had told Pharaoh in Egypt, Isaac gave the king his reason. Then the king told all his people to take great care of Isaac and his wife. Isaac worked very hard in the fields, and in time he had large flocks of sheep, and herds of goats and cattle, together with servants to look after them.

Abraham had dug many wells in that part of the land, but the king's men had filled them in again. They were jealous of Isaac, and eventually the king told him that he had better leave his land. Isaac journeyed on, opening the wells once more, and calling them by the names Abraham gave them.

The men of Gerar followed them, saying, 'That's our well!' and fighting with Isaac's servants. When Isaac dug a new well, they would say, 'The water is ours!', and then try to take it from him. At last Isaac dug a well that they did not take from him, and he said, 'Now the Lord has made room for us, and we shall do well in this land.'

He journeyed to Beer-sheba, and there he pitched his tent and built an altar to praise God, and his servants dug a well.

Then the king, and one of his friends, and the chief captain of his army, went to visit Isaac, who was surprised to see them.

'Why have you come,' he asked, 'when you sent me away?'

'We saw that God was with you,' they said, 'and we want to make a pact with you. Promise that you will be good to us and our people, as we have been good to you.'

So they all promised to be friends, and Isaac set a feast before them, and gave them shelter for the night.

The next morning they went home again, and when his servants told Isaac that there was water in the well, he was glad.

Jacob deceives Isaac

The years passed, and Isaac became an old man. His sight grew weak, and when his sons Jacob and Esau came in, he did not find it easy to see which was which.

One day, when he was feeling very old and tired, he called Esau – the clever hunter – to him, and said, 'Take your bow and arrows, and go out into the field and bring back some meat for my dinner. I am fond of stewed venison, and I would like you to make me a dish of it. Then, when you bring it to me, I will give you my blessing.'

Esau went away to do as his father asked. Meanwhile, Rebekah – who had heard what Isaac said, and who loved Jacob the better of her two sons – wanted Jacob to receive his father's blessing. So Rebekah told him what she had heard, and said, 'Go to the flock, and bring back two goat-kids. I will make a good dinner for your father from them, and you shall take it to him; then he will give you his blessing.'

Jacob looked down at his hands, and he said, 'Mother, Esau's hands are covered with hairs, and mine are very smooth. Even though our father cannot see well, he will feel my hands and know that I am not my brother, which will only make him angry.'

'I will bear the troubles, if they come,' said Rebekah. 'Just do as I say, my son.'

So Jacob went off, and soon returned with the meat, from which Rebekah cooked a fine dish. It was just the kind of food which Isaac loved.

Then Rebekah took Esau's best clothes and dressed Jacob in them; and to hide his smooth hands and neck, she covered them with kid-skin. Rebekah gave Jacob the good dinner she had cooked, and some bread, and told him to take it to his father.

Jacob went into the tent where Isaac was.

'Father!' he said.

'Here I am,' Isaac answered, peering at him. 'Who are you, my son?'

'I am Esau, your first-born,' replied Jacob, 'and I have done what you asked of me. Sit down and eat, and then bless me, father.'

'How did you find the meat so quickly, my son?' Isaac asked.

'The Lord God brought it to me,' Jacob told him.

'Come nearer,' Isaac said, 'so that I can feel you, and make sure that you are really my son Esau.'

Jacob went close to his father, and slowly

32

Isaac felt him. Then he said, in a puzzled way, 'The voice is Jacob's voice, but the hands are Esau's.'

He gave Jacob his blessing, as though he were Esau, his first-born son, but Isaac was still not quite sure in his own mind, and said, 'Are you truly my son Esau?'

'I am,' Jacob said.

'Bring the food close to me,' said Isaac, 'and I will eat it; and bring me some wine, too.'

When he had finished his meal, the old man said, 'Come now, kiss me, my son.'

Jacob went close to him and kissed him.

Isaac could not see that Jacob was wearing Esau's clothes, but he could smell the good smell of the earth, for Esau had worn them out-of-doors where he worked.

'See,' said the old man joyfully, 'the smell of my son is like the smell of a field which the Lord has blessed. Therefore may God prosper you and give you plenty of corn and wine. May people serve you and obey you. Be lord over your brethren. Blessed be everyone who blesses you.'

The Blessing of Esau

Jacob had hardly left his father before Esau came in from his hunting. He also had made a good meal with the meat he had brought, and hurried to take it to Isaac.

'Get up, father,' he said, 'and eat the meal I have brought you, and bless your son.'

'Who are you?' Isaac asked sharply.

'Why, I am your son – your first-born son, Esau.'

Isaac began to tremble.

'Who?' he cried. 'Where is the one who brought me a dish of meat, whom I blessed?'

When Esau heard his father's words, he gave a bitter cry. 'Bless me, even me also, O my father!' he begged.

But Isaac said, 'Your brother came to me with great cunning, and he has had the blessing that should have been yours.'

'He is rightly named Jacob,' said Esau bitterly, 'for it means "someone who has taken another man's place", and he has done that twice to me. He took my birthright, and now he has taken my blessing. Haven't you a blessing for me, too?'

'I have made him lord over you, and promised him corn and wine,' Isaac said. 'What can I give you, my son?'

Esau, man as he was, could not help crying, and he said again, 'Haven't you one blessing for me? Bless me, O my father!'

So Isaac said, 'By your sword shall you live, and you shall serve your brother; and it shall come to pass, when you are the stronger, that you shall free yourself from him!'

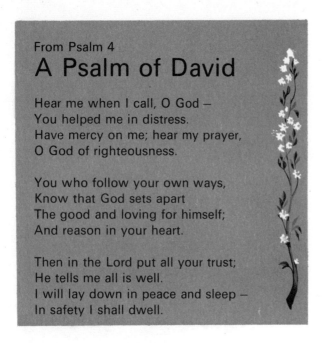

A Psalm of David

Hear me when I call, O God —
You helped me in distress.
Have mercy on me; hear my prayer,
O God of righteousness.

You who follow your own ways,
Know that God sets apart
The good and loving for himself;
And reason in your heart.

Then in the Lord put all your trust;
He tells me all is well.
I will lay down in peace and sleep —
In safety I shall dwell.

to heaven, and angels going up and down it. At the top of the ladder stood God, and he was saying, 'I am the Lord God of Abraham, and the God of Isaac. I will give the land on which you are lying to you and to your children's children. Your family shall spread north, south, east and west, and all men shall be blessed through you. I am with you and will keep you wherever you go, and I will bring you again to this land. I will not leave you till all this is done.'

Then Jacob woke up and looked about him. The ladder and the angels had vanished, but he said to himself, 'Surely the Lord is in this place, and I did not know it. How holy is this spot! This is the house of God, and this is the gate of heaven.'

Jacob's Dream

Because of what he had done to him, Esau thought of Jacob as his enemy; if he could, he would have killed him.

Rebekah found this out, and she went to Jacob and said, 'You had better go and stay with your Uncle Laban for a few days, until your brother's anger dies down and he forgets what you did to him. I will send for you as soon as it is safe to come home again.'

Then she went to Isaac and said, 'I don't want Jacob to marry a local girl. He should look farther afield for his wife.'

So Isaac sent for Jacob, blessed him, and said, 'You should not marry a girl from these parts. Go to your grandfather, Bethuel, and take one of your Uncle Laban's daughters as your bride. God will bless you and give you children.'

Jacob travelled a long way, and when the sun set, he knew he would have to spend the night where he was. After finding a suitable stone on which to rest his head, Jacob slept, for he was tired after his journey.

Then Jacob had a wonderful dream. He saw a ladder, set up on earth, which reached

Rachel at the Well

It was still very early in the morning, and Jacob got up and took the stone he had used for a pillow and set it up on end. Then he poured oil on the stone, because it now marked a holy place, and called it Beth-el, which means 'The House of God'. And Jacob made this vow: 'If God will be with me, and will keep me in this way that I go, and will give me bread to eat and clothes to wear, so that I come again to my father's house in peace, then shall the Lord be my God, and this stone, which I have set up as a pillar, shall be God's house; and of all that God gives me, I will give a tenth of it back to him.'

Then Jacob went on his way, and at last he drew near Haran, and saw the well, with three flocks of sheep lying beside it. Shepherds were waiting for the stone that covered the well to be moved, so that their sheep could drink before they put the stone back again. It was their custom to wait till all the sheep had arrived.

'My brothers, where do you come from?' Jacob asked them.

'From Haran,' they told him.

'Do you know Laban?' Jacob asked.

'Yes, we know him,' came the reply.

'And is he well?'

'Yes, he is well. Look, his daughter Rachel is just coming with his sheep,' the shepherds said.

Jacob thought that this would be a wonderful chance to get to know Rachel. He turned to the shepherds, and said, 'It is the middle of the day, and it is not yet time for all the cattle to be gathered together. Water your sheep at once, and then take them off and feed them.'

'We cannot do so,' said the shepherds, 'until all the flocks are gathered together, and till they roll away the stone from the well. Then we will water the sheep.'

By this time, Rachel was drawing near with her sheep, and Jacob made up his mind what he would do. He went up to the well and took off the stone himself. Then he gave Rachel's sheep water to drink.

After that, he kissed Rachel, and explained that he was her cousin. Rachel, very excited at this news, ran home to tell her father.

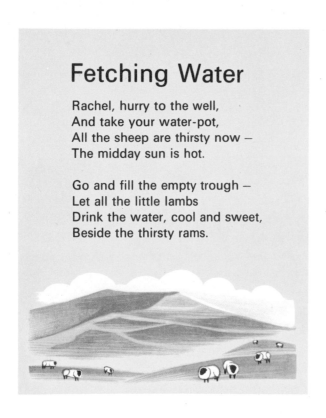

Fetching Water

Rachel, hurry to the well,
And take your water-pot,
All the sheep are thirsty now —
The midday sun is hot.

Go and fill the empty trough —
Let all the little lambs
Drink the water, cool and sweet,
Beside the thirsty rams.

Jacob and Rachel

When Laban, Rachel's father, heard that Jacob was waiting by the well, he ran out to welcome him. Then he took Jacob to his home.

Jacob told Laban his story, and the uncle said, 'You are indeed close to me – we are of the same family.'

So Jacob worked for him; then, one day Laban said, 'You are my nephew, but that does not mean that you must work for me for nothing. What shall your wages be?'

Now Laban had two daughters; the elder, Leah, was sweet and gentle; but Rachel, the younger, was very beautiful and Jacob loved her.

Jacob, therefore, replied, 'I will work for you for seven years, if you will give me Rachel for my wife.'

'I would rather give her to you than to any other man,' Laban told him. 'So stay with me.'

Thus Jacob worked for his Uncle Laban for seven years, so that he might win Rachel for his wife, and he loved her so much that the seven years seemed only a few days.

At last Jacob could say to his uncle, 'Give me my wife – the seven years are over.'

So Laban planned a splendid party and all their friends came; but he tricked Jacob, for it was Leah he gave to be his nephew's wife, and not Rachel.

When he realised what Laban had done, Jacob said, 'Did I not serve you seven years for Rachel? Why have you tricked me?'

'In our country,' Laban replied, 'the elder daughter must come before the younger; it would be wrong for Rachel to be married before her sister. Serve me another seven years, however, and Rachel shall be yours.'

In the end, Jacob won Rachel for his wife, and he loved her very dearly. He stayed with Laban's family for a long time.

Jacob goes Home

After he had spent twenty years with Laban, Jacob longed to go home again. He now had a favourite son whom he called Joseph, and he naturally wanted to show him to his own people.

But Laban did not want Jacob to go. 'God has blessed me while you have been with me,' he said.

He did not treat Jacob as well as he had done before, because he was angry with him for wanting to leave, but Jacob heard God telling him, 'Return to your own land, and I will be with you.'

So Jacob stole away secretly, taking with him his family, and his camels, and all that was his.

Of course, when Laban realised what Jacob had done, he was very angry, and he, with some of his relatives, went after Jacob.

God spoke to Laban, too, in a dream. He told him to treat Jacob with respect.

Laban caught up with Jacob at last.

'Why did you creep away like this?' he asked. 'Why did you not tell me that you were going, so that I could have sent you on your way with music and rejoicing? Why did you not let me kiss my relatives good-bye? You have been foolish, and if I wished I could make you pay for it; but God spoke to me last night and told me to be careful what I said to you.'

In the end, Jacob and Laban parted as friends, and they set up a heap of stones as a sign between them. They called it 'Mizpah' – which means: 'The Lord watch between you and me when we are away from one another.' And they agreed that they would not cross from one side of the heap of stones to the other, in order to do one another harm.

They had a meal together, and Laban spent the night there. Next morning, Laban got up early, kissed his relations and blessed them. Then he turned towards his own home, and Jacob and those who were with him went on their way.

Jacob's New Name

Jacob went on his way, and he felt that God's angels were taking care of him.

He began to think about his brother, Esau, and all that had happened since he last saw him. He decided to send messengers to let Esau know that he was on his way home.

'Tell him,' he said, 'that I have been staying with Laban, and now I am coming with my own oxen and asses and servants. I hope that he will be pleased to see me.'

The messengers did as they were told, and presently they came back to Jacob.

'We found Esau,' they said, 'and he is coming to meet you with four hundred men.'

Jacob was worried and afraid, because he thought that they were coming to fight him, so he divided all his men and camels, his flocks and herds, into two groups. 'If Esau comes and destroys one group,' he said, 'the other group may be spared.'

Then he prayed to God: 'Deliver me, I pray, from the hand of my brother Esau.'

He pitched his tents for the night, and got together a present for Esau: goats, sheep, camels, cattle and donkeys.

Jacob told his servants to drive the animals ahead in little groups. 'And when you meet Esau,' he said, 'and he asks you, "Who is your master? Where are you going? Who owns all these animals?" — tell him that they are my present to him, and that I myself am following behind.'

Jacob hoped that he might win Esau over with such a splendid present.

The men set off with the animals, and Jacob stayed behind for the night.

He sent his sons and Rachel, and the other women who were with them, to the other side of a brook, and Jacob remained alone.

In the night, Jacob dreamed he was wrestling until his thigh was sprained.

At last the man whom he fought said, 'What is your name?'

'Jacob!' he answered.

'You shall not be called Jacob any more,' the stranger told him. 'You shall have a new name – Israel.' His new name meant 'Prince of God'.

'What is your name?' Jacob asked.

'Why do you ask?' the stranger replied, and blessed him.

Then suddenly Jacob understood. He had been talking with God himself; and, although he was now lame, Jacob would be truly strong – he would not trust in his own strength, but in the power of God.

'I have seen God face to face,' he said, 'and my life is spared.'

Esau meets Jacob

Jacob looked up, and saw a great crowd drawing near. He knew that these people must be Esau and his four hundred men.

Then Jacob told the women and children who were with him to form groups, and for safety's sake he sent Rachel and Joseph right to the back; they were very precious to him, and he did not want them harmed.

Now Jacob himself went forward, and bowed low seven times.

Esau ran forward to meet him, and the two brothers fell into each other's arms, kissing one another and crying for joy. All their old quarrels were forgotten.

When Esau looked up and saw all the women and children who had come with Jacob, he asked his brother, 'Who are they?'

Jacob told him, and they came forward and bowed politely. The last to come were Rachel and Joseph, and of course Jacob told his brother who they were.

'What about those animals I saw on the way?' Esau asked him. 'Whose are they?'

'They are a present for you,' Jacob told him; but Esau shook his head.

'I have enough,' he said. 'Keep them for yourself.'

But Jacob begged him, 'Please take my present – we are so glad to see one another again. Take my blessing, too, because God has been very good to me, and I have enough.'

So, in the end, Esau took his present, and it was time to move on.

'The children are young,' Jacob told his brother, 'and the little lambs and other animals get tired. We must not drive them too hard. You go ahead, and we will follow gently, at a pace that suits the little ones. We shall find you at home.'

'Well, at least let me leave some of my men with you,' Esau suggested.

Jacob shook his head. 'There is no need,' he replied.

So Esau went on his way, whilst Jacob and his party followed more slowly.

Jacob's Sons

REUBEN is the eldest;
He has eleven brothers —
SIMEON and LEVI,
And, of course, nine others:
JUDAH, who is like a lion,
Very brave and strong;
ZEBULUN lives near the sea;
And to ISSACHAR belong
The burdens which strong backs can bear,
Although they heavy grow;
DAN is born to be a judge;
Whilst GAD can overthrow
His enemies; and ASHER has
The best of everything;
NAPTHALI speaks goodly words,
And wisdom he can bring;
JOSEPH is a fruit bough
That grows beside a well —
God made him strong and powerful,
The God of Israel;
BENJAMIN, the youngest,
Is a wolf out seeking prey,
Who shares what he has hunted
At the ending of the day.

Joseph's Dreams

Jacob and his followers settled down in the land of Canaan, and when Joseph was seventeen years old, he and his brothers used to take his father's flocks into the fields to graze.

Now Jacob loved Joseph best of all his sons, and he gave him a coat of many colours. It was a very special coat with long sleeves, like those given to important people, and his brothers were jealous of him.

One night Joseph had a dream, and he told it to his brothers.

'I dreamt we were binding sheaves in the field,' he said, 'and suddenly my sheaf stood upright, and all your sheaves bowed down to it.'

'Do you mean that you think you are going to rule over us?' his brothers asked scornfully. They hated him more than ever.

Joseph had another dream, and he told his brothers about that, too, saying,

'I dreamt that the sun, the moon and eleven stars were bowing down to me.'

He told his father about the dream, too.

'What is this dream?' Jacob said. 'Do you mean that you think that I and your brothers are actually going to bow down to you?'

They all laughed at him.

One day, the brothers were out feeding the flocks, and Jacob sent for Joseph.

'Go and see if your brothers and the flocks are all right,' he said, 'and then come back and tell me.'

The brothers had moved from one place to another, but a man told Joseph where they had gone, and he went after them.

His brothers saw him in the distance.

'Here comes the dreamer!' they said scornfully. 'Let's kill Joseph and throw him in a pit! Then we'll say that a wild beast caught him. We'll see what becomes of his dreams then!'

One of the brothers, Reuben, was kinder than the rest.

'Don't let's kill him,' he said. 'Let's just put him into this pit and leave him.'

Reuben hoped that, later, he might be able to rescue Joseph and send him back to his father.

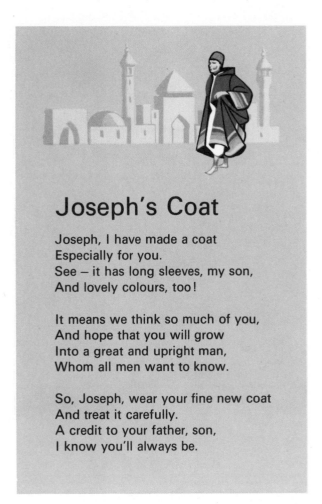

Joseph's Coat

Joseph, I have made a coat
Especially for you.
See – it has long sleeves, my son,
And lovely colours, too!

It means we think so much of you,
And hope that you will grow
Into a great and upright man,
Whom all men want to know.

So, Joseph, wear your fine new coat
And treat it carefully.
A credit to your father, son,
I know you'll always be.

Minding Sheep

Reuben, guard your father's flocks,
And keep them all from harm,
Carrying my little lambs
Within your sheltering arm.

Never let the prowling wolves
Give my sheep a fright,
And, Reuben, bring my precious flock
Safely home at night.

Joseph is taken to Egypt

When Joseph drew near to his brothers, they caught hold of him and took off the coat which his father had given him.

Then they put Joseph in the pit – a big hole in the ground – and left him there, while they sat down to have a meal.

Suddenly, they looked up and saw a band of men coming towards them, riding on camels. On the camels' backs were bundles of spices that were being taken to Egypt.

'Let's sell Joseph to those men,' suggested one of the brothers, whose name was Judah.

The others agreed; so they lifted Joseph out of the pit, and sold him to the passing travellers for twenty pieces of silver. Soon afterwards, the train of camels had disappeared, bearing Joseph away to Egypt.

Reuben – the brother who had wanted to save Joseph – was not with the others when this happened, and he was very sad when he came back, looked in the pit, and saw that Joseph was not there.

The brothers took Joseph's coat, dipped it in goat's blood and took it back to Jacob at home.

'We have found this,' they said. 'But we do not know if it is Joseph's.'

Jacob knew at once that it was the coat he had given his favourite son.

'It is my son's coat!' he cried. 'And surely some wild animal must have caught and killed him.'

Now Jacob was very sad; and although his family tried to comfort him, nothing could make up to him for the loss of Joseph, whom he had loved so dearly.

Joseph in Egypt

When they reached Egypt, Joseph was sold to Potiphar, who was a captain in Pharaoh's guard.

Joseph must have felt strange and lonely at first, so far from his home and his family, but he felt that God was with him, and he worked hard. His master was pleased with his young servant, and put him in charge of other men. As time went by, Joseph grew rich.

Then, one day, the captain's wife lied to her husband and told him that Joseph had done wrong. In fact, he had not done so, but the captain believed his wife and put Joseph in prison.

Soon after this, Pharaoh's butler and baker offended their master, and they were also put in prison with Joseph.

One morning, Joseph thought that they both looked very sad, and he asked them why.

'We dreamt strange dreams,' they said, 'and no one can tell us what they mean.'

'For that you need the help of God,' Joseph told them. 'But do tell me your dreams.'

So the butler said, 'In my dream I saw a vine with three branches. First it was as though it had buds, then the vine blossomed, and then there came fine grapes. I had Pharaoh's cup in my hand, and I pressed the grapes and filled the cup with wine from the grapes. Then I gave it to Pharaoh, the king.'

'I will tell you what your dream means,' Joseph said. 'The three branches are three days. Within three days, Pharaoh will take you back into his household, and you will give him a cup of wine, just as you have always done, because you are his butler. Think of me, when this happens, and ask Pharaoh to rescue me from prison, because I was stolen from my own land, and I have done no crime.'

Proverbs 6, 6–8
The Wise Ant

The ant is always very wise;
In summer she will store
Corn and seeds. When winter comes
She knows she'll need them more.
No one tells the busy ant
What she ought to do.
Lazy folk should watch her work,
And learn a lesson, too!

The Baker's Dream

When the baker saw how well Joseph had understood the meaning of the butler's dream, he too, asked for help.

'I was in my own dream, too,' he said. 'I had three white baskets on my head. In the top basket were all sorts of good things for Pharaoh to eat, but the birds ate them.'

'The three baskets are three days,' Joseph told him, 'and in three days' time Pharaoh will take your life.'

Two days went by, and the third day was Pharaoh's birthday. He gave a great party for his servants, and he let his butler out of prison and gave him his job back. Just as Joseph had prophesied, the butler filled Pharaoh's cup with wine. But the butler did not remember Joseph or ask his master to pardon him.

The baker's dream came true, too. He lost his life, just as Joseph had foretold.

Pharaoh's Dreams

Then Pharaoh himself had a dream. He dreamt that he was standing by a river, and seven fat, healthy cows came up out of the water and began to feed in the meadow.

Then seven other cows came up the river bank, but they were lean and hungry-looking animals. They stood beside the others, and it seemed to Pharaoh in his dream that the thin cows ate the fat ones.

It was such a strange dream, and at its end Pharaoh woke up.

But he went to sleep a second time, and dreamt about seven fat ears of corn on one stalk, and seven thin, withered ears on another. The seven withered ears seemed to eat up the seven fat ones, and again Pharaoh awoke. He began to wonder about his dreams, and what they could mean.

In the morning, he sent for all the wise men and magicians in Egypt and told them his dreams, but they only shook their heads; they could not tell if they had a meaning.

Then the butler went to his master.

'I remember, when you were angry and you put me in prison with the baker, that we both had strange dreams one night. There was a young man in prison with us, a Hebrew, servant to the captain of the guard, who explained the meaning of our dreams to us. What he said came true: I got my job back, and the baker lost his life.'

At once, Pharaoh gave orders that Joseph was to be brought before him.

When Joseph heard this, he changed his clothes and made himself ready to be brought before Pharaoh.

'I have had a dream,' Pharaoh told him, 'and they tell me that you will know the meaning of it.'

'I cannot tell you without the help of God,' Joseph said, 'but he can help you.'

So Pharaoh told Joseph his dream about the fat and lean cows, and his second dream about the good and the poor ears of corn.

'I told this to my magicians,' he said, 'but none of them knew what it meant.'

'The two dreams have the same meaning,' Joseph said. 'God is showing you what he is about to do. The seven fat cows and the seven plump ears of corn are seven good years; the seven thin cows and the poor corn are seven years of famine, when there will not be enough food in the land. Egypt is going to have seven years of plenty; but when they are over, seven very hard ones will follow.'

Then Joseph added, 'You should find a good, wise man and put him in charge of all the land. He should have men under him, so that they can gather up all the spare food during the good years and store it, and then there will be enough food to eat when the famine comes.'

And Pharaoh approved of Joseph's plan.

Joseph is made Ruler

After speaking with Joseph, Pharaoh began to look out for a wise and clever man who would arrange to store the food that would be needed in the years to come.

'Can we find such a man as this?' he asked his servants. 'He would need to have the Spirit of God in him.'

And then, suddenly, he realised that Joseph himself was the man he needed.

'There is nobody as wise as you,' he told him, 'so you shall be next to me in the land, and my people must do what you tell them. See, I have set you over all the land of Egypt.'

He took the ring from his own finger and put it on Joseph's. Then he gave him fine clothes, and placed a gold chain around his neck. Pharaoh also gave Joseph his second-best chariot to ride in, and all the people stood at the roadside to see him pass.

Everything happened just as Joseph had told Pharaoh that it would. For seven years the corn grew richly in the fields, and Joseph made the people store it in every city, to be used when the hard times came.

After seven years, a great famine started everywhere, and in many places there was not enough to eat. But there was bread for the Egyptians, because Joseph had told them to store their corn.

When the people became hungry, and cried to Pharaoh for bread, he told them to go to Joseph, who opened the store-houses and sold the corn to the Egyptians.

People in other lands began to hear about this, and many of them came to Egypt to buy corn from Joseph, because there was none in their own country.

The Brothers' Visit

When Jacob learnt that there was corn in Egypt, he said to his sons, 'Go to that land and buy corn for us to eat.'

Ten of Joseph's brothers set out, but Jacob kept one of them with him. His name was Benjamin, and Jacob felt that, if anything should happen to his other sons, he would at least have one left. He was still sad because he had lost Joseph.

There was famine in Canaan, where Jacob and his family lived, and many people went down to buy corn in Egypt. Joseph's brothers were among them.

Joseph was still governor over the land, and as it was he who sold the corn to those who came to buy, his brothers were brought before him. They bowed low before the governor, but of course they did not recognise him. Joseph knew them, but he pretended that they were strangers to him.

'Where do you come from?' he asked his ten brothers.

'From the land of Canaan, to buy food,' they answered.

Joseph remembered dreams that he had had about his brothers, and said, 'You are

spies, come to see how empty our fields are.'

'No, my lord,' they told him, 'we have come to buy food. We are all the sons of one man in Canaan; one brother, the youngest, stayed behind, and one is dead.'

'Well,' Joseph said, 'I say that you are spies; but, if you want to prove that you are not, send for your youngest brother, otherwise you will never leave this country. Let one of you go and fetch him, and the others will be imprisoned till he comes.'

He put them all under guard for three days. Then he said, 'If you are honest men, let one of your number be bound in prison. The rest, take corn for your hungry people, but bring your youngest brother to me – so will you prove that you are telling the truth, and will not die.'

Then the brothers began to remember Joseph, and to feel ashamed of what they had done to him.

'Because we behaved so badly then, this further sorrow has come, and we must risk the loss of another brother. We would not spare Joseph when he pleaded with us!'

'I told you,' said Reuben. 'But you refused to listen.'

The brothers did not realise that Joseph

46

understood what they were saying, for he had been pretending that he did not know their language, and had spoken to them through an interpreter.

Joseph felt so moved that he turned away to hide his tears. Then he went back, talked to his brothers, and bound the one called Simeon. He would keep him under guard until the others brought Benjamin.

Joseph told his servants to fill their sacks with corn, and, at the top of each sack, to put back the money which his brothers had paid. Then with food for the journey, they went on their way.

Inside the Sacks

Presently, the brothers stopped to feed their asses. One of them opened his sack of corn, and saw the money on top.

'Look!' he cried excitedly. 'My money has been given back!'

The brothers were puzzled: they could not think what this meant. They wondered whether it was a trick.

When they reached home, they told Jacob what had happened to them.

'The lord of the land spoke roughly to us and thought we were spies,' they said. And they told their father how they had been put in prison, and how the governor wanted them to take Benjamin to Egypt.

They all opened their sacks, and in every one of them there was money. The brothers felt afraid, because they did not know what it could mean.

Jacob, too, was troubled. 'I no longer have Joseph,' he said. 'Now I've lost Simeon, and you want Benjamin, too.'

'If we don't bring him back to you,' Reuben said, 'you may take the lives of my two sons.' Reuben felt it was safe to make such a bargain, for he was sure that he would being Benjamin home again.

But Jacob was firm – he would not let Benjamin go.

Then the famine grew worse, and in time they had eaten all the corn which the brothers had brought from Egypt.

'Go again,' said Jacob to his sons, 'and buy us a little more food.'

'We will, if you will let us take Benjamin,' Judah said. 'But the governor said that he would not see us again unless our brother came with us.'

'Why did you harm me by telling him that you had another brother?' Jacob wanted to know.

'The man asked us if we had another brother,' they said. 'How were we to know that he was going to ask us to bring him?'

'Send the lad with me,' Judah said. 'I will have him in my charge and, if I do not bring him back to you, may I for ever bear the blame. But if we do not take him, we shall all starve!'

So at last Jacob agreed. He told his sons to take what they had to give – fruit, honey, spices and nuts – and to carry double the amount of money.

'Take the money you found in your sacks,' he said. 'Perhaps it was put there by mistake. Take your brother, too, and go. May God be merciful to you when you meet this man, and may Simeon and Benjamin be brought home.'

Joseph and Benjamin

The brothers went to Egypt for the second time, taking Benjamin with them, and they all stood again before Joseph.

Joseph gave orders that a meal was to be prepared in his house, because he was going to take his brothers to his home to dine.

The brothers thought this was a trick to take away their asses and turn them into slaves; but, when they saw the head of Joseph's household standing at his door, they plucked up courage and told him about the money they had found in their sacks, and the gifts that they had brought.

'Do not be afraid,' the man said. 'God gave you treasure in your sacks.'

He brought Simeon to join them, and they were very glad to see one another again. Then the servant fetched water to wash their feet, and found food for their asses.

When Joseph came in, the brothers gave him their presents, and bowed before him.

Joseph's Plan

Soon after the brothers left, Joseph said to his steward, 'Go after those men, and when you catch up with them, say: "Why have you done wrong to those who have been kind to you? Is not this my master's cup from which he drinks? You have done wrong in taking it." '

The steward did as Joseph told him, and at once the brothers said, 'Why do you say that? We brought back the money we found in our sacks. Would we be likely to steal silver or gold from your master's house? If you find that any one of us has the cup, he shall die, and we will become your slaves.'

The steward answered, 'He who has the cup shall be my servant, and the rest of you shall go free.'

So each brother quickly took down his sack from the ass's back, and opened it. Joseph's steward searched all the sacks, beginning with the one carried by the eldest brother, and coming last of all to Benjamin.

He looked in Benjamin's sack – and there on the top lay Joseph's silver cup.

The brothers were dismayed. There was

'Are you well?' he asked. 'And how is your father – the old man you spoke about. Is he still alive?'

'Yes, and in good health,' they told him. How glad Joseph was to hear that news!

Then he caught sight of Benjamin. 'Is this your youngest brother, of whom you spoke to me? God be gracious to you, my son.'

Joseph was so moved at seeing Benjamin that he had to leave the room quickly, lest they should all see that he was crying for joy. But, presently, he washed his face and returned to them.

Joseph told the man in charge of his household to fill the brothers' sacks with corn, and once again to put their money on the top. But in Benjamin's sack they were to put Joseph's own silver cup, as well as his corn-money.

As soon as it was light next morning, the brothers loaded up their asses, and set out for home, with Simeon and Benjamin.

nothing they could do, except return to the city which they had just left so happily.

They came to Joseph's house, and bowed before him, wondering what was going to happen to them.

'What have you done?' Joseph asked them.

'What shall we say unto my lord?' said Judah sadly. 'How shall we clear ourselves? God has found out this wrong-doing, and we must become your slaves.'

'I will not ask that of you all,' Joseph told them. 'Only he who had my cup shall stay as my servant. The rest of you can go back to your father.'

Then Judah stepped forward, and began to plead with Joseph. He reminded him how he had told his brothers that they must bring Benjamin with them, when they came to Egypt a second time. 'But,' he said, 'our father has lost one son, and if he were to lose Benjamin as well, I am sure he would not want to go on living. I pray you, let the boy go back to our father, and keep me as a slave instead of my young brother.'

Joseph was very moved by Judah's words, and felt that he could not hide who he was any longer.

Sending everyone except his brothers out of the room, Joseph told them that he was the brother whom they had sold, and who had been carried away to Egypt so long ago.

'But do not be sorrowful, remembering what you did to me,' he said, 'because God has used me to save many lives. It was not really you who sent me to Egypt; it was God, who had work for me to do. Go back to our father, and tell him that his son Joseph wants him to come to Egypt. You shall all be near me, with your families and your animals, and I will look after you, even though there is famine in the land.'

He embraced his brothers and they wept for joy. Then they talked for a long time about everything that had happened, for there was so much to tell and hear.

Jacob goes to Egypt

Pharaoh was very pleased to hear about Joseph's brothers. 'Tell them to go back to Canaan,' he said, 'and fetch your father, and your brothers' families, and come back. They shall have the best land we can find, and we will see that they have plenty to eat. Let them take wagons with them, for their wives and children to ride in. Tell them not to worry about the things which they have to leave behind – we will see that they get all they need in Egypt.'

So Joseph gave his brothers wagons and food and clothes. To Benjamin he gave three hundred pieces of silver, and five changes of clothes. To his father he sent twenty asses, laden with corn and bread and meat, and all the good things of Egypt.

The brothers set out once more, and at last they reached their own home. Of course,

went on ahead to tell Joseph, who climbed into his chariot and went out to meet his father.

How happy they were to see one another again! 'I will go and tell Pharaoh that you are here,' Joseph said at last, 'and I will let him know that you are shepherds, and have brought your flocks and herds with you. When Pharaoh sends for you and asks you what your work is, tell him that you have looked after animals all your lives. Then he will let you stay where you are.'

Joseph took five of his brothers to see Pharaoh.

'What work do you do?' Pharaoh asked.

'We are shepherds,' they told him. 'We have come hoping to stay in your land, for there is nothing for our flocks to eat in our own country. Please let us all live in Goshen.'

Pharaoh told Joseph to settle his father and brothers in Goshen, and if any of them were specially good at their work, they were to have charge of Pharaoh's own animals.

Jacob wanted to hear of all their adventures. What a wonderful story they had to tell! At first, Jacob could not believe that his beloved son Joseph was still alive and well, and that now he was a great ruler in Egypt.

But when he saw the wagons which Joseph had sent, and all the presents, he said gladly, 'It is enough – Joseph is still alive! I will go and see him before I die.'

At last the great procession was ready. Jacob and the brothers' wives and children travelled in Joseph's wagons, and they took everything that could be packed on to their animals' backs. They said good-bye to the country which they now called their own, and set out on the long journey to a land that would be strange to them. But Joseph was there, and so they could begin a new life together.

When they reached Goshen, and were nearing the end of their journey, Reuben

Proverbs 30, 29–31

Four Things worth watching

See a lion, proud and strong;
See a greyhound race along.
See a billy-goat as he stands;
See a king rule all his lands.

Jacob's Blessing

Joseph brought Jacob to meet Pharaoh, and the old man blessed him.

As soon as he could, Joseph arranged for everyone who had come from Canaan to settle on good land; and, although there was still a famine, they had enough to eat, and settled down very happily.

Seventeen years went by, and then Jacob knew that his life was drawing to an end.

Joseph went to see him, as he lay in bed, and took with him his own two sons, Ephraim and Manasseh.

Jacob was nearly blind, and could not see their faces, but Joseph led the boys to their grandfather. Jacob stretched out his right hand and laid it on Ephraim's head, and his left hand he laid on Manasseh's head, and he blessed them. He blessed Joseph, too, and said, 'May God, before whom Abraham and Isaac walked – the God who fed me all my life long unto this day – bless these boys.'

Joseph noticed that Jacob had laid his right hand on Ephraim's head, and his left on Manasseh's. Manasseh was older, so Jacob should have laid his right hand on him.

Joseph tried to take Jacob's hand, as it rested on Ephraim's head, and lay it on the head of Manasseh.

'This is my elder son, father,' he said. 'Put your right hand on his head.'

But Jacob replied, 'I know that Manasseh is the elder. He shall be great, but his younger brother shall be greater.'

Afterwards, Jacob called all his sons to him and blessed them. He talked about what they had all done with their lives. Judah was strong and brave as a lion; Joseph was like a bough beside a well, that bore good fruit.

Then he said that, when he died, he wanted to be buried in the cave that Abraham had bought for Sarah: Isaac and Rebekah were there, too – he would rest among his own family.

Jacob did not live long after that, and his sons did as he asked; they took his body back to Canaan.

The Baby in the Bulrushes

Joseph lived to be a very old man, and when he died, a new king ruled in Egypt.

The families who had made the long journey from Canaan were known as 'the children of Israel', or Hebrews. And as the years passed, they grew strong.

The new Pharaoh was worried.

'The children of Israel are more and mightier than we are,' he said to his people. 'Come, let us deal wisely with them, before they become dangerous.'

So the Egyptians set the children of Israel hard tasks. They made them build wonderful cities for Pharaoh, and set over them strict taskmasters, who made their lives very hard.

Day after day the Israelites toiled, carrying bricks and making mortar, and always their taskmasters forced them on with harsh words and blows.

Pharaoh thought of a wicked plan to keep the Israelites from getting stronger. He gave orders to their nurses that all the baby boys who were born were to be killed. But the Israelite nurses saved the babies.

There was one Israelite and his wife who managed to keep their baby boy hidden from the Egyptians for three months. Then his mother had an idea. She made a cradle out of bulrushes stuck together with mud, and then she put her baby into his strange bed and carried him down to the reeds that grew by the river and left him there.

Then she asked his sister to stand a little way away and watch what happened.

Presently Pharaoh's daughter came down with her maids to wash in the river. They walked along the bank, and when the princess caught sight of the cradle, she sent one of her maids to fetch it.

The poor little baby was crying, and the princess felt very sorry for him as she watched him lying in his cradle.

'This is one of the Hebrews' children,' she said.

The baby's sister came timidly out of her hiding-place.

'Shall I go and find a Hebrew woman who would be a nurse for the baby?' she asked the princess.

'Yes, go!' said Pharaoh's daughter.

So the baby's sister ran home quickly to her mother, and brought her back to the princess.

'Take this child away and nurse him for me,' Pharaoh's daughter said, 'and I will pay you.'

How glad the baby's mother was when she heard that! Her own darling baby was being given back to her.

Happily she took her little son home with her, and watched over him as he grew sturdy and clever, until the day came when he was big enough to be handed over to the princess, and his mother knew that she would have to give him up.

Sadly she took him to the palace. Now he would be the son of Pharaoh's daughter, and she would bring him up herself. He would be someone special, not just a Hebrew baby in a simple home.

The Princess passed by

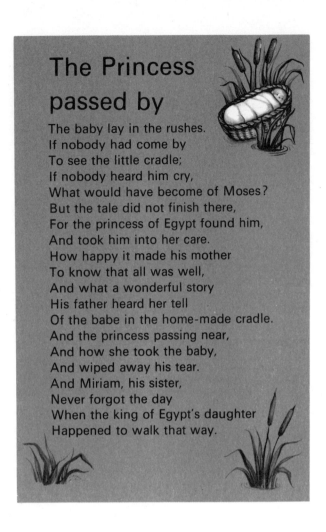

The baby lay in the rushes.
If nobody had come by
To see the little cradle;
If nobody heard him cry,
What would have become of Moses?
But the tale did not finish there,
For the princess of Egypt found him,
And took him into her care.
How happy it made his mother
To know that all was well,
And what a wonderful story
His father heard her tell
Of the babe in the home-made cradle.
And the princess passing near,
And how she took the baby,
And wiped away his tear.
And Miriam, his sister,
Never forgot the day
When the king of Egypt's daughter
Happened to walk that way.

The Burning Bush

The princess called the baby Moses, which means 'drawn out of the water'. He grew up in the palace, and the princess treated him as though he were her own son.

When Moses was a young man, he went one day and saw how the Egyptian task-masters were treating the Hebrews as they worked hard to build Pharaoh's cities, and he saw an Egyptian strike one of the Hebrews.

When Moses saw that no one was watching, he slew the Egyptian and buried him in the sand.

When he went out next day, he saw two Hebrews quarrelling.

'Why are you striking your fellow countryman?' Moses asked the man who seemed to be to blame.

'Who made you a prince and ruler over us?' the man asked rudely. 'Are you going to kill me, as you killed the Egyptian?'

Moses was frightened, because he realised that his secret was known after all.

When Pharaoh heard about it he was angry, and wanted to kill Moses, but Moses ran away to hide himself in the land of Midian.

He sat down by a well. Now the priest of Midian had seven daughters, and while Moses was resting there, they came to the well to draw water.

Some rough shepherds came up and tried to drive the girls away, but Moses went to their rescue, and helped them to fill their water pots, and the sheep troughs.

When the sisters got home, their father asked, 'How is it that you are early today?'

'An Egyptian saved us from some rude shepherds,' they told him, 'and he drew water for us and gave some to our flock.'

'Well, where is he?' asked their father.

'Why have you left him? Call him, that he may eat bread with us.'

So Moses joined the family meal, and in the end he stayed with them. He married one of the sisters, whose name was Zipporah, and they had a little son.

Moses looked after the flocks of Jethro, his father-in-law, and one day he led them to feed on a mountainside.

While he was there, the angel of the Lord appeared to Moses from the middle of a burning bush. The flames leapt up, but the bush was not burnt, and Moses said to himself, 'I will turn aside and see this. Why is the bush not burnt?'

Then God's voice called to him out of the burning bush, 'Moses! Moses!'

And he said, 'Here am I.'

'Do not draw near,' said the voice. 'But take off your shoes, for the place where you are standing is holy ground. I am the God of your father, the God of Abraham, the God of Isaac and the God of Jacob.'

And Moses hid his face, for he was afraid to look upon God.

God's Promise to Moses

God went on speaking to Moses from the burning bush.

'I have seen the sad things that have happened to my people in Egypt, and I have heard them crying. I have come to deliver them out of the hand of the Egyptians, and to bring them out of that land into another large land – a good place flowing with milk and honey. It is the country of the Canaanites and other tribes.

'Come now, and I will send you to Pharaoh, that you may bring forth my people, the children of Israel, out of Egypt. Certainly I will be with you, and this shall be a sign to you that I have sent you: when you have brought the people out of Egypt, you shall serve God on this mountain.'

Moses said, 'Behold, when I come to the children of Israel, and say to them, "The God of your fathers has sent me to you," and they say to me, "What is his name?" what shall I say to them?'

God said, 'I AM THAT I AM. Tell the children of Israel, "I AM has sent me to you. The Lord God of your fathers, the God of Abraham, the God of Isaac and

the God of Jacob has sent me to you."
This is my name for ever. Go now, and
gather the chief men of Israel together
and tell them that God appeared to you and
told you to do this, and they will listen to
you. You will go to the king of Egypt and
say to him: "Let us go, we beg of you, three
days journey into the wilderness, that we
may sacrifice to the Lord our God." I am
sure that the king of Egypt will not let you
go, but I will stretch out my hand, and
Egypt will suffer many things. After that, he
will let you go. I will see to it that the
Egyptians look on the children of Israel
with favour, and when you go, you will not
go empty-handed. Every woman shall
borrow jewels and clothes from her neighbour, and you will take from the Egyptians
to give good things to your own sons and
daughters.'

Moses was troubled. 'They won't believe
me,' he said.

'What is that in your hand?' God asked.

'A rod,' said Moses.

'Throw it on the ground,' God told him.

Moses did so, and it became a serpent.
Moses started back at the sight of it.

'Pick it up by its tail,' God said.

Rather timidly Moses did so, and it
became a rod again.

It was a sign to him that God could do
wonderful things, and he must trust him.

But Moses still did not feel equal to this
great task.

'O my Lord,' he said, 'I am not very good
at talking to people.'

'Who made man's mouth?' God asked
him. 'Who made the dumb people and the
deaf, the seeing and the blind? Was it not I,
the Lord? Now go, and I will watch over
your mouth, and give you the words to say.'

Then, when Moses still seemed doubtful,
God said, 'Your brother Aaron can speak
well. He is coming to meet you, and he shall
be your spokesman. Take this rod with you;
with it you shall do wonderful things.'

'Let My People Go'

Moses went to Jethro, his father-in-law,
and when he asked him to let him go back
to Egypt, Jethro said, 'Go in peace.'

So Moses took his wife and his sons and
returned to Egypt with his rod in his hand.
All his enemies were now dead, and a new
Pharaoh sat on the throne.

God told Aaron that he should go out and
meet his brother Moses, and Moses told
Aaron all the wonderful things that had
happened.

They went to the children of Israel and
gathered them all together. Then Aaron
told them what God had said to Moses, and
they were very glad, and gave thanks to God
who would deliver them.

Moses and Aaron went to see the new
Pharaoh, and said, 'The Lord God of
Israel says, "Let my people go, that they
may hold a feast for me in the wilderness."'

life even harder for the children of Israel.

But God told him that all would be well, and that Moses should call him JEHOVAH.

Yet still Pharaoh would not listen to Moses, and he would not let the people go.

The Plagues

'Pharaoh's heart is hardened,' the Lord said to Moses, 'and he will not let the people go. Go and stand by the river in the morning, until Pharaoh comes. Then tell him that because he would not let your people go, you will strike the water with your rod and it will turn red. And tell Aaron to do the same, wherever he finds water.

Moses and Aaron did as they were told, and the water in Egypt was changed so that none could drink it and fish could not live in it. For a week, the Egyptians had to dig for water when they wanted it.

Then God told Moses to go to Pharaoh and say, 'Let God's people go, that they may serve him. If you refuse, there will be a

'Who is the Lord?' asked Pharaoh scornfully, 'that I should obey his voice, to let Israel go?'

They answered, 'Let us go, we beg you, a three days' journey into the desert, and sacrifice unto the Lord our God.'

'Moses and Aaron, why do you stop the people from working?' Pharaoh demanded. 'Go and take up your burdens!'

He made the task of the children of Israel even harder, by telling the taskmasters that they should no longer give the Israelites straw with which the bricks were made: they must go out and find the straw for themselves.

The children of Israel were troubled. They could not find the straw to make the bricks, and they were beaten if the bricks were not made, and they said this was the fault of Moses and Aaron.

Moses could not see that God was helping him. Pharaoh only seemed to have made

plague of frogs in Egypt.' If Pharaoh refused, Aaron was to stretch out his rod once more.

Pharaoh did refuse, and again Aaron held out his rod over all the rivers and ponds and streams. Out came thousands of frogs, hopping everywhere: into the houses, and then into the ovens and the beds, and the troughs where bread was made.

Pharaoh sent for Moses and Aaron.

'Ask the Lord to take the frogs away,' he said, 'and I will let the people go.'

So Moses asked God to take the frogs away, and he did. But when they had gone Pharaoh still would not let the people go. After that there was a plague of horrible insects, and then a plague of flies, but although Pharaoh pretended that he would let the children of Israel go if the plague stopped, he did nothing of the kind.

After the flies, the animals all fell sick. Next the Egyptians themselves suffered from painful sores. Then there were hailstorms and thunder, and later a plague of locusts – small winged creatures that came down in clouds and ate up all the grass and the fruit.

Pharaoh kept on pretending he was going to let the children of Israel go if only the plagues were taken away, but every time God was merciful and brought an end to Egypt's troubles, he would not.

After the locusts, God sent a great darkness over the land that lasted for three days, and frightened the Egyptians.

Pharaoh called Moses to him, and said, 'Go, serve the Lord. Only leave your cattle behind, as a pledge that you will come back.'

'You must give us animals for sacrifice,' Moses told him. 'We shall have to take our beasts with us.'

But Pharaoh would not agree to this.

At last God told Moses, 'Just one more plague will fall upon Pharaoh and then he will indeed let you all go. About midnight, all the eldest sons in the land of Egypt will die, and Pharaoh's own son will be among them. The children of Israel will come to no harm, for they are my people.'

The Passover

God reminded Moses that the children of Israel were to borrow jewels from the Egyptians. Then they were to take a lamb for every home, or little group, and roast and eat it with herbs and flat pieces of bread. Before they ate it on a certain evening, they were to mark the door posts and the beams above their doors with the lamb's blood. It was to show that an Israelite lived there, and when trouble came to the Egyptians, these houses would be spared.

The children of Israel were to get ready for a journey, and they were to eat the lamb quickly, with their shoes on, dressed for travelling, and with their staves in their hands. This very special event was called 'the Lord's Passover'.

Moses told the children of Israel what God had commanded, and they all went away to get everything ready.

At midnight on the special day, the eldest son died in every Egyptian family, and Pharaoh's own son was among them.

Then Pharaoh said to Moses and Aaron, 'Rise up and go, you and all the children of Israel. Go and serve the Lord, as you have said. Take your flocks and herds and be gone; but bless me before you go.'

All the Egyptians were eager to see the Israelites go, before any more troubles fell on them.

So the children of Israel quickly gathered up the bread they were making, not stopping to put yeast in it. They took the Egyptians' jewels and garments which God had told them to borrow, and set off.

They were a very big company – about six hundred thousand men on foot, as well as children. They had all their flocks and herds with them, and they baked their bread without yeast as they went.

The night that God brought the children of Israel out of Egypt was a very special night; it is always remembered.

Crossing the Red Sea

God led his people Israel
Across the wilderness
That they might know he cared for them,
And would their journey bless.
He went before them in a cloud
That they could see by day;
At night, a pillar of bright fire
Was there to lead the way.
When Pharaoh followed, people cried,
'Will troubles never cease?'
But Moses said, 'God fights for us,
And you should hold your peace.'
God told him to stretch out the rod
He carried in his hand.
The Red Sea parted, and they crossed
In safety to dry land.
But when Egyptians would have crossed,
No dry land there was found.
Pharaoh's men were overcome,
And all of them were drowned.
Then the people feared the Lord,
And Moses sang a song.
He knew that all things would be well
When men to God belong.

The Song of Moses

When the children of Israel had crossed the Red Sea, Moses sang a song of praise to God who had delivered them.

I will sing unto the Lord,
Who triumphed gloriously.
The horse and rider, overthrown,
Were cast into the sea.

The Lord, he is my strength and song
And he is my salvation.
He is my God, and I will make
For him a habitation.

He is my father's God, and I
Will sing his praise alone.
The Red Sea drowned all Pharaoh's men —
Each sank there like a stone.

And who is like to thee, O Lord,
Who hast stretched out thine arm
And brought thy fold to safety here,
And kept them from all harm.

In the Wilderness

So Moses led the children of Israel into the wilderness, but soon they grew thirsty. At last, after three days, they caught sight of some water, and ran joyfully towards it. But the water was too bitter to drink.

Moses prayed to God to help them, and the Lord showed him a tree. Moses threw a branch into the water which at once became pure and sweet. Everybody drank eagerly.

They went on, but the journey was hard, and they began to grow hungry, for they had finished the food they took with them. Some of the people even began to murmur: 'In Egypt we had food, at least! Now we shall all starve to death.'

God told Moses that the people should have meat in the evening, and bread in the morning, and so they would know that he was the Lord God.

At evening time, hundreds of small birds called quails appeared. They were all over the camp. They were good to eat, and the hungry Israelites had a wonderful meal.

The next morning, the ground was covered with small round pieces of something that tasted like wafers made with honey. It was called manna.

On the sixth day, Moses said, 'Gather up enough for two days, because tomorrow is the sabbath, when we shall all rest.'

Some of the people disobeyed and went out to look for manna on the sabbath, but they did not find any.

Another time, when the children of Israel were very thirsty, Moses struck a rock with his staff, and water gushed out.

In a Thirsty Land

The desert was a barren, hot, dry land,
And as the Hebrews marched through the
waterless sand,
They longed for melons and the fruits which
had grown
On the banks of the Nile, from whence they
had flown.

The Ten Commandments

The children of Israel had been in the wilderness for three months. Some of them must have wondered if they were ever going to reach the end of their journey.

At last they saw in front of them a great mountain. It was Mount Sinai, and all the Israelites pitched their tents at the foot of it and rested for a while.

God called Moses to climb the mountain, and he told Moses that if the children of Israel would keep his commandments, they would be his chosen people.

In three days time, God told Moses, he would come to meet his people, although a cloud would hide him from their sight. They were to get ready to meet him, but they were not to go on to the mountain.

The third day came, and the people waited eagerly at the foot of Mount Sinai, which was covered with a thick cloud.

Moses himself climbed up the mountain, and there God gave him his ten commandments.

'I am the Lord, your God,' he said, 'who has brought you out of the land of Egypt, and you shall have no other gods before me.'

They were not to worship carved images.

They were not to use God's name lightly.

They must keep the sabbath day holy, and not do any work on it.

They must honour their parents.

They must not kill.

They must not take away another's husband or wife.

They must not steal.

They must not say what is untrue about their neighbours.

Last, they were not to envy their neighbour for his house, or anything else that was his – his ox or his ass, his wife or his servant.

The people waited there, with their eyes fixed on the mountain. All they saw was smoke coming from the mountain. All they heard was thunder, and the noise of the trumpet; but they knew their leader was there, talking with God.

The commandments were written on tablets of stone, which Moses showed to the people, when he came down from the mountain.

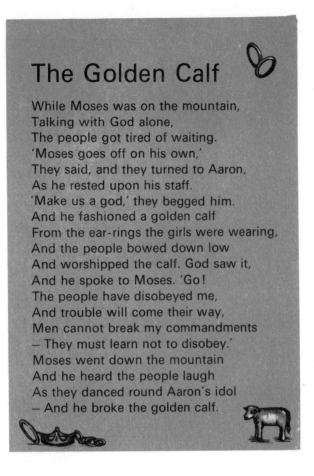

The Golden Calf

While Moses was on the mountain,
Talking with God alone,
The people got tired of waiting.
'Moses goes off on his own,'
They said, and they turned to Aaron,
As he rested upon his staff.
'Make us a god,' they begged him.
And he fashioned a golden calf
From the ear-rings the girls were wearing,
And the people bowed down low
And worshipped the calf. God saw it,
And he spoke to Moses. 'Go!
The people have disobeyed me,
And trouble will come their way,
Men cannot break my commandments
— They must learn not to disobey.'
Moses went down the mountain
And he heard the people laugh
As they danced round Aaron's idol
— And he broke the golden calf.

Moses covers his Face

When Moses came down the mountain and saw his people dancing round the golden calf which his brother Aaron had made, he was so angry that he broke the tablets on which God's commandments were carved.

God told Moses that the next morning he was to climb to the top of the mountain to speak with him, and then God would give him the commandments afresh on the new stones. Moses was to go alone.

So in the morning Moses climbed the mountain, taking two stone tablets which he had made ready. A cloud surrounded him on the mountain, and God spoke to him out of the cloud.

Moses stayed there for forty days, and he wrote out the commandments again on new tablets of stone.

When at last he came down to his people again, carrying the commandments with him, he did not know that a new light shone from his face, reflecting the glory of God, in whose presence he had been.

But Aaron and all the others saw it as they gathered round their leader, and they were afraid to come near him.

When Moses realised what had happened, he covered his face while he was talking to the people. He took off the veil he wore whenever he went to talk with God, and put it on again afterwards. His new, dazzling radiance was a secret between the Lord and his servant Moses, and other people were not meant to share it.

Making the Tabernacle

Out in the wilderness there was no temple in which the people could worship, but God told Moses to make a tent or tabernacle that they could carry with them on their wanderings.

So they made a tabernacle. It was a long, flat-topped tent made of tapestry, with three covers, and a frame of wood. The tabernacle was in two parts divided by a curtain. One of them was called the Holy Place, and the other was called the Holy of Holies. Here they put the Ark, which was a wooden chest covered with gold. Inside was a copy of the Law which Moses had been given. The Ark, they believed, was really God's dwelling-place.

There was to be a golden lampstand with seven branches, and altar for burnt offerings, and a table for special bread called 'shewbread'. Aaron was high priest, and Moses lighted the lamps before the Lord, and burnt sweet incense on a golden altar. He also laid sacrifices on the altar, for burnt offerings.

He set a basin between the tent of the congregation and the altar, and Moses and Aaron and their sons washed their hands and feet because they were going into a holy place.

So the people worshipped God, and their tabernacle was full of the glory of God.

The Spies go out

Moses sent out men as spies
To view their promised land.
They were to see what it was like,
And if the wandering band
Would find themselves with friendly folk.
So much they had to know —
Did they dwell in towns or tents?
And what crops could they grow?
Were they strong or were they weak?
Many — or only a few?
The spies were told to bring back fruit,
And this they swore to do.
They came back after forty days.
'A goodly land,' said they,
'Flowing with milk, and honey, too.
But as we made our way,
We saw the Canaanites were strong.
Their cities have stout walls.'
'Fear not,' said Moses, 'for our God
To us, his people, calls.'

Aaron's Rod

Moses divided the children of Israel into twelve tribes – one for each of Jacob's sons. At the head of each tribe was a leader.

One day, God told Moses, 'Take a rod from each tribe, and write the leaders' names on them. Write Aaron's name on the rod of Levi. Lay them all in the tabernacle, where I will meet with you. And it shall come to pass, that the man's rod whom I shall choose shall blossom; and I will make the children of Israel stop murmuring against you.'

Moses knew that his followers had indeed been doing this, for they sometimes felt discontented and disheartened.

He told the twelve leaders to give him a rod each, and Aaron's rod was among them.

Moses took them into the tabernacle and laid them there before the Lord.

In the morning he went back to see what had happened. The rod of Aaron, for the house of Levi, was no longer just a stick – it had buds and flowers and almonds on it,

just as though it were still growing on the tree.

Moses brought out all the rods and showed them to the waiting people.

Then the Lord said to Moses, 'Bring Aaron's rod back into the tabernacle, and let it be kept there to remind the rebels of their murmurings against me. Stop their grumbling, and they will not be harmed.'

Balaam's Ass

When at last the children of Israel drew near the land of Moab, the king of that country, whose name was Balak, became afraid of the reports of this crowd of strangers about to enter his kingdom. He decided to ask a wise man, Balaam, to say that evil would fall on the travellers. Men from Moab took some money to pay him, and set out to ask him to do as the king wanted.

Balaam asked God what he should do, and God told him that he should do nothing to harm the children of Israel. The messengers had to go back to King Balak, and tell him that Balaam would not come, nor would he say what the king asked.

The king would not give in. He sent bigger presents of money to Balaam.

But Balaam's answer was, 'I can only do what God wants. A whole house of gold and silver would not tempt me to disobey God.'

But the next morning, he decided he would set out with the messengers from Moab.

He was travelling along the road on the back of an ass, when suddenly the ass turned aside, refusing to follow the way to Moab.

Balaam tried to urge the animal out of the field into which she had trotted, but she refused to go back to the road, so he struck her with the stick he carried. He did not know that the ass had seen an angel with a flaming sword who stopped her.

The angel then stood in a narrow path between two walls, and when the ass saw him, she pushed against the wall and Balaam hurt his foot. So he struck his ass again.

The angel moved to a place which was so narrow that the animal could not move.

When the ass saw the angel she fell in the narrow path, and because Balaam could not see the angel, he hit his ass again, thinking she was just being stubborn.

Then the ass was given power to speak.

'What have I done to you,' said the ass, 'that you have hit me three times?'

'It was because you were mocking me,' Balaam said angrily. 'If I had a sword I would kill you.'

'Am I not your ass,' asked the animal, 'on whom you have ridden, ever since I belonged to you? Did I ever harm you?'

'No, you did not,' Balaam admitted.

Then the Lord enabled Balaam too to see the angel standing in the way, with his drawn sword in his hand. Balaam fell to the ground before him.

'Why have you beaten your ass three times?' the angel asked. 'I wanted to stop you taking that road, and the ass saw me, and turned from me three times. Otherwise you would have died. She saved your life.'

Balaam said how sorry he was. The angel told him to go with the men from Moab, but only to say what he was told to.

Of course Balaam told King Balak that he could not harm the children of Israel.

Rahab and the Spies

Moses died before he could enter the promised land, but he saw it in the distance, and knew that the children of Israel had not much farther to go.

Their new leader was Joshua, and God promised to be with him as he was with Moses. Joshua must be strong, and very brave, God told him.

The Israelites came to the River Jordan, and knew that in three days' time they would cross it, and enter into the land they had come so far to find.

Joshua wanted to know what the country was like, so he sent two spies to Jericho.

The spies did as Joshua told them, and when they reached Jericho, they stayed in the house of a woman whose name was Rahab.

The king of Jericho heard they had come.

'Men came here tonight,' he was told.

'They came from the children of Israel, and they want to spy out the land.'

The king told Rahab to bring out the men who were staying with her, but she told Joshua's men to go up to the flat roof of her house and hide under some flax that she had laid there to dry in the sun.

Then she sent a message to the king.

'The men were here,' she said, 'but I did not learn where they came from. They went out, when it was dark, and I don't know where they were going. Go after them quickly, and you will catch them up.'

The king's men hurried off to the Jordan, where they thought they would find the spies, and the city gate was shut behind them.

When they were safely out of the way, Rahab climbed the stairs to the roof where the men were hiding.

'I know the Lord has given you the land,' she said, 'and that we are all afraid of you.

We have heard how the Lord dried up the water of the Red Sea for you, when you came out of Egypt, and how you overcame your enemies by the way. I pray you, because I have been good to you, be good to my father's house in return, and give me a sign that you will keep us all alive.'

'Let it be our lives for yours,' said the men. 'Keep quiet about us, and when the Lord has given us the land, we will deal kindly with you.'

Rahab's house was built on the city wall, and she let them out of a window with a rope.

'Go to the mountains and hide there for three days,' she whispered, 'until the men who have gone after you have returned. Then you can go on your way.'

'When we come into your land,' the spies said, 'put this scarlet thread in your window, and gather all your family together in your house. They shall be safe as long as they stay indoors.'

Joshua takes Jericho

Joshua led his people to Jericho, and they stood gazing up at the city walls. The gates were shut. How were they going to get inside, when the men who lived there were all ready to defend their town?

Then God gave Joshua his orders.

'March round the city once a day for six days,' he said. 'Your men of war will be there, and right in the front will be seven priests blowing trumpets made of rams' horns; and behind them, will come the Ark.

'On the seventh day, you will march round Jericho seven times, and then the priests are to blow their trumpets.

'When the people hear the trumpets, they are to shout loudly, and the walls will tumble down.'

So Joshua told the priests to take up the Ark, and bring their trumpets. Armed men walked in front and behind, and all the people followed them.

Crossing the Jordan

Joshua came to Jordan.
The river overflowed —
It was the time of harvest.
The priests took up their load.

It was the Ark they carried —
The sign that God was here.
The people followed after,
But did not draw too near.

The priests' feet touched the water;
It parted, and they trod
On dry land, and the people
Knew that they walked with God.

When they had crossed the Jordan,
And reached the farther shore,
The path they took was covered;
The river flowed once more.

'You mustn't shout or speak until I tell you to,' Joshua told them.

For six days, they all walked round the city once. The people inside the walls peered out of the windows, wondering what was happening, and feeling rather frightened.

On the seventh day, Joshua got up early, and the procession set out once more. This time it went round the city seven times, and then, when the priests blew their trumpets, Joshua cried to the people, 'Shout, for the Lord has given you the city!'

The people shouted, the trumpets rang out, and the walls fell down flat.

The children of Israel went in and captured Jericho. Rahab and her family were not harmed. And the Lord was with Joshua, so that his fame spread throughout all the country.

The People who Pretended

Not very far from Jericho was another city, Gibeon, and when the people who lived there heard of Joshua, they were afraid.

They sent messengers to him, but they dressed them up in ragged clothes and put worn shoes on their feet. They gave them stale bread to take with them.

These things were done to make it seem that their home was very far away, and they had come on a very long journey.

The messengers had old sacks on their asses, and old, torn wine skins. In their ragged clothes they looked a wretched group of men, as they limped into Joshua's presence in their broken, shabby shoes.

'We have come from a country far away,' they told him, 'so we want you to make a pact with us. When we left home we took bread hot from the oven, but we have come such a long way that it has gone mouldy. These bottles of wine were new when we set out, but look at them now, and at our clothes, which are ragged. We come because we have heard of the Lord your God, and all that he has done. We are your servants.'

Joshua made them a promise that there should be peace between them, and told them that they would not be killed.

But three days later, Joshua learnt that the men had tricked him. They did not live far away, but were his neighbours. Their cities were quite close.

Joshua's men went to Gibeon and the towns near by, but they did the people no harm, because they had given their promise.

'We have given our word,' the children of Israel said, 'and so we may not touch them. We will let them live, but we will make them saw wood and draw water for us all.'

The Day the Sun stood still

Joshua said to the sun, 'Stand still!'
And he said the same to the moon.
'Until I have beaten my enemies;
May victory come soon.'

The sun stayed still, and the moon stayed still,
And neither climbed the sky
Till Joshua's men were conquerors,
And their enemies turned to fly.

The Call of Gideon

After Joshua died, many of the children of Israel turned away from God.

They fought many battles, and were often conquered by their enemies, and life was hard for them. The Lord appointed judges to rule over them, and at times the judges helped them but still many of the people turned away from God.

Among the enemies were the Midianites, who ruled them for seven years. The children of Israel were driven into the mountains, where they had to make their homes in dens and caves.

When they had sown their corn, the

Midianites came up in great numbers and destroyed all the crops and livestock of the Israelites, so that they cried to the Lord for help.

There was a young man named Gideon, who threshed wheat near a wine-press. He was going to hide the wheat from the Midianites.

There was an oak tree near by, and Gideon looked up from his task, and saw an angel of the Lord sitting under a tree.

'The Lord is with you, you mighty man of valour,' the angel said.

Gideon answered, in amazement, 'If the Lord is with us, why has all this trouble fallen on us?'

'Go in your strength,' the angel said to Gideon, 'and you shall save Israel. Has the Lord not sent you?'

Gideon answered humbly, 'How could I save Israel? My family is poor, and I am the least important person in my father's house.'

The angel told Gideon, 'The Lord will be with you, and you shall conquer the Midianites.'

'Then if I have favour in his sight,' Gideon said, 'give me a sign that you have talked with me. Don't go away till I have

gone to fetch a present for you and brought it back again to set before you.'

'I will wait till you come back,' said the angel, who had spoken for the Lord.

Gideon hurried home and made ready a kid and some cakes. He put the meat and cakes in a basket and the broth in a pot, and brought them out to give to the angel as he waited under the oak tree.

'Take the meat and the cakes,' the angel told him, 'and lay them on this rock, and pour out the broth.'

Gideon did as he was told.

Then the angel of the Lord held out the staff he was carrying and touched the meat and the cakes, and fire rose out of the rock and burnt them up.

The angel disappeared from sight, and then Gideon knew that this was a sign from God.

He built an altar to the Lord, and waited to see what he should do next.

Gideon and the Fleece

The Midianites camped in the valley,
And Gideon watched them there.
Then he blew his trumpet loudly,
And to God he did declare,
'You said you would save all Israel,
And by my hand alone.
Now grant me a certain sign, Lord,
By which this may be known.
I will spread out the coat of a sheep here,
And if there is morning dew
On the coat, but the earth is dry still,
I will believe it true.'
He rose up early next morning;
The fleece was soaking wet.
But Gideon was not certain.
He said, 'Grant one sign yet.
If the fleece is dry tomorrow
And the ground is wet with dew,
Then I will hold for certain
That what you have said is true.'
God gave him his sign in the morning
And Gideon knew full well
That the strength of God was upon him,
When he fought for Israel.

Gideon chooses his Men

Gideon rose up early, and all his men with him, and camped by a well. The hosts of Midian were in a valley under a hill.

The Lord said to Gideon, 'You have too many men with you. I do not want Israel to feel that they win because they are so strong. Go and tell the people that if any of them are afraid, they may go home again.'

Gideon did as God told him, and twenty-two thousand people went home. But there were ten thousand people left, and again God said it was too many.

'Bring them down to the water,' he told Gideon, 'and I will tell you who shall go with you, and who shall not.'

Gideon took his men to the water, and God said, 'Put into one group all those who lap the water up in their hands to drink, and put all those who go down on their knees into another group.'

Three hundred men lapped the water, and the rest went down on their knees to drink.

'By the three hundred men who lapped I will save you,' God said. 'Tell the others to go home.'

The men who took water from their hands would be able to keep watch for the enemy, but those who knelt down could not see what was happening.

That night, Gideon crept with his servant to the edge of the Midianite camp, and saw how great their numbers were. They seemed like a cloud of grasshoppers, and their camels were without number, like the grains of sand on the sea shore.

One man had a dream, and he told it to his companion. 'I dreamt that a cake of barley tumbled into the host of Midian,' he said. 'It fell in a tent and overturned it.'

'This means that Gideon is coming to conquer the Midianites,' the other man said.

Pitchers and Trumpets

When Gideon heard about the dream, and what it meant, he gave thanks to God, and then went back to the Israelites.

'Get up,' he said, 'for the Lord has delivered the host of Midian into your hand!'

He divided the three hundred men into three groups, and to every man he gave a trumpet, an empty jar, and a lamp to put inside it.

'Watch me,' he said. 'When we come near the camp, I shall blow my trumpet. You must do the same, and you must cry, "The sword of the Lord and of Gideon."'

So Gideon, and the three hundred men who were with him, crept through the darkness to the camp of the Midianites.

Suddenly they blew their trumpets and broke their jars, and all their comrades did the same, shouting:

'The sword of the Lord and of Gideon!'

The Midianites heard the noise and saw the lights, and they woke up and rushed out of their tents, startled and afraid.

They fled from their camp, with Gideon's men after them. It was a great victory for a small band of Israelites against Midianites.

The Story of the Trees

When Gideon's life-work was done, his son Abimelech took his place. Gideon had another son called Jotham.

When Jotham heard that Abimelech had been chosen, he told the people this story:
'Once on a time the trees all met
To choose themselves a king.
They said to the olive, "We choose you,
So govern everything."
But the olive said, "Should I leave my work
Of making oil for men?
No, I cannot come and be your king."
So they asked the fig tree then.
"Can I leave my sweetness?" asked the fig.
Then next they asked the vine,
Who said, "Can I turn aside to rule?
I am busy making wine."
At last they turned to the bramble,
Who didn't belong to these,
And the bramble said, "If you make me king,
Then trust me, if you please,
Or fire may come from the bramble,
And burn up the cedar trees."'

Samson's Riddle

Samson was an Israelite. He was very strong and brave, and God blessed him.

One day, when Samson was walking in some vineyards, a young lion sprang at him. Samson had no spear or sword with him, but he killed the lion with his own hands. Afterwards, he did not tell his mother and father what he had done.

Some time later, Samson saw that a swarm of bees had made their nest in the body of the lion he had killed. He took some honeycomb to eat, and carried some home for his parents, but he did not tell them where he had found it.

Samson was soon going to be married. He gave a wedding feast, and invited thirty young men from his wife's country. He said to his guests, 'I will tell you a riddle. If you can guess the answer in a week, I will give you thirty sheets and thirty sets of new clothes; but if not, then you must give those things to me.'

'Well, go on – tell us your riddle,' said the guests.

Thinking of the incident with the lion, Samson said, 'Out of the eater came food, and out of the strong came sweetness.'

The young men who had been at the party tried for three whole days to find an answer to Samson's riddle, but they could not.

On the fourth day the young men went secretly to Samson's bride.

'Coax your husband to tell us the answer to his riddle,' they said, 'or we'll set you and your father's house on fire.'

She went to Samson, and began to cry.

'You don't really love me,' she said. 'You

have told a riddle to my people, but you haven't told me what the answer is.'

'I haven't told my father and mother,' Samson said, 'so why should I tell you?'

She kept on crying, until, on the seventh day, Samson gave in and told her. Then she went to the men and told them.

Just before the sun went down on the seventh day, the young men said to Samson, 'What is sweeter than honey? And what is stronger than a lion?'

It was the answer to the riddle, but Samson knew that they had not found it out for themselves.

He went down into their country and killed thirty men and took away what they owned. He gave the clothes to the men who had solved the riddle, but he was very angry about the way they had found out the answer.

Samson was Strong

Samson was so very strong.
When his enemies found him,
They took him as their prisoner,
And with new cords they bound him.
But Samson heaved his mighty arms
And snapped the cords in two.
Then, with the jawbone of an ass,
A thousand men he slew.
He wrenched out doorposts with his hands,
And took the city gate
Upon his back; he carried it
As though it had no weight.

Samson's Secret

Samson's enemies wanted to find out why he was so strong. He must have some special power, they thought, and perhaps they could take it away from him.

Samson's wife was dead, and now he loved a woman called Delilah.

The Philistines, who were the Israelites' enemies, said to her, 'See if you can find out why he is so strong, and how we can make him our prisoner and bind him, and we will give you eleven hundred pieces of silver.'

Delilah was tempted by so much money, so she went to Samson and asked him what they wanted to know.

'If they bind me with seven green willow twigs that have never been dried,' Samson said, 'then I shall be as weak as any man.'

Delilah told the Philistines, and they gave her seven green willow twigs. With them she tied Samson up.

Some of the Philistines hid in the room, and Delilah called out, 'The Philistines are after you, Samson!'

'Come at once,' she said. 'This time he has given me the true answer.'

While Samson was asleep with his head in her lap, Delilah called for a man who shaved off Samson's long hair.

Then she said again, 'The Philistines are after you, Samson!'

He woke up, but his great strength had gone, and the Philistines took him prisoner.

The Philistines' Prisoner

The Philistines took Samson to Gaza in their own land, and made him work very hard grinding at the mill in the prison. It meant that to do this he had to walk round

He broke the willow twigs as if they had been a strand of cotton.

'You didn't tell me the truth,' said Delilah. 'You were mocking me. Now this time, tell me how you can be bound.'

'If they bind me fast with new ropes that have never been used,' said Samson, 'I shall be as weak as any other man.'

Delilah bound him with new ropes, and again she said, 'The Philistines are after you, Samson!'

But he broke them easily.

'How can you say you love me,' Delilah said, 'when you won't answer me properly? You mock me again and again.'

She kept on begging and pleading, and at last Samson had to tell her the truth.

'I have never cut my hair,' he said. 'I have been a Nazarite since I was born. If I used a razor on my head, my strength would go, and I should be as weak as any other man.'

Samson's mother had vowed before her baby was born that he would be a Nazarite – a man devoted to the service of God – and that his hair would never be cut.

Delilah knew he had told her the truth at last, and she sent for the Philistines.

and round turning a big, heavy stone. The Philistines put out his eyes, and mocked him cruelly.

One day they decided to offer a great sacrifice to their god Dagon, for delivering Samson into their hands.

They were making merry, when someone said, 'Let's get Samson. It's fun to watch him blundering about! He'll make us laugh.'

Samson was brought from his prison, and a boy led him by the hand because he could not see. They took him to stand between the pillars, and then they waited to see what he would do. A great crowd of men and women was there, many of them on the flat roof of the house, watching Samson.

Samson spoke to the boy who was his guide.

'Let me feel the main pillars supporting the house,' he said, 'and I will lean on them.'

The boy led the blind man over to them, and Samson put out his hands and felt them.

Then he prayed. 'O Lord, remember me, I pray, and strengthen me, only this once, O God, that I may be avenged on the Philistines.'

Then he took hold of the two middle pillars in the house, crying:

'Let me die with the Philistines!'

He bent his back with all his might, and the house came tumbling down. It fell on all the people, and Samson died too.

The Story of Ruth

Once more there was famine in the land, and a farmer decided to move his family from Bethlehem, where they lived, to Moab, where it was easier to grow corn.

The farmer and his two sons died after a time, and the farmer's wife, Naomi, made up her mind that she would go back home.

The two sons had married in Moab. Their wives were called Orpah and Ruth, and when Naomi told them she was going home, they said they would go part of the way with her.

Presently Naomi told them it was time for them to go back. Orpah kissed her, and was ready to return to Moab, but Ruth said, 'Don't ask me to leave you, or to go back again. Where you go, I will go, and where you live, I will live. Your people shall be my people, and your God my God.'

When Naomi saw that Ruth's mind was made up, she let her stay with her, and they went on till they reached Bethlehem.

It was the time of the barley harvest, and Ruth said to her mother-in-law, 'Let me go to the field, and glean ears of corn.'

The part of the field she chose belonged to a rich man named Boaz, who was a relation of Naomi's husband. When the reapers had finished their work, they would leave a little for the gleaners, and this was what Ruth hoped to gather up for herself and Naomi, for they were poor.

Boaz came to watch his men at work.

'The Lord be with you,' he greeted his reapers.

'The Lord bless you,' they answered.

Then Boaz caught sight of Ruth, gathering up what the reapers left behind.

'Who is that girl?' he asked.

The man in charge explained, 'It is the Moabite girl who came back with Naomi, and she asked if she might glean in the field after we had made up the sheaves. She has been here all day.'

Boaz went up to Ruth and spoke to her.

'Stay here working with my own girls,' he said. 'Don't go to any other field. You will be safe here. And if you are thirsty, share the water that the young men have drawn for the workers.'

Ruth bowed before him, for he was a great man.

'Why are you so kind to me,' she asked, 'seeing that I am a stranger?'

'I have heard how good you have been to your mother-in-law,' Boaz said. 'May God reward you.'

'You have comforted me,' Ruth said gratefully. 'And you have been kind to me, though I am not one of your own servants.'

'Come here and share our food,' Boaz said to her at mealtime, so Ruth sat down by the reapers and ate with them.

The Fields of Bethlehem

Sing a song of Bethlehem —
The town where Christ was born.
Round about the city stood
The fields of waving corn.

Ruth went gleaning in those fields
For grain to make her bread
When harvest time came round once more;
The sun shone overhead.

But oh, we know another tale
Of night time, and a star,
And shepherds watching in those fields,
And wise men from afar.

It was to fields near Bethlehem
That angels came, we know;
Was it the field where Ruth once stood,
So very long ago?

Boaz helps Ruth

When Ruth had finished eating, and got up to go on working, Boaz said to his reapers, 'Let her glean among the sheaves – don't turn her away – and drop some corn specially for her to pick up. Don't scold her when she does.'

Ruth was able to gather a heap of barley for Naomi, because of Boaz's kindness. When evening came, she took it back to the city and gave it to her mother-in-law. She was tired after her long day's work, but very happy.

'Where did you get all this?' Naomi wanted to know, for there was far more barley than a gleaner usually found.

'The name of the man I worked with today is Boaz,' Ruth told her.

'He was kind to those who are gone,' Naomi said happily, 'and he goes on being kind to those who are living! The man is a near relation of ours.'

'He told me to stay by his young men till the harvest is all gathered,' said Ruth.

'That is good, my daughter,' Naomi said.

So Ruth went on working in Boaz's field till the barley harvest and the wheat harvest were all gathered in.

Boaz began to love Ruth, and one day they were married. Naomi was so happy. The day when Ruth came to Bethlehem had been a good day for them both.

Samuel is Born

There was a woman named Hannah, who longed for a little son. One day, when she went to worship God in the temple, she began to cry, and then she prayed, 'O Lord, if you will grant my wish, and give me a son, I will give him to you, and he shall serve you all his life.'

Sitting on a seat near Hannah was a priest, whose name was Eli. He watched Hannah, and saw that her lips were moving, but he heard no words. She was weeping, so Eli asked her why.

Hannah said, 'My lord, I am very unhappy, and I have been talking to God about it.'

'Go in peace,' Eli said, 'and may God grant your wish.'

Hannah went home feeling much happier, and prepared a meal for her family.

Her prayer was answered, and she had a baby boy. How happy she was! She called him Samuel.

Hannah did not forget her promise to God. When Samuel was old enough, he would have to go and help the priest in the temple, as young boys used to do.

At last the day came for her to take him to the temple. Hannah packed up food and wine, and set off with her little boy.

When they reached the temple, she took him to Eli.

'O my lord,' she said, 'I am the woman who stood by you here, praying to the Lord. For this child I prayed, and the Lord has answered my prayer. So I have lent him to the Lord, as long as he lives.'

Samuel stayed with Eli, and learnt to help him in the temple services. Hannah must have missed him very much, but every year she made him a little coat, and went to see him.

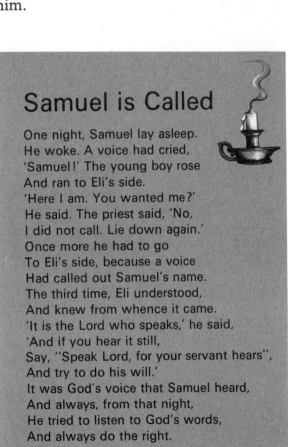

Samuel is Called

One night, Samuel lay asleep.
He woke. A voice had cried,
'Samuel!' The young boy rose
And ran to Eli's side.
'Here I am. You wanted me?'
He said. The priest said, 'No,
I did not call. Lie down again.'
Once more he had to go
To Eli's side, because a voice
Had called out Samuel's name.
The third time, Eli understood,
And knew from whence it came.
'It is the Lord who speaks,' he said,
'And if you hear it still,
Say, "Speak Lord, for your servant hears",
And try to do his will.'
It was God's voice that Samuel heard,
And always, from that night,
He tried to listen to God's words,
And always do the right.

The Ark of The Lord

Israel was at war with its neighbours, the Philistines, and the Israelites were gradually being overcome.

Then one of them had an idea.

'Let us fetch the Ark of the Lord,' he said, 'and take it into battle with us, then we shall win.'

So the people sent a message to the temple at Shiloh, and asked if they might take the Ark into battle with them, and Eli's sons, Hophni and Phinehas, took the Ark to the battle front. It was the very precious chest covered in gold, with two carved angels bending above it, and inside were the laws God had given Moses.

When the Israelites saw the Ark being carried towards them, they gave a great shout. The Philistines heard them, and wondered what the noise was.

When they were told that the Ark had

The Philistines fought, and Israel was overcome. Then the Philistines killed Eli's sons, and captured the Ark.

A man from the tribe of Benjamin, who was in the Israelite army, ran to Shiloh to tell the people what had happened. He tore his clothes and put earth on his head, as a sign of great sorrow.

Eli was sitting by the roadside; his heart trembled for the Ark of God.

When the man reached the city, he told the bad news, and everyone cried out in dismay. They thought that having lost the Ark, God would no longer be with them.

When Eli heard the shouts and wailing, he wanted to know what had happened.

Quickly the messenger told him.

'Israel has fled before the Philistines,' he said. 'And many of our men have lost their lives. Your sons are dead, and the Ark has been taken.'

Poor Eli! It was sad news indeed.

arrived, they were afraid. 'God has come to the camp,' they said. 'Woe unto us! Such a thing has never happened before. These are the gods that smote the Egyptians with all the plagues in the wilderness. Be strong, and stand up for yourselves like men, O you Philistines, that you may not become slaves of the Hebrews as they have been to you. Stand up for yourselves like men, and fight!'

The Ark comes Home

The Philistines took the Ark of God,
And carried it home in glee.
They set it down by their own false god
And said, 'Now we shall see!'
But Dagon, the false god, fell to the ground
Before the Ark of the Lord,
And he was destroyed. Said the Philistines,
'Such things we can't afford.
We'll send the Ark to another place.'
But the people suffered sore,
So they said they could not keep it there,
And sent it on once more.
'What shall we do with the Ark of the Lord?'
They said when ill befell,
And at last they thought they must send it home,
Then again all might be well.
They put the Ark on a fine new cart,
And they added presents, too,
And they sent it back to the Israelites —
It was all that they could do.

Samuel and Saul

When Samuel grew up, he became the ruler of his people, and he tried to get them to follow God and obey his commandments. But when he was an old man the people decided that they would like a king to reign over them.

They asked Samuel to find them one, and he agreed, but he warned them that they would not enjoy his rule.

'He will take your sons and make them soldiers,' he said. 'He will take your daughters to cook for him. He will take your fields, your best vines and olives, your servants, your sheep and asses. Everything will be pressed into his service, and you will wish you had never asked for him.'

But the people were quite sure they wanted a king, so in the end Samuel had to give in to them.

Now a man named Kish had a son, Saul, who was tall and good-looking.

One day Kish's asses were lost, and he told Saul to take one of the servants and go and look for them.

They hunted high and low, but they couldn't find the asses anywhere. In the end,

Saul said to the servant, 'Let's go back home, in case my father starts to worry.'

'In this city lives a very wise man,' the servant said, 'and all that he says will happen, comes true. Perhaps he knows which way we ought to go. Let us go and see him.'

'But if we go,' Saul objected, 'what can we take this man? We've eaten all our bread, and we've nothing to give him!'

'I have got a coin here,' said the servant. 'We could give him that.'

'Well said,' cried Saul. 'We'll go!'

As they went up the hill to the city, they saw some girls setting out to fetch water. They asked them, 'Is the wise man here?'

'Yes, he is,' the girls said. 'He came to the city only today, because there is to be a special sacrifice. You will find him here.'

They hurried on, and presently they met Samuel.

God had told Samuel the day before that a man was coming whom he should anoint as ruler of the Israelites, so when Samuel saw Saul, God told him, 'Here is the man. He shall reign over my people.'

Saul went up to Samuel, and not knowing who he was, he asked the way to the wise man's house.

'I am the man you are looking for,' Samuel said. 'Eat with me now, and then I will talk with you. As for the asses, don't worry about them, they are found.'

Saul went with Samuel, and was given the best place at the table, and afterwards they sat on a flat roof-top together, and talked of all that was in Samuel's heart.

King Saul

Very early next morning, Saul and Samuel and the servant set out together.

As they were leaving the city, Samuel said, 'Tell your servant to go on. Then stand still for a while, and let me show you what God wants of you.'

When they were alone, Samuel took out a flask of oil and anointed Saul's head, and kissed him.

'I have done that because the Lord has anointed you to be leader of his people,' he said. 'When you leave me, you will meet two men near Rachel's tomb, and they will tell you, "The asses which you went to look for are found. Your father is not worrying about them any more – he is troubled about you."

'Then you will go on, and presently, by Mount Tabor, you will meet three men, one carrying three kids, another carrying three loaves of bread, and another carrying a bottle of wine. They will greet you, and give you two loaves.

'After that, you will come to the hill of God where the Philistines are; when you reach the city, you will meet a group of prophets who will be chanting and playing musical instruments. Then God's Spirit will fill you, and you will prophesy, too.

'When these things happen, do as seems best, for God is with you. In seven days, I will come and join you, and show you what you shall do.'

It all turned out just as Samuel had said, and people found it hard to understand, for to them this man was just Saul, the son of Kish.

'Do you see the man God has chosen?' Samuel cried. 'Is there anyone else like him?'

Everyone shouted, 'God save the King!' They had got what they wanted.

Jonathan and his Armour-Bearer

Saul had a son whose name was Jonathan. He was a soldier in Saul's army, and one day he said to the young man who carried his armour, 'Come on, let's go over to the Philistines' camp. It may be that the Lord will work for us, because it is as easy for him to work through a small number of people as through many.'

'Do whatever you feel you should,' said the armour-bearer. 'I am with you.'

'We will go and show ourselves to the Philistines,' Jonathan told him. 'If they say, "Wait until we come to you," we will stay where we are. But if they say, "Come up to us," then we will go, for it would be a sign that the Lord has given them into our hand.'

So they went forward and showed themselves to the Philistines, and the Philistines cried mockingly, 'Look, the Hebrews are coming out of the holes where they hid themselves!' Then they shouted to Jonathan and his armour-bearer, 'Come up here, and we'll show you how to fight!'

'Come on after me,' Jonathan said to his armour-bearer. 'The Lord has delivered them into the hands of Israel.'

Together, they killed about twenty Philistines. Saul's watchmen saw the crowd running in all directions.

Saul told his men to see who was missing from the ranks, and they discovered that it was Jonathan and his armour-bearer.

'Bring out the Ark,' Saul told them. The Israelites went up to the Philistines, and found everyone fighting everyone else, and great confusion everywhere. Saul attacked his enemies and won a great victory.

Saul told his men that they were to vow not to eat anything until the evening when he hoped that his enemies would be overcome. Trouble would fall on anyone who broke this vow, he said.

Presently they came to a wood, and found honey dripping from a honeycomb, but no one would touch it.

Jonathan did not know anything about the vow, and he was hungry, so he dipped a stick he was carrying into the honeycomb and ate honey. After that, he was able to see things much more clearly.

The others told him what his father had said, and they were afraid that trouble would come to Jonathan, but he said, 'See how I see everything more clearly because I tasted a little honey. If you had eaten what you took from the Philistines, might there not have been much greater destruction among them?'

When Saul found out that it was Jonathan who had broken the vow by eating honey, he said that, even though Jonathan was his own son, he must die.

But the people would not let that happen.

'Jonathan has brought us a great victory today,' they said. 'Not a hair of his head must be hurt.'

So they rescued Jonathan.

Samuel chooses David

Saul was not a good ruler, and Samuel felt that the time had come for him to find someone better to reign over the Israelites as their next king.

One day he heard God's voice telling him to fill a horn with oil, ready to anoint one he had chosen, and to go to the house of a man named Jesse, who lived in Bethlehem. One of his sons would become the next king.

Samuel was afraid of what would happen when Saul found out, but he did as God commanded him, and journeyed to Bethlehem.

The elders of the town were rather alarmed when they saw him, for they wondered why he was there. But Samuel told them that he came peaceably.

He offered a sacrifice to God, and invited Jesse and his sons to attend it. When they came, he blessed them.

He wondered very much which of the sons was to be king, and he looked first at Eliab, the eldest, who was tall and good-looking. Surely he was the one? But God told Samuel, 'Do not look at his appearance, for he is not the one I choose. A man looks at the outside, but the Lord looks at the heart.'

Then the next son, Abinadab, was called forward by his father, and made to walk where Samuel could watch him.

Samuel shook his head.

'God has not chosen him, either,' he said.

Then Jesse brought forward his third son, Shammah, and again Samuel said, 'The Lord has not chosen him.'

Jesse brought out his seven sons, one after

the other, but every time Samuel said, 'That is not the one.'

'Is this everyone?' he asked at last.

'Well, there is just the youngest,' Jesse said doubtfully. 'He is in the fields, minding the sheep.' They had not even thought it worth while to bring him.

'Send for him!' Samuel said.

So they sent for the youngest son, whose name was David. He was a strong, good-looking boy, and God said to Samuel, 'Arise, anoint him, for this is he.'

Samuel took the horn of oil, and anointed David's head, while his brothers watched in amazement. David, their little brother, a king?

The Spirit of the Lord was on David from that day onwards, although the choice of the new king was kept secret.

Saul and David

King Saul's heart was heavy,
And his world looked very black.
His servants said, 'Sweet music
Might bring his spirits back,
And make him more good-tempered.'
So they went to Saul. Said they,
'We know a man in Bethlehem
Whose shepherd son can play.
He's also good and clever,
A valiant man of war,
Wise, and good to look at,
And God goes his ways before.'
So King Saul sent for David,
And on his harp he played.
Saul's bad temper left him,
And the shepherd boy was made
The king's own armour-bearer.
And when Saul had a spell
Of melancholy, David plucked
His harp-strings — all was well.

David and Goliath

Now the Philistines were gathered together for battle on a mountain, and the Israelites pitched their tents on the mountain opposite, so there was a valley between them.

One of the Philistines was a giant named Goliath. He was ten feet tall, with a helmet of brass and a huge spear. His legs were also covered with brass, and he wore a coat of mail. Another soldier bearing a shield walked before him.

He swaggered out, and cried across the valley to the Israelites, 'Why have you come out to fight in your numbers? Am I not a Philistine, and you servants of Saul? Choose one man from among you, and let him come down to me. If he is able to fight me and kill me, we shall all be your servants; but if I win and kill him, you will be our servants. I defy the armies of Israel this day! Give me a man, that we may fight together!'

When the Israelites heard Goliath's words, they were very frightened.

The giant shouted his challenge day after day, but no one answered it.

Jesse's three eldest sons were in Saul's army, and David was still minding his father's sheep.

One day, Jesse said to David, 'Take this corn and these loaves to your brothers, and carry these ten cheeses to their captain, and find out how your brothers are getting on.'

So David found someone else to mind the sheep, and went to the valley where the two armies were fighting.

He left the food he had brought with an Israelite, and went to find his brothers.

While he was talking to them, Goliath came out, and shouted his usual challenge.

The Israelites told David who he was.

'If someone kills Goliath,' they said, 'the king will give him great riches, as well as his daughter to be his wife.'

Eliab, his eldest brother, heard David talking to the soldiers, and he was angry.

'What have you come here for?' he demanded. 'Who is looking after your few sheep? I know well how proud you are.

You have just come to watch the fighting!'

But David was making up his mind to face Goliath, and the soldiers saw what he was thinking. They took him to Saul.

'Do not let anyone be afraid because of Goliath,' David said to the king. 'Your servant will fight this Philistine.'

Saul looked at the young boy standing so confidently before him.

'You can't go against this Philistine and fight with him!' he said. 'You are only a youth, and he has been a man of war since he was a boy.'

'I kept my father's sheep,' David told the king, 'and if a lion or a bear came which took a lamb out of the flock, I went out after him at once and smote him, and killed him. I have killed both lions and bears, and this Philistine shall be as one of these because he has defied the armies of the living God. The Lord that delivered me out of the paw of the bear will deliver me out of the hands of this Philistine.'

So Saul gave in. 'Go', he said, 'and the Lord be with you.'

Five Small Stones

Saul armed David with his own armour. He put a helmet of brass on his head, and helped him on with the coat of mail. David fastened on the sword, but he had never worn armour before, and when he tried to walk, it felt very heavy and weighed him down.

'I am not used to these things,' he told the king. 'I cannot wear them.'

He took the armour off, put down the sword, and went outside to the brook that ran through the valley.

There he stooped and picked up five smooth stones. He put them in the shepherd's bag he wore, and took the sling he used when he was keeping wild animals from the flock, and his shepherd's staff.

Then he was ready to face the giant.

When Goliath saw him coming, he laughed mockingly:

'Am I a dog,' he cried, 'that you come to me with sticks? Come here, and I will give you up to the birds and beasts of the field!'

'You come to me with a sword,' David called back, 'and a spear and a shield, but I come to you in the name of the Lord of hosts, the God of the armies of Israel, whom you have defied. All these people shall know that the Lord does not save by the sword and the spear. The battle is the Lord's, and he will deliver you into our hands.'

Goliath, angry at such words, rushed towards David, and bravely the shepherd boy went out to meet him.

Then David put his hand into his bag, and took out a stone. He put it into his sling, and aimed at the giant.

The stone hit Goliath in the forehead, and he sank to the ground, dead at once.

David ran forward, and with the giant's own sword, he cut off Goliath's head.

When the Philistines saw what had happened to their champion, they turned and fled. The men of Israel chased their enemies out of the valley shouting victoriously.

David and Jonathan

David had won the prize that Saul had offered to anyone who could get rid of the giant. He took him to live at his court, and put him in charge of a regiment.

Soon Jonathan met David and he and David became very close friends. Jonathan gave David his own robe and girdle, and his sword and bow. Nothing was too good for his new friend.

David came back from defeating the Philistines, and the women came out of their houses, singing and playing musical instruments. As they danced for joy as King Saul passed by, they sang:

'Saul has slain his thousands,
And David his ten thousands.'

Saul heard them, and grew very jealous of David.

The next day, Saul was still in a bad mood, and David went to him to play his harp, to soothe his temper. But Saul picked up a spear and flung it at David.

Now Michal, Saul's younger daughter, loved David.

Saul said she could become David's wife, if he killed a hundred Philistines. He hoped that David himself might lose his life killing them. David, however, killed two hundred Philistines, and Saul had to let him marry Michal. But he grew even more afraid of David, and thought him his enemy.

He tried to get Jonathan to kill him, but Jonathan warned David, and told him to hide. Then he himself went to his father, and spoke well of David, and Saul listened to what he had to say. For a time the king showed no ill will, and took him back to the court.

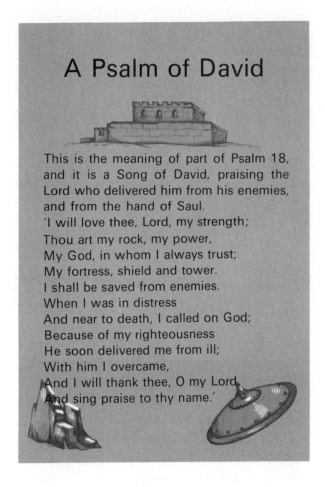

A Psalm of David

This is the meaning of part of Psalm 18, and it is a Song of David, praising the Lord who delivered him from his enemies, and from the hand of Saul.

'I will love thee, Lord, my strength;
Thou art my rock, my power,
My God, in whom I always trust;
My fortress, shield and tower.
I shall be saved from enemies.
When I was in distress
And near to death, I called on God;
Because of my righteousness
He soon delivered me from ill;
With him I overcame,
And I will thank thee, O my Lord,
And sing praise to thy name.'

David Escapes

Saul was so eager to get rid of David that he sent messengers to his house to wait for their chance and kill him.

Michal, David's wife, discovered what her father, Saul, was doing, and she said to David, 'Unless you save yourself tonight, tomorrow you will lose your life.'

She let him down by a rope from a window, and he escaped in the darkness, and hid.

Then Michal took a carved image, and laid it in the bed, with a goat's hair pillow, and covered it up. It looked just as though David were asleep in bed.

When Saul's messengers arrived, and said they had come to take David away, Michal said, 'He is ill.'

The messengers went back and told Saul, and he sent them to David's house once more.

This time they made their way to the bedroom, meaning to kill him, but of course when they lifted the covers, there was only a wooden image in the bed.

'Why have you deceived me so?' Saul asked Michal angrily, when he had heard what had happened. 'Why have you sent away my enemy, so that he escaped?'

'He told me to let him go,' Michal said.

So David escaped, and he went to Samuel, and told him all that Saul had tried to do to him. He stayed with Samuel for a time, and Saul could do him no harm.

After a while, he went to Jonathan, his great friend, and Jonathan promised to do what he could to protect him from Saul.

David was to hide himself in a field, and Jonathan would tell a boy to go and find three arrows he had shot into the air.

'If I say, "The arrows are on this side of you, take them," Jonathan told David, 'then come, for everything is all right. But if I say to the boy, "The arrows have gone beyond you, go your way," it means the Lord is sending you away.'

So David hid himself and waited and watched.

Presently Jonathan appeared with his bow and arrows, and a little lad was with him.

Jonathan shot an arrow into the air, and when the boy went to pick it up, he cried, 'Is not the arrow beyond you? Make haste, run away.'

The boy did not know that Jonathan's words had a special meaning. He gathered up that arrow and the others Jonathan had shot, and brought them to his master. Then Jonathan gave his weapons to the boy and told him to take them home. Obediently, the lad ran off.

As soon as he had gone, David came out of his hiding place, and he and Jonathan pledged their faithfulness to one another, for as long as they lived. Then David hurried off across the field, and Jonathan went back to the city.

David the Outlaw

David was now an outlaw, always hiding and hoping that Saul would not find him.

A band of men joined him, and together they wandered about the country. Saul was always trying to track them down.

One day, the outlaws were very hungry, for it was a long time since they had had anything to eat.

David went to a priest named Ahimelech. He saw that Ahimelech had a pile of loaves in front of him, and David begged him to give him five of them, or all the bread, if he could spare it.

'This isn't ordinary bread,' the priest told him. 'This is holy bread, set aside for the priests.' It was the shewbread, which no one else was allowed to eat. But because David and his men were starving, Ahimelech said he might take the loaves.

'Have you a spear or a sword?' David asked. 'I left so hurriedly that I did not bring my sword, or any weapon with me.'

'The sword of Goliath, the Philistine you slew, is here,' the priest said. 'It is hidden away, wrapped in a cloth. Take that, if you wish – it's the only one here.'

'There is none other like it,' David said, and he went off with Goliath's sword.

For a time, David hid in the Cave of Adullam, and many of his old comrades joined him there, so that in the end he had a band of four hundred men.

They wandered about, escaping from Saul, or fighting with the Philistines.

One day, when Saul was resting in a cave, he fell asleep. He did not know that David and his men were there too. David's followers wanted him to kill Saul, now he had the chance, but David would not. Saul was the king, anointed in God's name, he told his followers. However, David cut off part of Saul's robe with Goliath's sword, and when Saul woke up, he showed it to him.

Saul was touched that David had spared his life, so he did no harm to David.

Psalm 124
A Psalm of David

If God had not been on our side
When enemies arose,
Then had we all been overwhelmed,
As Israel surely knows.

And when their anger was aroused,
It was as though we drowned
In deepest waters – but the Lord
In time his servants found.

And like a bird who has escaped
From an imprisoning net,
We are set free; the Lord's great help
We never can forget.

David and Abigail

There was a man named Nabal, who owned a great many sheep and goats, and he used to shear his sheep near Mount Carmel. He was not a very kind or good man, but he had a beautiful wife named Abigail, and everybody liked her.

One day David heard that Nabal had three thousand sheep, and was busy shearing them. He called ten of his young men, and said to them, 'Go to Nabal and say, "Peace to you, and your house. I hear that you have shearers; we never hurt your shepherds. So please spare anything you can for David."'

David's men did as he told them, and when they had finished speaking, they waited for Nabal's answer.

'Who is David?' Nabal asked scornfully. 'Who is Jesse's son? Many servants these days run away from their masters; I expect he is one of them. Must I take my bread and my water, and the meat I have prepared for my shearers, and give them to men when I don't know who they are or where they come from?'

So David's men turned away, angered by Nabal's words, and went back to David.

But a young man had gone to Abigail and told her what had happened.

'David's men were very good to us,' he said. 'They never took anything that was ours, and they protected us and our sheep from harm. We thought you would do the right thing, but our master is so bad-tempered that a man cannot speak to him.'

Quickly Abigail packed two hundred loaves, two bottles of wine, the meat from five sheep, five measures of corn, a hundred clusters of raisins and two hundred cakes of figs, and fastened them all on to the backs of asses.

'You go on first, and I will follow,' she said

to her servants; but she did not tell Nabal anything about it.

She herself mounted an ass and rode off after the men. Soon she saw David and his followers coming towards them, brandishing their swords, for David was ready to kill Nabal's men, whom he now thought of as his enemies because he could get no help from them.

But when Abigail saw him, she got down from her ass and knelt at his feet.

'Let me speak to you,' she said. 'Do not take any notice of Nabal, for he is foolish. Do not harm them, though they would harm you. When good comes your way and you are ruler of Israel, you might be grieved to think that you had avenged the wrong done to you. And when the Lord has dealt well with you, then remember me, your handmaid.'

David was moved by her words.

'Blessed be the Lord God of Israel,' he said, 'who has sent you to meet me today. Thank you for your advice, which has kept me from avenging myself on my enemies.

Truly, if you had not come and talked to me, I would not have left one of Nabal's men alive by the morning.'

So David received the food she had brought and said, 'Go home in peace; see, I have listened to you, and taken your advice.'

Saul's Spear

Peace between David and Saul did not last very long. Once again some men told Saul where David was, so Saul set off to find him.

One night, David and one of his men called Abishai crept into Saul's camp.

They found him asleep behind a row of wagons. Now was their chance, thought Abishai, and he begged David to let him kill the king. But again David said, 'We cannot kill the man whom God has anointed.'

There was a jar of water beside King Saul, and before he went to sleep he had stuck his spear in the ground beside his pillow, in case his enemy woke him suddenly.

David took the spear and the water bottle, and he and Abishai crept away.

In the morning, David climbed up a hill, on the other side of the valley and held up the bottle and the spear. He called out mockingly to Abner, the captain of Saul's army, 'Are you not a brave man? Who is like you in Israel? Why have you not protected your lord and king? Someone could have taken his life, and you have failed to do your duty. Now see where the king's water bottle is, and the spear that was beside his pillow!'

Saul knew David's voice, and he called out, 'Is that you, my son David?'

'It is my voice, my lord, O King,' David answered. 'Why do you hunt down your servant? Listen to me, my lord.'

Saul listened, and then he said, 'I have done wrong. Return, my son David, and I will harm you no more.'

Then David held up the spear again.

'Behold,' he said, 'the king's spear! Let someone come over and fetch it. The Lord delivered you into my hand today, but I would not harm his anointed one. As I spared you, do you spare me.'

'Be happy, my son David,' said Saul. 'The Lord is with you and you shall prosper.'

So David went on his way, and Saul returned to his camp.

Saul and the Witch of Endor

Samuel was dead, and all Israel had grieved for the wise old man. About this time, Saul had ordered that no one was to try to practise magic, or to read the future.

But when the great army of the Philistines was gathered together against him, Saul felt he must know what was in store for him.

So in spite of his new law, he said to his servants, 'Find me a women who has the power to tell the future for me.'

'There is a witch living at Endor,' they told him.

So Saul put on someone else's clothes, and disguised himself, for he did not want the witch to know who he was.

He and two servants waited till nightfall and then they went to the witch.

'I want you to call up a spirit for me,' he said. 'I will tell you who it is.'

'Surely you know King Saul has told us we must not do this,' the witch said. 'Are you laying a trap for me? I don't want to lose my life.'

'I swear you won't be punished for it,' Saul promised.

So the witch gave in.

'Whose spirit do you want me to call up?' she asked.

'Samuel's,' said Saul.

It seemed as though the witch could indeed see the spirit of Samuel, and then she cried, 'Why have you deceived me? You are Saul!'

'Don't be afraid,' Saul told her. 'What did you see?'

'I saw an old man covered with a cloak,' said the witch.

Saul knew that it was Samuel, and he bowed to the ground.

'Why have you disturbed me and brought me here?' Samuel said to King Saul.

'I am very troubled,' Saul said. 'The Philistines make war against me, and God is no longer with me so I have come to you, to ask what I ought to do.'

'Why do you ask me when you say that God is no longer with you?' Samuel asked. 'You did not obey his voice, and he has taken the kingdom away from you and given it to David. Tomorrow you and the Israelites will be overcome by the Philistines, and you and your sons will be with me.'

Saul fell to the ground in fear, when he heard that. He had eaten nothing all day, and he was faint with hunger.

The witch tried to help him.

'I have done what you asked,' she said, 'and my life is at your mercy. Now let me get you some food, to give you strength.'

Saul shook his head, but the witch and the servants insisted, so he got up and the witch baked bread and meat for him.

As soon as they had eaten, Saul and his servants crept away through the darkness.

It all happened as Samuel had said. There was a great battle between the Israelites and the Philistines. Saul saw three of his sons killed, and in his sorrow he killed himself.

David was king after Saul's death, but his heart was heavy, for he had lost his greatest friend, Jonathan, Saul's son.

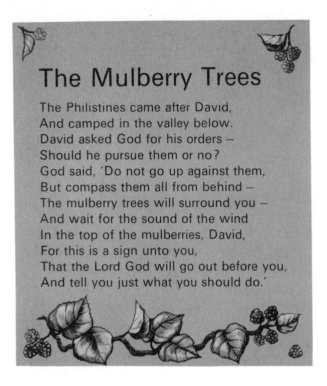

The Mulberry Trees

The Philistines came after David,
And camped in the valley below.
David asked God for his orders –
Should he pursue them or no?
God said, 'Do not go up against them,
But compass them all from behind –
The mulberry trees will surround you –
And wait for the sound of the wind
In the top of the mulberries, David,
For this is a sign unto you,
That the Lord God will go out before you,
And tell you just what you should do.'

God's Promise to David

David became king of Israel and Judah, and he decided to make Jerusalem the most important city in his kingdom. He had the Ark taken there, and the king of Tyre sent cedar wood and carpenters and masons to build King David a palace.

One day the King said to his prophet, Nathan, 'You see, I dwell in a house of cedar wood, but the Ark of God is kept only behind curtains.'

'Do what you feel is right,' Nathan told him, 'for the Lord is with you.'

That night, God spoke to Nathan.

'Go and say to my servant David, "The Lord says: Will you build a house for me to dwell in? My Spirit has dwelt first in a tent, and then in the tabernacle. Have I ever asked any of the Israelites to build me a house of cedarwood?"

'Tell David that I took him from his work as a shepherd to be a ruler over my people Israel. I have been with him always, and have made his name great. I will see my people Israel settled in their own land, so that they need not move about any more. Their enemies will not trouble them.

'When his life is over, I will look after his son. He shall indeed build a house for me, and I will be like a father to him, and he will be my son.'

Nathan went to David and told him all that God had promised. David went into the tabernacle and thanked God for all the care he was offering to him and his family.

'With your blessing,' David prayed, 'let my house be graced for ever.'

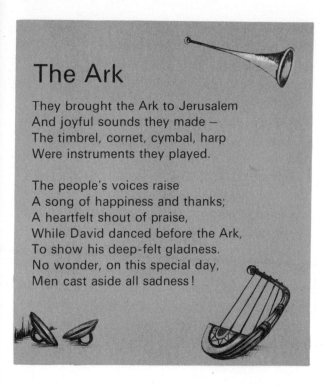

The Ark

They brought the Ark to Jerusalem
And joyful sounds they made —
The timbrel, cornet, cymbal, harp
Were instruments they played.

The people's voices raise
A song of happiness and thanks;
A heartfelt shout of praise,
While David danced before the Ark,
To show his deep-felt gladness.
No wonder, on this special day,
Men cast aside all sadness!

David and Mephibosheth

David never forgot his friend Jonathan, and one day he said, 'Is there any one of Saul's household left? If so, I should like to be kind to him, for Jonathan's sake.'

There was one man named Ziba, who had been Saul's servant, and David sent for him, and asked him if there was anyone he could help, in memory of his friend Jonathan.

'Jonathan had a son who is lame,' Ziba told the king.

'Where is he?' David asked, and Ziba told him where he lived.

So David sent for Jonathan's lame son. His name was Mephibosheth and he had been lame since he was five years old.

He came hobbling into the king's presence and bowed before him.

'Do not be afraid, Mephibosheth,' David said, 'for I will look after you for your father's sake, and you shall be welcome to eat at my table.'

'Why should you bother about me?' asked Mephibosheth.

But David called for Ziba.

'You and your sons and servants must look after the land I am going to give to Mephibosheth,' he said. 'It is my wish that you should do so.'

'I will do what you ask,' Ziba answered. So all his household looked after Jonathan's lame son, and Mephibosheth's life was made much happier by David's kind thought.

Water from Bethlehem

The Philistines were in Bethlehem
And David was heard to say,
'O that someone would give me to drink
Bethlehem water today!
There is a well beside the gate.'
Three men said, 'We'll go,
And bring back water for you, sire,
Though the enemy's there, we know.'
They crept through the ranks of the Philistines,
And fetched water for their lord.
But he would not drink it when it came.
They saw it all was poured
On the dusty earth, and David said,
'In dangerous spots they trod.
These risked their lives to bring me drink —
I pour it out to God.'

95

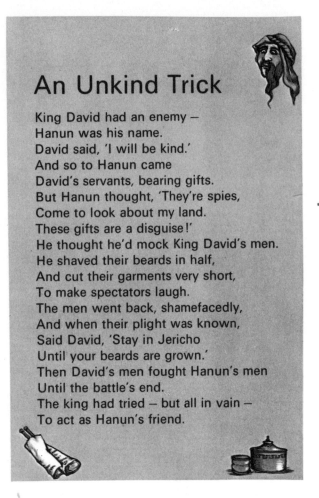

An Unkind Trick

King David had an enemy —
Hanun was his name.
David said, 'I will be kind.'
And so to Hanun came
David's servants, bearing gifts.
But Hanun thought, 'They're spies,
Come to look about my land.
These gifts are a disguise!'
He thought he'd mock King David's men.
He shaved their beards in half,
And cut their garments very short,
To make spectators laugh.
The men went back, shamefacedly,
And when their plight was known,
Said David, 'Stay in Jericho
Until your beards are grown.'
Then David's men fought Hanun's men
Until the battle's end.
The king had tried — but all in vain —
To act as Hanun's friend.

Solomon the Wise

When David died, his son Solomon became king.

One night Solomon had a dream. He felt that God was promising to give him whatever he wanted most.

'I want to have an understanding heart,' Solomon said, and he asked for wisdom.

God was pleased that Solomon did not ask for riches or for long life, or a victory over his enemies, and his wish was granted. Solomon was very wise in everything he thought and did.

One day, two women came to him, and one of them had a little baby in her arms.

'O my lord,' one woman said, 'we both live in the same house, and we both had babies. This woman's baby did not live, and she took mine and said it was hers. She said that it was my baby that died, but it was not, it was hers! This baby is mine.'

'No,' said the other woman. 'The baby is mine. It was her baby who died.'

'One says one thing, and the other says the opposite,' said wise King Solomon. He turned to one of his men. 'Bring me a sword,' he said.

A sword was brought. Then the king said, 'Divide the baby between them.'

He did not really mean any such thing to happen, but it was his clever way of finding out which was the true mother of the baby, and his plan worked.

At once, one of the women sprang forward.

'O my lord, don't do that!' she cried. 'Give the baby to her!'

The second woman said, 'Don't give the baby to either of us. Do as you said. It is the fairest way.'

Then the king said, 'Give the child to the woman who spoke first!' He knew the baby was hers, because she would rather the other woman should have her precious baby than that any harm should come to it. That was true mother-love.

So Solomon sent the woman away with her own baby in her arms. And everyone said what a wise king he was.

Building the Temple

King Solomon knew that his father David had wanted to build a beautiful temple in Jerusalem, and he knew that God had said that although David would not live to see it, his son would indeed build the temple.

One day, Solomon felt that it was time to begin the great work, and first of all he sent a message to King Hiram of Tyre.

'You know how my father David could not build a house of the Lord, because he was always busy fighting. Now I have no enemies to trouble me, I plan to build a temple, just as God said I would when he spoke to my father.

'We cannot cut down trees and work with wood like your people can, so I ask you to let your men hew down your fine cedar trees, and then come and work with my own men.'

Hiram was very pleased when he heard this.

'Of course I will give you cedar trees and fir trees to build your temple,' he answered.

So Hiram gave Solomon the wood he needed and Solomon gave Hiram wheat and oil in return.

Then a great number of men began to saw the wood, and others brought big stones, and they began to build the temple.

It was the most wonderful building, with many carved figures of angels and flowers. The whole temple was covered with gold.

A man named Hiram came from Tyre. He made beautiful brass pillars, with carved fruit and lilies on top. He made brass chains and basins, pots and shovels.

The altar was gold, and so was the table where the shewbread was kept. There were gold candlesticks and lamps; even the hinges of the doors were gold.

They put the Ark in the most holy place of all. At last the wonderful temple was finished, and it stood gleaming in the sunshine. It had taken seven years to build.

Then all the people came together to see Solomon dedicate the temple to God. It was a very special day, and one which they would remember all their lives.

Solomon's Riches

King Solomon had rich treasure,
And he made many things —
Gold shields and targets; drinking cups,
Fit for the wine of kings.
From ivory he made a throne,
All overlaid with gold,
And lions were carved to stand nearby.
As well as this, we're told,
Ships came from Tarshish, and they brought
Gold, silver, peacocks many hued,
Spices and ivory, even apes,
Proud horses, mules, harness too,
Raiment from Egypt, precious vessels.
Mighty in wisdom, wealth — his fame
Spread o'er the world.
All glorified his name.

The Visit of the Queen of Sheba

Solomon's fame spread far and wide, and the Queen of Sheba heard how wise he was. She lived a long way from Solomon, but she decided to find out how clever he was.

She travelled with a great number of camels carrying gifts for the king: sweet spices, gold and precious jewels, and when she reached Jerusalem, everyone stood to watch the procession go by.

When the Queen of Sheba found how much he knew, and saw the house that he had built, and how many servants he had, and the beautiful temple, she knew that all she had heard about Solomon was true.

'I did not believe all I was told until I came and saw it with my own eyes,' she told the king. 'But I was not told even the half of it, for your wisdom and riches are even greater than I heard they were.'

Then she gave King Solomon the presents she had brought – the gold, the spices and the precious stones.

King Hiram's navy from Tyre also brought gold and jewels and wood, and Solomon's workmen made pillars for the temple from the wood, and for his palace, and they also made harps and other musical instruments.

King Solomon gave presents to the Queen of Sheba, and she and her servants left Jerusalem with their camels, and went back to their own country.

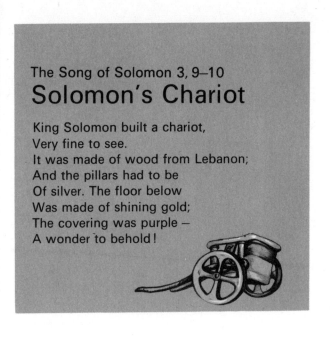

The Song of Solomon 3, 9–10

Solomon's Chariot

King Solomon built a chariot,
Very fine to see.
It was made of wood from Lebanon;
And the pillars had to be
Of silver. The floor below
Was made of shining gold;
The covering was purple —
A wonder to behold!

Elijah and the Ravens

After King Solomon died, the kingdom was divided again: Israel had its own ruler, and so did Judah.

When King Ahab was on the throne of Israel, an old man named Elijah came to see him. Elijah was a prophet and he said to the king, 'As the Lord God of Israel lives, before whom I stand, there shall not be dew nor rain these years, unless I say so.'

Ahab was a bad king; he worshipped a false god named Baal, and did many wrongs. He was alarmed to hear what Elijah told him, because if there was not going to be any rain or dew the crops would die, and food would be scarce.

Elijah went away and hid himself, as God had told him to do; otherwise, the king might have tried to harm him. The hiding-place was very lonely, but there was a little brook from which Elijah could drink, and every day the big black ravens flew down with food for him in their beaks.

After a while the little brook dried up, and God told Elijah to move to another place, where he would find a widow who would look after him.

He made his way to the city and, when he reached the gate, Elijah saw the woman he sought gathering sticks for her fire.

'Please fetch me a little water to drink,' Elijah asked her.

Water was, of course, very precious, but the woman still wanted to share the little drop she had. As she turned to fetch it, Elijah called after her, 'Please bring me a scrap of bread, too.'

'As God lives,' said the woman, 'I have no loaf. All I have left is a handful of flour in a barrel, and a little oil in a jar. I am trying to find a couple of sticks for my fire, so that I may cook the last of our food for my son and me. After we have eaten it, we shall have no more.'

'Do not be afraid,' Elijah told her. 'Go and do as you said, but make a little cake for me first, and then cook for yourself and your son. For this is what the Lord God of Israel says: "The barrel of flour shall not grow empty, nor the jar of oil, until the day on which the Lord sends rain on the earth."'

The woman did as Elijah told her, and he stayed in her house. All that he had told her came true, and there was enough food for them all.

Elijah and the Widow's Son

One day, the son of the widow with whom Elijah was staying fell ill. His mother watched over him and did all she could to make him better; but then there was no more anyone could do, and it was not long before the boy died.

His mother was so distraught that she hardly knew what she was saying, and she told Elijah that it was his fault.

'Give your son to me,' Elijah said quietly.

He took the boy out of her arms and carried him up to the loft, and laid the lad on his own bed.

Then he turned to God for help. Three times he covered the boy's body with his own and breathed on him. Three times he prayed: 'O Lord my God, I pray you, let this child's soul come into him again.'

Elijah's prayer was answered. The boy

sat up and looked about him wonderingly. He was quite well again.

'See, your son is alive!' Elijah said gently.

The woman hugged the boy to her; she was overjoyed.

Then the widow looked up at Elijah, her eyes filled with tears of happiness.

'By this I know that you are a man of God,' she said, 'and the things you say are true.'

Elijah on Mount Carmel

Still there was no rain, and the crops and fruit would not grow.

Ahab thought that it was Elijah's fault, but Elijah reminded the king that he had disobeyed God's laws.

Then Elijah said, 'Bring all the prophets of your god Baal to the top of Mount Carmel.'

The king did as the old prophet told him, and a great crowd of the worshippers of Baal climbed up the mountain, wondering what was going to happen.

Then Elijah went to the people and said, 'When are you going to make up your minds? If the Lord be God, follow him; but if Baal is God, then follow him.'

The people said nothing in reply.

So Elijah spoke to them again. 'I am God's prophet, and I am alone; there are four hundred and fifty prophets of Baal. Let them give us two bullocks for sacrifice. They shall kill one and lay it on wood, but they shall not light a fire; and I will do the same with the other. You must call on your gods to send down fire, and I will call on my God in the same way. Whoever answers will be the true God.'

All the people agreed to this. The prophets of Baal made an altar of stones, gathered wood, and arranged it in a pile for burning. Then they laid the sacrifice on top, and all through the morning they stood round it, chanting: 'O Baal, hear us! O Baal, hear us!' But nothing happened.

They even jumped on the altar that they had made, so eager were they; but still nothing happened.

At midday, Elijah began to mock them.

'Cry aloud,' he said, 'for he is a god! Perhaps he is talking, or out hunting. Maybe he is on a journey, or asleep, and you must wake him up.'

So the followers of Baal cried even louder, and in their excitement they cut themselves with knives, but still nothing happened.

At last it was evening, and Baal's followers were getting very tired.

Then Elijah told all the people to draw near, and they crowded round him. He stooped down and put back some stones which had been knocked down from God's altar. He took twelve stones, one for each of the tribes of Israelites, and built up the altar and made a trench all round it. Elijah rearranged the wood, laid the sacrifice on it, and then said, 'Fill four barrels with water, and pour it over the sacrifice and the wood on the altar.'

Some men did so, and he told them to do it a second time, and then a third. The water ran all round the altar and filled the trench, soaking the wood. The people must have murmured about it, for water was so precious.

It was the time when an evening sacrifice was offered to the Lord, and Elijah prayed: 'Lord God of Abraham, Isaac and of Israel, let it be known this day that you are God in Israel and I am your servant, and that I have done all these things at your command. Hear me, O Lord, hear me, that these people may know that you are the Lord God, and that you have turned their hearts back again!'

Then the fire of the Lord fell, and burnt up the sacrifice, and the wood, and the stones and the dust, and licked up the water in the trench.

And when all the people saw it, they fell on their faces and said, 'The Lord, he is God! The Lord, he is God!'

Then Elijah said to King Ahab, 'Eat and drink, for there is the sound of heavy rain.' Their time of trouble was drawing to a close.

Then Elijah took his servant to the top of Mount Carmel, and fell on his knees.

'Go and look out over the sea,' he told his servant.

The man did so, but when he came back, he said, 'I can't see anything.'

'Go again seven times,' his master said.

The servant must have thought this was a strange order, but he did as Elijah told him, and the seventh time he hurried back.

'There is a little cloud over the sea,' he said, 'just the size of a man's hand.'

'Go and tell the king to get into his chariot,' Elijah said, 'lest the rain holds him up.'

By this time the sky was black with storm clouds, and there was a fierce wind. Then it began to rain – sheets of heavy, life-giving rain. Soon, the crops and the trees would revive, and there would be enough for the animals and all the people to drink.

The Still Small Voice

Elijah sat under a juniper tree,
And prayed that his life might end;
But he fell asleep, and in his dream
It seemed that God did send
An angel, who said, 'Arise and eat,'
And set before him bread,
With water in a jug. Again
The angel stooped and said,
'Elijah, eat, for your way is long.'
He ate the food the angel gave,
Then journeyed onward forty days
Until he reached a lonely cave.
God asked him what he was doing there
And Elijah said, 'I grieve
Because so many have gone astray;
Your most holy way they leave.'
'Come and stand on the hill,' said God,
And his prophet the Voice obeyed;
A whirlwind rushed through the mountains,
But Elijah was not afraid.
There followed a terrible earthquake,
And later a fire it brings,
But Elijah knew that the Lord, his God,
Was not to be found in these things.
Then to his ear came a still, small Voice,
That thrilled his sad heart through;
Elijah poured out his fears and doubts,
And God told him what he must do.

Naboth's Vineyard

Close to King Ahab's palace was a very fine vineyard belonging to a man whose name was Naboth. Ahab wanted it for his own, and he said to Naboth, 'Give me your vineyard so that I may have it for a herb garden, because it is close to my house! I will give you a better vineyard in exchange, or, if you would rather, I will pay you what it is worth.'

But Naboth loved his vineyard, because it had belonged to his family for a very long time. He would not do as the king asked.

Naboth angered Ahab very much, and the king flung himself on his bed, turned his face to the wall and sulked, because he could not get his own way. No one could make him take any food.

His wife, Jezebel, tried to get him to eat. 'Why are you so sad that you won't eat anything?' she asked.

So King Ahab told her the reason.

'I asked Naboth to sell me his vineyard, or to change it for another, but he will not do it.'

'And you are King of Israel!' Jezebel teased him. 'Get up and eat, and I will see that you have your vineyard.'

So she wrote letters in Ahab's name, sealed them with his seal, and sent them to the important men in the city. In them she wrote: 'Send two men to say that Naboth has spoken evil against God and the king, so that he will be put to death.'

Jezebel's orders were carried out, and presently messengers came to say that Naboth was dead.

Then the wicked queen said to her husband, 'Go and take Naboth's vineyard, for he is dead.'

So Ahab went out to do so, but God spoke to Elijah and told him to meet the king in the vineyard.

When Ahab saw Elijah coming, he called out, 'Have you found me, O my enemy?'

'I have found you,' Elijah said sternly, 'because you have done wrong in sight of the Lord, and evil will fall upon you.'

When Ahab heard that, he was sorry for what he had done. He tore his clothes, wore sackcloth, and would not eat, to show that he repented. So God forgave Ahab, but he told Elijah that trouble would come to the land when Ahab's son became king.

Elijah's Chariot

Elijah's work was nearly done, and he had found a man named Elisha to take his place. Elisha had been ploughing with his father's oxen when Elijah stopped and threw his own mantle over Elisha, to show that he was to carry on his work.

Elisha had said goodbye to his father and mother, and left his home to follow Elijah and look after him.

One day, Elijah took Elisha with him to a place named Gilgal.

'You stay here,' Elijah said, 'for the Lord is sending me to Bethel.'

'As the Lord lives, and as your soul lives, I will not leave you,' Elisha answered: so they went on to Bethel.

When they reached it, some wise men's sons met them.

'Do you know that the Lord is going to take away your master today?' they asked Elisha.

'Yes, I know it,' said Elisha, quietly.

'Elisha, you stay here,' Elijah said, 'for the Lord is sending me to Jericho.'

'As the Lord lives, and as your soul lives, I will not leave you,' Elisha answered again.

So they went on to Jericho, and again wise men's sons came out with the same news for Elisha, and again he said that he knew it, and that they should be quiet.

'Stay here, I pray you,' Elijah said, 'for the Lord is sending me to Jordan.'

But Elisha gave him his usual answer, and they went on together. Nothing would make Elisha desert his master.

When they came to the River Jordan, a little crowd of men came out to watch.

Elijah took off his cloak and bundled it up, and hit the water with it. The river parted, and Elijah and Elisha crossed on dry land.

Then Elijah said, 'Ask me anything that I can do for you, before I am taken from you.'

Very humbly, Elisha said, 'Let a double

portion of your spirit fall on me, I beg you.'

'You have asked a very hard thing,' Elijah told him. 'Nevertheless, if you can see me when I am taken from you, it will happen. But if you cannot do so, then it will not.'

As they were talking, a chariot – drawn by horses and surrounded by fire – drew near and came between them, and it seemed as though Elijah, in the chariot, was being caught up in a great wind to heaven.

When Elisha saw it, he cried, 'My father! The chariot and horsemen of Israel!'

Elisha and the Spring

The men of Jericho came out
Saying 'Elisha, look at our land
Withered, wasted, dry with drought,
It is barren and useless sand!'

Elisha took a pot and cast
Salt into the spring.
He cried 'The Lord says now at last
The water is healed again!'

At once the spring began to flow
The grass again was green,
The trees and flowers would always grow
And drought no more be seen.

The Woman of Shunem

One day, as Elisha was passing through Shunem, a woman begged him to take a meal in her house. After that, he often called there, and then the woman – who was quite wealthy – had an idea.

'I can see that this man who so often passes through Shunem is a holy man,' she said to her husband. 'Let us make a little room for him on the roof, and put in it a bed, a stool, a table and a candlestick. Then he can stay with us when he comes.'

Her husband agreed, and he built the room, and they put in it all the things Elisha would need.

Elisha was very pleased when he knew what they had done, and he made use of his own little room. He wanted to show the woman his gratitude, so he asked her if there was anything he could do for her.

'Would you like me to speak about you to the king?' he asked. 'Or to the captain of the army?'

But she shook her head. 'I live happily among my own people,' she said.

'Then what can I do for her?' Elisha asked his servant, Gehazi.

Then he saw Elijah no more. Only his cloak was left behind, the chariot had disappeared, and he was alone beside the river.

Elisha picked up Elijah's cloak. Then, just as his master had done, he struck the water, and it parted so that he could cross to the other side.

When Elisha reached Jericho, and the wise men's sons saw him, they said, 'The spirit of Elijah rests on Elisha.'

And they came to meet him, and bowed before him to do him honour.

'She has no child,' Gehazi said.

Elisha called the woman, and told her that she would have a little son.

'I must believe you, for you are a man of God,' the woman said.

It came true, and the woman had a son and was happy; but one day, when the boy was older, he went to the fields where his father was, with the reapers.

The sun blazed down, and the boy's head began to ache very badly.

'My head! My head!' he wailed.

'Carry him to his mother,' his father said to a lad who was standing by.

His mother held the boy on her lap for a while, and then he died. She carried her son up to Elisha's room and laid him on the bed. Then she shut the door and went out, calling to her husband, 'Send one of the young men to me with an ass. I must go and find the man of God.'

'Why do you want to go to him today?' he asked. 'It is not a special day.'

'It will be,' said his wife, and she saddled the ass and rode as quickly as she could to Mount Carmel, where Elisha was at that time.

Elisha saw her coming, and he said to Gehazi, his servant, 'Look, here comes the woman from Shunem! Go quickly and meet her, and say "Is all well with you, and your husband? Is all well with the child?"'

Gehazi did as he was told, and all the woman said was, 'It is well.'

When she reached Elisha, she flung herself at his feet.

Gehazi would have made her get up, but Elisha said, 'Leave her alone. She is troubled about something, and the Lord has not told me what it is.'

'Did I not ask for a son?' said the woman. 'I begged you not to deceive me!'

Elisha realised something had happened to her boy. He turned to Gehazi.

'Take my staff and go,' he said. 'Do not let anyone stop you on the way. Lay this

staff of mine quickly on the child's face.'

'As the Lord lives,' said the woman, 'I will not leave you.'

So Gehazi hurried ahead with the staff and Elisha and the woman followed.

Gehazi went up to the boy in Elisha's room, and laid the staff on his face – but he did not stir.

Gehazi ran back to meet Elisha. 'He is not awake,' he said.

Elisha then went up to the room, shut the door and prayed. He, like Elijah, covered the child with his own body, and put his mouth on the boy's mouth, and his hands on the boy's hands, and warmed him.

Presently he rose, went down the stairs, and paced up and down. Soon, Elisha went back to the boy and breathed on him again.

The child sneezed seven times, and opened his eyes. All was well!

Elisha gave the woman back her son, and she fell at Elisha's feet, full of gratitude. Then she took up her son and went out.

Naaman and the Little Maid

Naaman was captain of the king of Syria's army. He was a great man and a brave one, but he was not well. Naaman had leprosy, and he longed to be cured.

When the Syrians were fighting the Israelites, Naaman's men had taken some prisoners, and among them was a young girl who became a maid in Naaman's house, and waited on his wife.

She saw that Naaman was ill, and she longed to do something to help him.

'How I wish my master lived in Samaria!' she said to her mistress one day. 'There is a prophet there who could cure him.'

A servant who heard what the little maid had said went to tell his master. Then when the king of Syria also heard about the

prophet he wanted to help his captain.

'I will send a letter to the king of Israel,' he said.

Soon Naaman was hurrying off with the letter, together with presents of gold, silver and new clothes.

When he was shown in to the king of Israel's presence, the king read the letter and was vexed.

'Am I God,' he demanded, 'who has power to make life and take it away, that this man sends to me, to cure someone of leprosy? No, it is a trick; he is trying to quarrel with me!'

But when Elisha heard about it, he sent a message to the king.

'Let this man come to me,' he said, 'and he shall know that there is a prophet in Israel.'

The messenger went back and told Naaman what Elisha had said.

Elisha lived in the land of the people whom the Syrians thought of as enemies, and it was not easy for Naaman to obey humbly and go to visit an Israelite. But he was so anxious to be made well that he climbed into his chariot, urged on his horses, and came to Elisha's house.

He expected the prophet to come and

greet him, but Elisha sent out a servant to meet this great man from Syria.

'Go and wash in the River Jordan seven times, and you will be cured,' Naaman was told.

Naaman was very cross. 'Well,' he said, 'I thought he would come out himself, and stand there and call on the name of the Lord his God, and put his hand on me and heal me. And why should I go to their river, Jordan? Are not our rivers of Damascus better than all the waters of Israel?'

Naaman turned away and went off in a rage. But his servants reasoned with him persuading him to do as he was told.

'If the prophet had told you to do something big and important, would you not have done it? How much better it is to carry out this simple order: "Wash and be clean!"'

Naaman knew that they were right, so he went down to the River Jordan and dipped himself in it seven times. He was cured!

Naaman went back to Elisha and stood before him humbly. 'Now I know there is no God in all the earth but in Israel,' he said.

The Axe is Found

The young men wished to build a house
Close to the river-side.
'We'll make some wooden beams,' they said,
'And build it large and wide.'
Elisha also went with them,
And watched them cut down trees.
Oh, it would be a splendid house,
With fine beams such as these!
But as they cut wood with an axe
Upon the Jordan's brink,
An axe-head fell into the depths,
And they all saw it sink.
'Alas, alas!' the young man cried,
'That axe was only borrowed.
However shall I get it back?'
And for its loss he sorrowed.
'Show me the place,' Elisha said.
They showed the spot to him.
He threw a stick in after it.
The axe came up, to skim
The surface of the river's flow.
Gladly the young man bent
To rescue, very thankfully,
The axe that had been lent.

Elisha and the Syrians

The king of Syria made war on the Israelites, and chose a place to pitch his camp.

Elisha sent a message to the king of Israel, telling him where it was, and the Israelites were victorious.

The king of Syria was worried by this, and asked his servants which of them had been disloyal enough to give away the Syrians' hiding-place to the Israelites.

'None of us, my lord,' they told him, 'but the prophet of Israel knows everything. He even tells the king of Israel the secrets that you whisper in your own room.'

'Go and spy out where he is,' said the king, 'and we will take him prisoner.'

The Syrian soldiers found where Elisha

108

was, and they told the king that he was in Dothan.

So the king of Syria sent chariots and horses and a great number of men, and they surrounded the city walls.

The next morning, Elisha got up early and saw what had happened.

'Alas, my master! What shall we do?' wailed his frightened servant.

'Don't be afraid,' Elisha said, 'for those who are with us are more than those who are with them.' Then he prayed: 'Lord, open the young man's eyes.'

The young man looked round him and he could see what Elisha saw: the mountain seemed full of horses and chariots of fire.

Then, as the Syrians drew near, Elisha prayed again, and asked that his enemies might not be able to see for a time.

The Syrians began to grope about, not knowing where they were, and Elisha went out to them.

'This is not the way,' he said. 'Follow me, and I will bring you to the man for whom you are looking.'

He led them away from Dothan to Samaria, and then he prayed again; and the Syrians opened their eyes and saw that they were in a strange place.

'Shall I smite them?' the king of Israel asked Elisha. 'Shall I smite them?'

'No,' Elisha said. 'Give them food and drink, and then send them back to their master.'

Flour and Barley

The king of Syria sent his army against Samaria, and there was not enough food for the Samarian people to eat, because of their enemies' siege.

They were all hungry, and searching everywhere for food. Yet Elisha told them that, the very next day, fine flour and barley would be on sale at the city gates. But no one could believe him.

Four poor lepers were sitting by the city gate.

'Why do we sit here until we die?' they said to one another. 'If we go into the city, there is famine and we shall not live; and neither shall we live if we go on sitting. Let us go and give ourselves up to the Syrians –

they may perhaps at least save our lives.'

So they got up, as dusk was falling, and made their way to the Syrian camp. But all was silent; there was not a single man there. The Lord had made the Syrians hear a noise of chariots and horses and many soldiers, and they had told each other that the Israelites had sent for the Hittites and the Egyptians to fight for them. Thus the Syrians had taken fright and fled, in the twilight, leaving their tents, their horses and asses, and their camp, just as they stood.

When the lepers peeped into the first tent and saw that it was empty, they grew bold, went in, and ate and drank eagerly. They took gold, silver, and clothes, and hid them, and did the same in another tent.

Then they said to each other, 'We are not doing right. This is a glad day for us, and we are not taking back the good news. If we wait till morning light, some trouble may befall us. Let us go and tell the king's household now.'

They hurried back to the city gate.

'We came to the camp of the Syrians,' they said excitedly, 'and there was nobody there – only horses and asses, tethered.'

Messages were sent to the king's household at once. The king got up, although it was in the middle of the night, and said to his servants, 'Now I will show you what the Syrians have done to us. They know we are hungry, so they have left their camp to hide in the fields, saying: "When they come out of the city, we shall catch them."'

'Let some of us take five of the horses that are left, and let us go and see,' suggested one of his servants.

They took two of the chariot horses, and set off. All the way to Jordan, the road was strewn with clothes and pots, which the Syrians had dropped in their haste to get away. The servants came back and told the king.

Then all the people went out and took what the Syrians had left behind in the camp. They took flour and barley, and sold it at the city gates, as Elisha had foretold.

The Lesson of the Arrows

Elisha fell ill, and when it was known that he had not very long to live, King Joash of Israel went to see him, his heart heavy.

To the king's surprise, Elisha suddenly said, 'Take a bow and arrows!'

The king did as he was told.

'Put your hand on the bow,' said Elisha; and when the king had done so, the old prophet laid his hand on that of the king.

'Now open the window that faces east,' Elisha said.

King Joash opened it. The window looked towards Damascus, which was the capital of Syria.

'Shoot!' said Elisha.

The king pulled the bow-string and, as it twanged, the arrow flew in the direction of his enemies' country.

'It is the arrow of the Lord's deliverance,' said the old prophet. 'It is a sign of your victory over Syria, which will surely come. Take the arrows!'

King Joash did as he was told.

'Now strike the ground with them,' Elisha ordered.

King Joash struck three times, and then he stopped.

'You should have struck the ground five or six times,' Elisha said; he knew that the king could not overcome the Syrians, unless he learned not to give up too soon. 'You would have beaten Syria, because you would not stop until you had done so. Now you will only go up against her three times.'

The King they Hid

Queen Athaliah was on the throne of the kingdom of Judah, and did not want to give up her crown, which she would have to do if there were any royal princes who could claim the throne. So she ordered that all the boys in the royal family were to be slain.

Yet one baby boy escaped; his name was Joash, and the priest's wife hid him, with his nurse, in a room in the temple. Joash stayed there for six years, and no one ever found him. The queen knew nothing about this, and thought that nobody could now take the throne from her.

When little Joash was seven, the high priest sent for the captains and leaders of the army, and told them about the little boy who was in hiding.

Then he brought out King David's own spears and shields, and gave them to the soldiers. They stood on guard around the temple, and then the little boy was brought out and crowned king. The high priest put the crown on Joash's head, and anointed him, and all the people clapped their hands and shouted: 'God save the King!'

When the wicked Queen Athaliah heard

the noise, and saw the soldiers and crowds gathering round the temple, she came out to see what was happening.

Athaliah saw the little boy with the crown on his head, and all the people shouting for joy, and the trumpeters blowing their instruments.

'Treason! Treason!' cried the queen furiously, and tore her clothes in anger. Then the priest gave an order, and the soldiers came forward to take Athaliah away. After that, the priest told the people to break down the altars to Baal which had been used during the wicked queen's reign.

King Joash had learnt about God and his servants in the temple, and thus would be a good king – living and serving God – although he was only seven years old. He reigned under the name Jehoash.

Repairing the Temple

The beautiful temple was needing repairs;
The stonework was broken in places.
The woodwork was marked, and the statues looked faded,
Gilding was needed to beautify faces.
'Now make a big chest with a slit in the top,'
Said the priest, 'and I think you will find
That the money collects in a wonderful way.'
They all knew what he had in his mind.
People dropped in their coins: 'twas counted with joy,
And put into bags that they had.
Then the masons and carpenters all got to work,
And the priests and the people were glad.
The temple grew gleaming and lovely once more,
And they had enough money to pay.

The King of Assyria

While King Hezekiah was reigning in Judah, a very powerful king called Sennacherib came from Assyria, and captured the cities of Judah.

King Hezekiah sent a message to him, saying, 'I have offended; what you demand of me, I will hand over to you.'

Sennacherib asked for a great deal of gold and silver, and Hezekiah gave him all the silver that was found in the Lord's temple, and in the king's treasury. He cut off all the gold from the temple doors, and from the pillars, and gave it to the king of Assyria.

King Sennacherib sent three leaders, with a great host of men, against Jerusalem. On reaching the walls of the city, they called to the king, who sent out the head of his household and two others, to meet them.

Rab-shakeh, one of the Assyrian leaders, spoke to Hezekiah's men. 'Go to Hezekiah,' he said loftily. 'Tell him, "Thus says the great king, the king of Assyria: In what do you put your trust? You say – but they are vain words – that you have help and strength when you fight. Whom do you trust, that you can dare to rebel against me? You trust Egypt, which is like a broken reed; if you lean on it, it will pierce your hand.

'"But if you say, we trust in the Lord our God, is not that he whose high places and altars Hezekiah has taken away, telling his people that they must worship only in Jerusalem?" Now, I pray you, give pledges to my lord, the king of Assyria, and I will let you have two thousand horses – that is, if you can find men to ride them. How can you turn away the least of my master's servants, and put your trust in Egypt to send you chariots and horsemen? Am I come up against this land to destroy it without the Lord's help? The Lord told me to do it.'

Then Hezekiah's men said, 'Please speak to us in the Syrian language and not in the Jewish language, which the men sitting on the wall can hear.'

'Has my master sent me to your master, and to you, to speak these words?' Rabshakeh answered. 'Has he not sent me to the men who sit on the wall, that they may hear?' And he called out at the top of his voice, in the Jewish language: 'Hear the words of the great king – King Sennacherib of Assyria! The king says: "Do not let

Hezekiah deceive you, for he shall not be able to deliver you out of his hand." Neither let Hezekiah make you trust in the Lord, saying: "The Lord will surely deliver us, and this city shall not be given into the hand of Assyria." Do not listen to Hezekiah, for thus says the king of Assyria: "Make an agreement with me. Come out to me, and then every one of you shall eat the fruit of his own vine, and drink water from his own supply – until I come and take you away to a land like your own land, with corn and wine, bread and vineyards, olive oil and honey, that you may live and not die." '

But the people did not answer, for the king had told them to keep silent, and the three men went and told Hezekiah what Sennacherib had said.

Hezekiah's Prayer

When King Hezekiah heard of King Sennacherib's boastful words, he put on sackcloth as a sign of mourning, and went to the temple.

He told his three leaders to go to the prophet Isaiah, and say to him, 'Hezekiah says that this is a sad day for us all. It may be that the Lord your God will hear what Rabshakeh has been saying, and will reprove him for his words. Pray for those who are left.'

When Isaiah received this message, he replied, 'Say this to your master: "The Lord says, do not be afraid because of what you have heard; I will send the king of Assyria back to his own land, and there he will perish by the sword."'

Rab-shakeh sent messengers with a letter to Hezekiah, saying yet again that it was useless for him to trust in God, since no one could hold his own against the king of Assyria.

When Hezekiah had read the letter, he took it into the temple. Then he prayed, and said, 'O Lord God of Israel, you are God, even you alone, of all the kingdoms of the earth. You made heaven and earth. Lord, bow down your ear and hear. Lord, open your eyes and see.

'Hear the words of Sennacherib, who reproaches the living God. Truly, Lord, the Assyrians have destroyed other nations and lands, and thrown their gods into the fire. Now, O Lord, I beg you, save us so that everyone may know that you are the Lord God, and you alone.'

Soon afterwards, Isaiah sent a message to King Hezekiah, saying, 'The Lord God of Israel has heard your prayer. The king of Assyria shall not come into this city, nor shoot an arrow into it. I will defend the city and save it, for my own sake, and for my servant David's sake.'

That night, the Assyrians were overcome, and thousands were slain, and King Sennacherib returned to his own country.

Hezekiah is made well again

King Hezekiah of Judah fell very ill, and no one thought he would get better.

The prophet Isaiah went to see him. 'Thus says the Lord,' he told the king, '"Put your affairs in order, for you will not live."'

King Hezekiah turned his face to the wall and prayed to the Lord.

'Remember now, O Lord, I beg you,' he said, 'how I have walked before you in truth and with a perfect heart, and have done what is right in your sight.'

Isaiah came to him again, and this time he said, 'Thus says the Lord, the God of David: "I have heard your prayer, and seen your tears. I will add fifteen more years to your life. I will deliver you and this city out of the hand of the king of Assyria, and I will defend this city. And this shall be a sign to you from the Lord – I will put the sun-dial back by ten degrees."'

Then it happened just as the Lord had said.

Isaiah said that a plaster of figs should be lain on the place where the king felt pain, and it would heal him.

When Hezekiah was better, he wrote a hymn of thanksgiving.

'The living, the living shall praise you, as I do this day,' he sang joyfully. 'The Lord was ready to save me; therefore we will sing my songs to stringed instruments, all the days of our life in the house of the Lord.'

A Gift from Babylon

The king of Babylon heard that Hezekiah was better, and he sent him letters and a present. King Hezekiah was very pleased to receive them, and he took the messengers who brought them to see all his treasures.

Hezekiah showed them the many precious things in his palace: silver, gold, spices and costly, sweet-smelling ointments.

Once more, Isaiah came to see him.

'What did these men say?' he asked Hezekiah. 'Where did they come from?'

'They came to me from a far country,' the king told him. 'Even from Babylon.'

'What have they seen in your house?' Isaiah wanted to know.

'They have seen everything,' Hezekiah answered. 'I have shown them all my treasures, and kept nothing back.'

'Hear the word of the Lord of hosts,' said Isaiah the prophet. 'The days shall come when your house and your treasures will be carried off to Babylon. Nothing will be left, says the Lord. They will take away your sons to serve in the palace of their king.'

But King Hezekiah said to Isaiah, 'There shall be peace and truth in my days.'

The Book is found

Josiah was only eight years old when he became king of Judah. As he grew up, he tried to be a good ruler, and keep God's laws, and rule as King David had done.

It was not easy, for many people had set up altars to false gods.

Josiah made up his mind to repair the temple, and bring it back to the beauty of holiness of other days. He told Hilkiah, the high priest, to see that the work was done, and once again the carpenters and stonemasons were busy.

Then, one day, Hilkiah came hurrying to Shaphan in great excitement. Shaphan was a writer who could copy out books.

'We have found the book of the law, hidden away in the house of the Lord!' he said, and held out a scroll.

Shaphan took the scroll and opened it. He began to read, and then said, 'We must take this to the king.'

The scribe went straight to King Josiah. 'Hilkiah, the high priest, has given me a book,' Shaphan said, and he began to read the laws on the scroll aloud to the king.

As he listened, the young king grew more and more dismayed, for the scribe was indeed reading the laws of God, but the people had forgotten them.

'Everyone must hear the laws which God gave us,' he said, and he himself took the scroll into the temple and read it to all the people who gathered there. Then Josiah stood by a pillar and made a promise to God to walk in his ways, and to keep his commandments as they were written in the book they found.

And all the people cried: 'Amen!'

Then King Josiah told the priests to bring out all the vessels that had been made for the false god, Baal, and he took them to the fields outside Jerusalem and burned them.

Then Josiah told his people to keep the feast of the Passover. This had been forgotten for a long time, but the king had read about it in the book.

Josiah was a very good king, who turned to the Lord with all his heart, and tried to teach his people to keep the laws which Moses had given to the children of Israel.

To Babylon

Nebuchadnezzar of Babylon
Was a great and mighty king.
He fell upon Jerusalem,
And broke down everything.
He took the temple's precious gold
Away to Babylon;
The vessels of the house of God,
The silver — all were gone.
The king was taken prisoner,
And many people, too;
They were enslaved in Babylon,
And had hard work to do —
It was a sad and bitter day
When they were carried far away.

Psalm 137
Far from Home

The people who were taken away from Judah to slavery in Babylon often thought longingly of home. This is a song they sang about it:

We sat down in Babylon,
At the river's side,
Remembering Jerusalem —
How often we have cried.

We even hung our silent harps
Upon the willow trees.
'You used to sing such joyful songs,
Now sing us one of these.'

So say the men of Babylon;
They do not understand.
How can we sing the Lord's own song,
Here in this foreign land?

If I forget Jerusalem,
Let my right hand grow weak;
And if I fail to talk of her,
My tongue shall cease to speak.

Jeremiah and the Potter

Wise men, known as prophets, tried to help the people by their words of wisdom, and by the visions they saw.

There was a prophet called Jeremiah. One day, Jeremiah heard God telling him to go down to the potter's house, where he had something to say to him.

Jeremiah did as he was told, and he watched the potter shaping clay pots on his wheel. Presently, he saw him make a pot that turned out to be the wrong shape; the potter would not let it go, and patiently formed it all over again.

Then God gave Jeremiah a message to take to his people: 'O house of Israel, cannot I do with you as this potter has done? As the clay is in the potter's hand, so are you in my hand, says the Lord.'

God went on to tell Jeremiah that he could make, or break, a nation or a kingdom. If the people repented of the wrong things they had done, God would take them and make them anew.

117

Jeremiah and the Figs

Another time, when the king of Babylon had taken the princes of Judah, and the carpenters and workmen of Jerusalem, as his prisoners, and carried them off to his own country, Jeremiah had a vision of two baskets of figs, set down before the temple of the Lord.

In one basket were fresh, ripe figs, and in the other the fruit was bad, so that it could not be eaten. Then God told Jeremiah that the good figs stood for the people who would remain faithful to him in a strange land, and who would one day return to their own country. The bad figs were a sign of the people who would do wrong, and fall away from God, and who would therefore not return from Babylon.

Jeremiah took his messages to the people. At first they did not want to listen to him, but in the end they said, 'This man has spoken to us in the name of the Lord our God.'

Jeremiah in Prison

King Zedekiah would not listen to what Jeremiah the prophet said. All the same, he sent a message to him one day, asking him to pray to God for the people of Judah.

Then God told Jeremiah: 'Say this to the king of Judah who sent to you to ask a boon of me – "The Egyptians, who have been helping you, will go back to their own land, and the Chaldeans will come up against your city and take it."'

The princes did not think Jeremiah was helping them at all by announcing such bad news. 'Let this man be put to death,' they begged the king, 'for he is weakening the spirit of the soldiers who are left in the city, by saying such things. He is not working for the welfare of the people, but in order to harm them.'

'He is in your hands,' said King Zedekiah. 'For the king cannot go against you.'

So they took Jeremiah, and let him down into a deep dungeon, by a rope. There was mud at the bottom, and poor Jeremiah sank into it.

Jeremiah had a friend in the court who went to the king, his master.

'My lord the king,' he said, 'these men have sinned in everything that they have done to Jeremiah the prophet, whom they have cast into the dungeon. He is likely to die of hunger, for there is no more bread.'

Then the king told his chamberlain to take thirty men, and rescue Jeremiah from prison. First, they had to pull Jeremiah out of the mud. They took with them a bundle of old clothes and rags, and let them down tied with cords to Jeremiah, in his deep, muddy dungeon.

'Put these old rags under your arms,' the chamberlain told him, 'and then tie the cord round you, over them.'

Jeremiah did as he was told, and then the men up above pulled hard, and raised him out of the mud.

The Scroll is Burnt

One day, Jeremiah heard the voice of God telling him to take a scroll, and write in it all that God had told him.

Jeremiah asked a man named Baruch to write down everything he told him so that he might obey God.

When at last the task was finished, Jeremiah told Baruch to read the scroll to the people in the Lord's House on a fast day. 'Maybe,' said Jeremiah, 'they will listen, and be sorry for all the wrong things they have done.'

So Baruch did as the prophet asked him.

A man named Michaiah was among those who listened in the Lord's House, and presently he hurried away to the scribes' room in the king's palace, and told them what he had heard.

The scribes wanted to know more about it, and they sent a messenger to ask Baruch to bring the scroll and come before them.

When he arrived, they said, 'Now, sit down and read it to us.'

Baruch did as they commanded, and they listened. Presently, however, they began to feel afraid, and said to Baruch, 'We shall tell the king about this.' Then someone asked Baruch, 'Tell us – how did you write all this down?'

'Jeremiah spoke the words,' Baruch explained, 'and I wrote them down.'

'You and Jeremiah had better hide,' they said, 'and do not tell anyone where you are!'

They left the scroll in the scribes' room; then they went to the king, and told him what they had heard.

The king sent a messenger to fetch the scroll; and when he had brought it, the messenger began to read it to the king.

It was winter, and there was a big fire burning in the room. When the messenger had been reading for some time, the king took the scroll from him, and threw it into the fire and waited until it was all burnt.

Then the king sent men out to capture Jeremiah and Baruch, but they could not find their hiding-place. When they heard all that had happened, Jeremiah took a fresh scroll and, together with Baruch, he began to write everything down again.

Building the Temple again

It was a joyful day indeed
When home the captives went.
To build the temple once again
Was their desired intent.
They took back to Jerusalem
The treasures that were brought
To Babylon, when enemies
Against their land had fought.
Once more they brought the wood and stone;
And with foundations laid,
They sang glad praises to the Lord,
While their musicians played.
It was a splendid sight to see,
After their weary captivity!
And now they wished no more to roam —
Ezra the priest had led them home.

Nehemiah's Plan

Nehemiah had a very important job; he was cup-bearer to the king of Persia. Now Nehemiah was a soldier on duty at the king's winter palace, when news reached him from Jerusalem that the great temple had been rebuilt, but that the ancient city walls and gates were broken down or crumbling away.

Because his own people were in Jerusalem, Nehemiah loved the city, and he was very sad upon hearing the news. When he took in the king's wine, his sad expression was noticed, for Nehemiah had never looked so unhappy before.

'You are not ill, I know,' said the king to Nehemiah. 'What is troubling you and making you look so very sorrowful?'

'Is it so surprising that I am sad,' asked Nehemiah, 'when the city of my own people is lying in ruins, and the gates are destroyed?'

'What do you want me to do?' asked the king.

First, Nehemiah sent up a swift prayer to God, and then he said, 'If it please the king – and if I, your servant, have found favour in your sight – let me go back to Judah, to build a new wall around Jerusalem.'

'How long will it take?' asked the king. 'When will you get back?'

Nehemiah named a time, and the king said he might go. He gave him a letter to the keeper of the king's forest, telling him to give Nehemiah the timber he needed, and letters to the governors to give him safe conduct until he arrived at Judah. And so at last Nehemiah set off for Jerusalem.

Nehemiah builds the Wall

Nehemiah rode round the walls of Jerusalem, seeing how much needed to be done. Then he went into the city, and told the priests that he had come to help them build a new wall around Jerusalem.

Some who heard him were very pleased. 'Let us rise up and build,' they said, and they were ready to begin. But others laughed at Nehemiah, and mocked at those who set to work so eagerly.

They could not daunt Nehemiah, however. While half the men got on with the work, the others watched for those who might try to hinder their task.

At last the great wall was finished, and the new gates set in place. There was much rejoicing; the people blew trumpets, and sang and played their harps and cymbals. It was a happy day for everyone, but Nehemiah was the happiest of them all.

The Valley of Dry Bones

Ezekiel was a prophet who was carried off into exile, and never returned to his home. One day, he had a vision with a wonderful meaning.

He thought he saw a valley between hills, and in the valley lay many dry bones.

'Son of man, can these bones live?' God's voice asked him.

Ezekiel could not tell, but he answered, 'O Lord God, you know.'

Again, the voice spoke. 'Speak to them! Say to them: "O you dry bones, hear the word of the Lord. Thus saith the Lord God – Behold, I will make breath enter into you, and you will live; I will lay muscles and flesh and skin over you, and breathe into you, and you will live, and know that I am the Lord."'

So Ezekiel did as he was told; and, as he spoke, the bones came together and were covered as the voice had said, and became men; but there was no life in them.

Then the voice said, 'Speak to the four winds, and tell them to breathe upon these men, that they may live.'

Ezekiel did as God commanded, and the breath came into the bodies, and they lived and stood up in the valley – a great army.

Then God told Ezekiel what it meant.

'Son of man,' he said, 'these bones stand for the whole company of Israel. They say that their hope is lost; but tell them that God will bring them into the land of Israel. You shall live, and I will place you in your own land. Then you will know that I, the Lord, have spoken, and done as I promised.'

121

A Promise of Peace

One day, Ezekiel heard God say,
'The people are my sheep,
And I their watchful shepherd am,
Who all my flock will keep.

'I will seek out the wandering lambs,
And find them food to eat;
They shall lie down within my fold,
And feed in pastures sweet.

'I will bind up my wounded sheep
And they shall live in peace.
One shepherd shall watch over them,
And all their troubles cease.'

Queen Vashti disobeys

There was a king named Ahasuerus, who ruled over a great stretch of land from India to Ethiopia.

One day, the king held a feast for all his princes, nobles and servants. It lasted a long time, and was held in the courtyard of the palace garden, which was decorated with white, green and blue hangings, and pillars of marble. The couches were gold and silver, and the floor was marble. The guests drank the wine out of gold cups, each cup was carved differently. Ahasuerus displayed all his treasures.

At the same time, the queen, whose name was Vashti, gave a party for all the women in the royal palace.

Presently, the king sent seven chamberlains to bring Queen Vashti to him. She must wear her crown, so that everyone could see how beautiful she was. But the queen refused to obey him, and it made the king very angry to think that she would not do as he asked.

'What shall we do to the queen for disobeying the king's orders?' he asked his wise men.

'Vashti has not only done wrong to the king,' said one of them, 'but she has wronged everybody, because, if she disobeys her husband, all the other wives will feel that they can act in the same way. Therefore, let the king send Vashti away and find a new queen, who is better than she. Then all the wives will honour their husbands.'

The king agreed, and Vashti was no longer queen. A new queen would have to be found, so officers were sent throughout the kingdom to find all the beautiful young girls, and then bring them to the palace for the king to choose one of them.

Esther is Crowned

In the palace there was a Hebrew whose name was Mordecai, who had been carried away from Jerusalem to Babylon by King

Nebuchadnezzar. Mordecai had brought up his beautiful cousin, Esther, because she was an orphan.

When all the girls had been brought to the palace of Ahasuerus for the king to choose the new queen, Esther was sent to join them.

As soon as King Ahasuerus saw her, Esther became his favourite, and he gave her seven maids, and they had the best places in the women's house.

Mordecai was longing to know if the king was going to choose Esther, and every day he walked up and down near the women's court, wondering how she was, and what would become of her.

Then the king saw every girl in turn, and told them that they might ask for any gifts they wanted; but when it came to Esther's turn, she asked for nothing at all.

The king loved Esther dearly, and chose her to be his queen. He set the royal crown on her head, and made a great feast.

A Time of Trouble

There was a man at the court of King Ahasuerus named Haman, and the king made him more important than any man there. Everybody paid great respect to him, as the king had commanded, except Mordecai, who refused.

When Haman realised this, he was angry. He knew that Mordecai was a Jew, and so he turned against all the Hebrew people in the kingdom. He went to the king and said, 'There are certain people scattered throughout the land whose laws are different from yours. They do not keep the king's laws; so, if it pleases the king, let it be written that they shall be destroyed, and I will give a large sum of money to those who have charge of the business, to go into the king's treasury.

So the king took the ring off his finger and gave it to Haman, and he said, 'The money is given to you, and to the people, to do as seems right to you to those who do not abide by my laws.'

Then the scribes were called, and the letters were written to all the governors and rulers of every part of the kingdom. The letters said that on a certain day all the

When she had listened to his tale, the queen said, 'Go back to Mordecai and tell him that I dare not go into the king's throne room without being sent for – no one does that and lives. Only if the king holds out his sceptre, for his visitor to touch, will his life be spared; that means that he has found favour in the king's sight. I have not been called to go before the king for a whole month.'

Mordecai sent a message back to Esther to tell her that she ought not to be afraid to plead with the king for the Jews. 'Who knows,' he said, 'whether you were not sent to the kingdom for this?'

Esther's Request

On the third day, Queen Esther made up her mind to be brave, and to try to help Mordecai and the Jewish people. She put on her royal robes, and went and stood in the inner court of the king's house, not far from the throne.

The king saw Esther standing there, and was pleased. He held out his golden sceptre as a sign that she should come to him.

Esther drew near, and touched the top of the sceptre.

'What is your wish, Queen Esther?' asked the king. 'It shall be granted, even to the half of my kingdom.'

'If it seems good to the king,' Esther answered, 'let the king and Haman come today to a banquet I have prepared.'

'Tell Haman to come quickly,' said King Ahasuerus, 'so that we may do what Queen Esther wishes.'

So the king and Haman went to the queen's banquet, and while they were feasting, the queen invited them to another banquet the next day. Haman was very pleased, until he saw Mordecai sitting at the king's gate, and once again the Jew would not get up or move for him.

Jewish people were ordered to be slain.

When Mordecai learnt what was happening he was very sorrowful. He put on sackcloth and ashes as a sign of mourning, and went into the city, crying aloud. As the news spread, all the Jews began weeping and wailing, and Queen Esther's servants told her about the people's distress.

The queen was troubled, and she sent clothing to Mordecai, that he might put it on instead of the sackcloth; but he would not take off his sign of mourning. Then the queen called Hatach, one of the king's chamberlains, and told him to go and ask Mordecai what was the matter.

Mordecai told Hatach all that had happened, and the chamberlain hurried back to the palace to tell Queen Esther. Mordecai sent her a copy of the decree, and begged her to ask the king to spare his people.

Haman went home full of indignation, and told his wife all about it. 'I was the only guest at the banquet prepared by the queen, except the king himself,' he said. 'The king has heaped honours on me, and tomorrow I'm invited to another feast – but I cannot feel glad about it whilst Mordecai is sitting at the king's gate.'

'Make preparations for him to die,' his wife and his friends said to him. 'Then tomorrow go and enjoy yourself at the feast, and speak to the king about Mordecai.' And Haman did this.

The King's Question

That night, the king could not sleep. He called for diaries of happenings in his kingdom to be read to him, and he heard of a time when Mordecai had gone to Queen Esther about a plot against him.

'What was done to reward Mordecai?' asked the king, and his servants told him: 'Nothing!'

Just then, Haman arrived to ask for Mordecai to be put to death. A servant told King Ahasuerus he was there, and the king ordered Haman to be brought in. Then the king asked him a question. 'What shall be done to the man whom the king delights to honour above everyone else?' he asked.

Now Haman thought: 'Whom would the king delight to honour more than myself?'

So he replied, 'For the man whom the king delights to honour, let the royal garments be brought which the king used to wear, and the horse the king rides, and the crown which is set on his head. And let the clothes and the horse and the crown be given to one of the most noble princes, that he may dress up the man whom the king delights to honour, and bring him on horseback through the city and proclaim before him: "This is done to the man whom the king delights to honour!"'

Then said the king, 'Quickly, take the royal clothes and the horse, as you have said, to Mordecai the Jew, who sits at the king's gate.'

Haman was dismayed and angry, but there was nothing he could do about it. He was obliged to do to Mordecai as he himself had suggested. He dressed Mordecai in the king's robes, put the crown on his head and set him on the horse, and led him in triumph through the city.

But afterwards he hurried home and told his wife and friends everything that had happened.

'It looks as though you will have to bow before Mordecai and his people,' they said. They were still talking when chamberlains arrived to take Haman to Queen Esther's second banquet, and he was forced to go with them.

A Great Day

When King Ahasuerus and Haman were at Queen Esther's second banquet, the king said to her, 'What is your greatest wish, Queen Esther? It shall be granted, to the half of my kingdom.'

'If I have found favour in your sight, O king,' Esther answered, 'I ask for my life, and for the life of my fellow Jews, for someone is plotting to kill us all.'

'Who is he, and where is he who dares to do this?' the king asked angrily.

'Our enemy is this wicked Haman,' said Queen Esther.

The king rose from the table and strode out into the garden. Haman, feeling very frightened, stood up to ask the queen to spare his life, for he was certain that King Ahasuerus would not let him live.

Haman was right, for the king ordered him to be put to death, and gave his house to Queen Esther. She, in turn, gave it to Mordecai, and then Ahasuerus gave him the royal ring which he had once given to Haman.

Again the king held out his sceptre for his queen to touch, as she made her wish. 'If it please the king,' she said, 'let letters be sent to all the governors, telling them that the Jews are to live in safety.'

The king did as she asked. Scribes were called to write letters, and Mordecai and Queen Esther saw that they were sealed with the king's ring, which meant that no one would dare to disobey.

Then the letters were carried in all directions by men riding on camels, horses and mules; they took the news to every province, from India to Ethiopia.

Mordecai left the palace wearing royal robes of blue and white, and a great crown of gold, and all the Jews were proud and happy when they saw him, and planned a feast in honour of this great day, and all that Queen Esther and Mordecai had done for their people.

A Man named Job

There was a man whose name was Job. He loved God, and lived a good life, and was always kind to his neighbours. Life was not easy for him, however, and Job had many troubles which tested him. He lost his flocks, his camels, and even his beloved children; but Job trusted in God through it all.

'The Lord gave, and the Lord took away,' Job said. 'Blessed be the name of the Lord.'

Then he himself fell ill, and it seemed that everything had now been taken from him. Sometimes Job found it hard to understand why he should have to suffer so, and three of his friends tried to explain why troubles came to him, but he knew that they had not found the right answer.

At last, the voice of God spoke to Job, reminding him of all the wonderful things that the Creator had done, which no man could do: man could not guide the Great Bear, and all the other stars, along their way; man did not give the horse his strength, or the peacock his fine feathers – only God could do these things.

'I know, O Lord, that you can do everything,' Job said. 'Nothing is impossible to you. I have spoken of things I do not understand; but now I have seen you.'

Job prayed for his friends, who had not understood God's ways, and he became a great man again, with more sheep and camels that he had ever had before. He had other sons and daughters, too, and life was full for Job again.

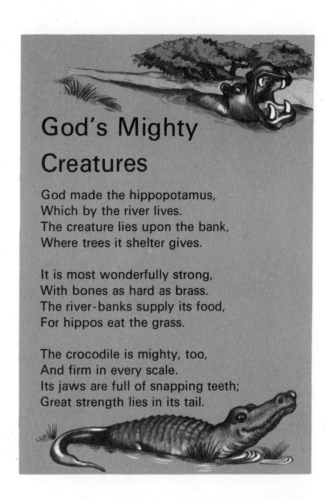

God's Mighty Creatures

God made the hippopotamus,
Which by the river lives.
The creature lies upon the bank,
Where trees it shelter gives.

It is most wonderfully strong,
With bones as hard as brass.
The river-banks supply its food,
For hippos eat the grass.

The crocodile is mighty, too,
And firm in every scale.
Its jaws are full of snapping teeth;
Great strength lies in its tail.

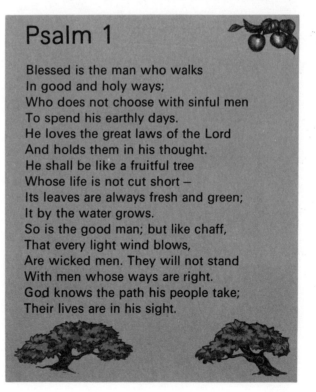

Psalm 1

Blessed is the man who walks
In good and holy ways;
Who does not choose with sinful men
To spend his earthly days.
He loves the great laws of the Lord
And holds them in his thought.
He shall be like a fruitful tree
Whose life is not cut short –
Its leaves are always fresh and green;
It by the water grows.
So is the good man; but like chaff,
That every light wind blows,
Are wicked men. They will not stand
With men whose ways are right.
God knows the path his people take;
Their lives are in his sight.

Psalm 8

O Lord, our Lord, how excellent
Your name, throughout the earth.
Your glory is above the heavens;
Small children know your worth,
And speak of you, to overcome
Your enemies. You plan
The heavens, with moon and stars.
I ask then, what is man?
You care for him, and visit him —
Almost an angel he;
You honour him, and give him charge
Of birds, beasts, fish at sea.
O Lord, our Lord, how excellent
Your name will always be!

Psalm 15

Lord, who shall in your temple dwell,
And in your holy hill?
Who walks uprightly, he it is,
And he who does your will;
Who does not speak an unkind word
Behind another's back;
Nor to his neighbour is unjust,
Nor in himself would lack
The heart that always fears the Lord;
Who would not money lend
For gain; nor ever take a bribe
For false words of a friend.
This righteous man shall not be moved
From God's ways, to the end.

Psalm 24

The earth is God's, and all the folk
Who on the round world dwell;
He founded it upon the seas,
And on the waters' swell.
Who shall climb the Lord's own hill?
Who in God's house soon stands?
He who knows his heart is pure;
Who uses not his hands
For wrongful deeds; who is not vain,
Nor speaks deceitfully —
The blessing of the Lord is given
To good men such as he.
Lift up your heads, then, O ye gates,
The God who fights to win,
The King of glory, Lord of hosts,
'Tis he, who will come in.

Isaiah's Vision

Isaiah was a prophet who sometimes saw strange visions. One of these he knew that he would always remember, because it came to him in the year that King Uzziah died.

In the vision, he saw God, sitting high up on a throne above which stood angelic creatures, each with six wings: two wings covered the face of the angel, two covered the feet, and two were used by the angel for flight.

They called aloud to each other, 'Holy, holy, holy, is the Lord of hosts; the whole earth is full of his glory.'

The sound seemed to shake the very doors, and the smoke of incense filled the temple.

'Alas,' cried Isaiah, 'and woe is me! I am a sinful man; my lips do not always speak

truth, and I dwell among other men who are like me but now my eyes have seen the king, the Lord of hosts.'

Then one of the angelic beings flew towards Isaiah. In his hand he held a burning coal, which he had taken with tongs from the altar. He laid it on Isaiah's mouth, and said, 'Lo, this has touched your lips, your wrong-doing is taken away; your sins are forgiven.'

Then Isaiah heard the Voice of the Lord himself. He was saying, 'Whom shall I send? And who will go for us?'

So Isaiah said, 'Here am I – send me!'

Isaiah tells of a Vineyard

Isaiah wrote a parable about a vineyard: it was a very fruitful vineyard, planted on a hill. The owner put a fence around it, and picked up all the stones from the ground. He planted the very choicest vines, and built a tower in the middle of his vineyard, together with a winepress where the grape-juice could be squeezed out. Then the owner watched his vineyard very carefully to see what fine fruits were brought forth; he was very sad, however, when he saw that the vines did not bear large, sweet grapes at all, but only small wild ones.

The grapes were like the people of Jerusalem, said Isaiah. They could not have had more done for them, and yet they did not do well. What would become of them? The 'vineyard' would meet with a sad end: the wall would be broken down, the land laid waste, thorns and briars would grow there, and the soil would become parched with drought.

Then Isaiah explained his parable, and its lesson for the people:

The house of Israel was like the vineyard, and sad things would happen to those within it, too, because they had not heeded the law of the Lord, and had despised God's word.

From Psalm 78

God brought our fathers to this place
And caused them to pass through
The sea, when all the waters were
Divided into two.
In daylight, he would lead them on
By cloud. A fire at night
Went on before them; thus they knew
The way they took was right.
He smote rocks in the wilderness
And brought forth waters sweet,
And when of hunger they complained,
He gave them food to eat.
Yet, very soon, they all forgot
The plagues, and every sign
By which their God had plainly said:
'I guide you – you are mine.'
He chose the men of Judah's tribe;
His sanctuary stood
On Zion's mount. A shepherd boy
Grew up both wise and good.
He fed his people as his sheep –
David, this servant's name;
He led them all most skilfully,
And Israel knew his fame.

Isaiah Looks Ahead

One day, the fierce wolf shall lie down
Beside the lamb so mild.
The calf and kid shall take their rest
Near lion and leopard wild,
And all fierce beasts shall meekly walk
Behind a little child.

Isaiah 35, 1–10
A Glorious Day

In the desert, flowers shall grow,
And the blind shall see.
The lame and crippled men will leap;
The deaf hear perfectly.
The thirsty ground shall water hold.
A highway shall appear —
Its name, 'The way of righteousness',
No wild beast may go near.
The Lord's own people shall walk there,
With glad songs day by day.
They shall be filled with happiness —
While sorrow flies away.

Isaiah's First Promise

The valleys shall be lifted up,
The mountains all brought low.
The roughest places will be smooth,
In straight ways men shall go.

Isaiah's Second Promise

He shall care for his flock like a shepherd;
He shall gather the lambs with his arm.
He shall carry them safe in his bosom,
And keep all his sheep free from harm.

Isaiah's Third Promise

The youths shall faint and weary grow,
And strong young men shall fall —
But they that wait upon the Lord
Shall not grow tired at all.

With him, they shall renew their strength,
And mount, as if on wings,
As eagles do; they shall not tire.
The Lord such vigour brings.

Isaiah's Fourth Promise

When the poor and needy thirst,
And long for cooling springs,
The Lord will open streams for them,
For pools and founts he brings.
He plants trees in the wilderness —
The cedar, fir and pine —
That men may see his handiwork,
And take it for a sign.

Isaiah 42, 10–13
A New Song

Sing a new song to the Lord
And from the mountains shout.
You who go to sea in ships,
Spread all his praise about.
From cities and from desert lands,
The Lord's song shall arise.
From rocks and islands sound it forth —
He's glorious in our eyes.

The Men who made Idols

One day, Isaiah wrote down what he felt about the men who made idols.

The blacksmith works among the coals with his tongs, making the idol. He does not stop, even when he is hungry or thirsty.

Then the carpenter stretches out his rule and measures. He marks the wood with his compass, and shapes the wood until it is like the figure of a man.

He cuts down cedar trees, and the cypress and the oak, he plants an ash tree, and the rain helps it to grow.

Then he takes the wood to burn, to keep himself warm, and bake his bread. He also makes a god, and falls down before the image he has made, and worships it. With the same wood, he makes a fire, and says, 'Aha! I am warm – I have seen the fire.' He roasts his meat and is satisfied – and he makes a god and prays to it, 'Deliver me, for you are my god.'

He does not see what he is doing, and that his god is only the wood that kept him warm, and cooked his dinner.

Daniel and his Friends

The king of Babylon had taken many of the children of Israel away to his own land.

One day, the king – whose name was Nebuchadnezzar – commanded that the wisest and most handsome young men among the prisoners should be brought to his court, to learn the language and the ways of his part of the world. For three years they were to eat meat and drink wine which the king provided, and then they would be ready to stand before the king himself.

A group of young men was chosen, and among them was one whose name was Daniel. Daniel did not want to take the king's food for he was proud of being from Judah.

'You will get me into trouble, if you refuse to eat it,' said the chief of the men who had chosen him; he liked Daniel, and did not want any harm to come to him.

'Please,' Daniel begged, 'for ten days let us have only lentils to eat, and water to drink. Then take a good look at us – and at those who eat the king's food – and see if

there is a difference between us. Then decide what you must do.'

So, for ten days, Daniel and three friends of his ate nothing but lentils and drank only water, whilst the others ate the rich food and drank the wine provided by the king. At the end of that time, Daniel and his friends looked healthier and fitter than all the others, so they were allowed to eat what they had chosen.

The four friends were all very clever and Daniel had a special gift: he could tell what dreams meant.

At the end of the time appointed by the king, the men were brought before him, and Daniel and his friends were the finest and wisest of them all. Indeed, when the king asked them questions, he found that they answered ten times better than all his own magicians and wise men.

The King's Dream

King Nebuchadnezzar began to have strange dreams that troubled him; and then he could not sleep, so he called all his magicians and wise men together, so that he could learn from them what his dreams meant.

They came and stood before Nebuchadnezzar and he said, 'I have dreamed a dream, and my spirit was troubled to know the dream.'

'O king, live for ever,' said the magicians, bowing low. 'Tell your servants the dream, and we will tell you its meaning.'

'It has gone from me,' said the king. 'If you cannot tell me what I dreamt, and what it means, you shall be cut into pieces, and your houses knocked down and turned into a rubbish heap; but, if you tell me my dream, and its meaning, you shall receive from me gifts and rewards and great honour.'

None of the wizards knew what the dream was, so they said, 'Let the king tell his servants the dream, and we will tell you what it means.'

'I cannot remember it,' the king said again. 'You must tell me, and then give me its meaning.'

'There is not a man on earth who could do that,' said the wise men. 'No king, lord or ruler has ever asked such a thing. You have asked something so difficult that only the gods could answer it.'

The king was angry, and commanded that all the wise men in Babylon should be slain. Daniel and his friends were known to be very wise, so the king's men went to search for them, in order to kill them with the others.

When Arioch, the captain of the king's guard, told Daniel what had happened, and that he must lose his life, Daniel said, 'Why has the king made up his mind in such a hurry?' And he went to see him.

'Give me time,' he told him, 'and I will explain your dream to you.'

'The wise men, the astrologers, the magicians and the soothsayers cannot tell you,' Daniel said, 'but there is a God in heaven who knows all things.

'Your dream, and the visions that came to you as you lay in bed, foretell what will happen. The secret is not made plain to me because I am wiser than anyone else, but for the sake of others.

'You saw, O king, a great image, and it was very bright. Its head was gold, its breast and arms silver, its body and thighs brass, its legs iron, its feet partly iron and partly clay. Then a stone, which had not been cut out by hand, struck the feet of the image, and broke them in pieces. The gold and silver, the iron, brass and clay were broken up into dust, and the wind carried it all away: and then the stone became a huge mountain.'

Remembering the Dream

After seeing the king, Daniel went home and told his friends what had happened.

'Pray to God to help us understand the king's dream,' he said, 'lest we die with the other wise men of Babylon.'

That night, Daniel had a vision which explained the dream to him.

'Blessed be the name of God for ever and ever,' cried Daniel, 'for wisdom and might are his. I thank you and praise you, O God of my fathers, for helping us now.'

Then he went to Arioch, the captain of the king's guard. 'Do not destroy the wise men of Babylon,' he said. 'Take me to the king, and I will explain his dream.'

Hurriedly, Arioch brought Daniel before King Nebuchadnezzar. 'I have found one of the prisoners from Judah who will explain your dream,' he said.

The king turned to Daniel.

'Are you then able to tell me my dream, and explain what it means?' he asked.

What the Dream meant

'Now,' said Daniel, as he went on to explain Nebuchadnezzar's dream to the king, 'this is what your dream means. You are a very great king, for God has given you a great country, with power, strength and glory. You rule over many people, and the beasts and birds are given into your hand. You are this head of gold.

'After you, there shall arise another kingdom, not so great as yours – that is the silver. Then a third kingdom will follow – that is the brass – and it shall bear rule over all the earth. A fourth kingdom shall be as strong as iron, and shall break other nations, as iron can bruise. You remember that, in your dream, the toes were partly of iron and partly of clay. This means that the kingdom will be divided: it will be partly strong, and partly broken. Its people shall not mix with one another – for iron and clay do not mix – but they shall mingle with other nations. Then God will set up a kingdom which shall never be destroyed; it shall break up these other kingdoms, and it shall stand for ever – that was the stone, cut out of the mountain without hands, that broke up everything else: the iron, brass, clay, silver and gold. The great God has made known to the king what shall come to pass, the dream is certain, and the meaning sure.'

Then the king fell on his face before Daniel, so full of gratitude was he, and he ordered that offerings should be made to him.

'Of a truth,' he said, 'your God is a god of gods, and a lord of kings, and a revealer of secrets, seeing that you could reveal this secret.'

Then the king made Daniel a great man, and gave him many splendid gifts, and set him up as ruler over the whole of the province of Babylon, and chief of the governors over all his wise men.

Daniel asked the king if his friends, Shadrach, Meshach, and Abed-nego, might be set in charge of the affairs of the province of Babylon, and his request was granted. As for Daniel himself, he sat in the gate of the king.

The Golden Image

King Nebuchadnezzar built a great image.
It was golden, and shone in the sun.
And he sent for his captains, his princes and judges,
His treasurers, sheriffs – each one –
To stand round the image he'd made.
Then a herald cried out: 'Here, now!
When the cornet, flute, sackbut and psaltery sound,
You must worship the image, and bow.
For if you do not, then the king has decreed
You'll be cast in a furnace, for such a wrong deed.'

Three Brave Men

Some of King Nebuchadnezzar's subjects went to see him.

'O king, live for ever!' they cried. 'You, O king, have made a decree that every man who hears the sound of the cornet, flute, harp, sackbut, psaltery and dulcimer, and all kinds of music, shall fall down and worship the golden image; and that whoever fails to do this shall be thrown into a fiery furnace. There are certain Jews whom you have set over the affairs of the province of Babylon – Shadrach, Meshach and Abed-nego. These men, O king, have disobeyed you; they do not serve your gods, nor worship the golden image which you have set up.'

The king, in a rage, ordered Shadrach, Meshach and Abed-nego to come before him.

'Is it true, O Shadrach, Meshach and Abed-nego,' he asked, 'that you do not serve my gods, nor worship my golden image? Now, if you are ready – when you hear the sound of the cornet, flute, harp, sackbut, psaltery, dulcimer, and all kinds of music – to fall down and worship the image I have made, that is well. But if you will not do so, you shall be cast right away into the middle of the burning fiery furnace. And who is the God who can deliver you out of my hands?'

Shadrach, Meshach and Abed-nego replied, 'O, Nebuchadnezzar! Our God, whom we serve, is able to deliver us out of the burning fiery furnace, and he will deliver us out of your hand, O king; but, whatever happens, we will not serve your gods, nor worship the golden image that you have set up.'

Nebuchadnezzar was very angry, and he ordered that the furnace should be made seven times hotter.

Then Shadrach, Meshach and Abed-nego were bound, and cast into the burning, fiery furnace.

The flames were so fierce that the guards themselves could not live in the heat given off by the furnace – and Shadrach, Meshach and Abed-nego were right in the middle of the furnace itself.

The Fiery Furnace

King Nebuchadnezzar looked at the fiery furnace – and then he looked again; astonished at what he saw, the king hurried to his counsellors.

'Did we not cast three men, bound, into the fire?' he asked.

'True, O king,' they told him.

Then Nebuchadnezzar said, 'But I can see four men, unbound, walking about in the fire. Not one of them is hurt, and the fourth man is like the Son of God.'

Together with all his counsellors, Nebuchadnezzar went to the mouth of the furnace. 'Shadrach, Meshach and Abed-nego, you servants of the most high God,' he called, 'come out, and come here!'

The three brave friends walked out of the flames, and the princes, governors and captains, and the king's counsellors who were looking on, stared in astonishment. The fire had not touched the three men, not a hair of their heads was singed, their coats were not scorched and there was no smell of burning about them.

'Blessed be the God of Shadrach, Meshach and Abed-nego,' said the king, 'who has sent his angel, and delivered his servants who trusted in him, and defied the king, rather than worship strange gods. Therefore I make a decree, that anyone who speaks against Shadrach, Meshach and Abed-nego shall be cut in pieces, and their houses knocked down and turned into a rubbish heap, because there is no other God who can deliver his faithful servants like this.'

And Nebuchadnezzar gave Shadrach, Meshach and Abed-nego still more important work to do in Babylon.

Another Dream

King Nebuchadnezzar had another strange dream. This time, he dreamt that he saw a great tree, which grew to such a height that it reached heaven, and could be seen by all men. The leaves and fruit of the tree were very beautiful; and animals lay down in its shade, birds lived in its branches, and men ate its fine fruit.

Then an angel came and cried:

'Cut down the tree, cut off the branches, shake off the leaves, and scatter the fruit. Let the beasts and the birds go away from it, but leave the stump of its root in the ground, with a band of iron and brass, as it stands in the tender grass. Let it be wet with dew. This is in order that men may know that the most high God rules in the kingdom of men, and gives it to whom he will, and puts the lowliest of men in charge of it.'

None of the wise men in the king's court was able to tell him what the dream meant, so Nebuchadnezzar turned to Daniel for help.

Daniel thought about the dream, and his thoughts troubled him. He did not speak for some time, but at last Daniel explained.

'You yourself are the tree, O king, for you have grown strong, and your kingdom reaches far and wide. But you will be driven out into the fields, and you will dwell with oxen, and be obliged to eat grass, as they do. The dew shall fall on you, and these things will go on until you realise that the most high God is greater than any earthly king. As for the stump that remained – that means that your kingdom shall be left to you, after you have accepted the rule of God. Therefore, O king, you must do good, that your sins may be forgiven.'

A year later, the dream came true. One day, when King Nebuchadnezzar was walking in his palace in Babylon, he spoke to those about him, saying proudly, 'Has not this great city of Babylon been built up

for the honour and glory of my majesty?'

But even as the king spoke, he heard a voice saying, 'O King Nebuchadnezzar, you have lost your kingdom. You will be driven into the fields to eat grass with the oxen, until you realise that God rules over the kingdom of men, and gives it to whom ever he chooses.'

King Nebuchadnezzar had to leave his beautiful palace, and he had nowhere to live but the fields, and nothing to eat but the grass. His thoughts were muddled; his hair and his nails grew long. He did not look like the mighty king of Babylon any longer.

Then, one day, Nebuchadnezzar's mind cleared, and he realised that God was greater than any earthly ruler. He blessed and praised his maker, and when his counsellors and lords heard him, they saw to it that he returned to his palace, to reign over his kingdom once again.

From that day, Nebuchadnezzar praised and honoured the King of Heaven, for he knew that God's ways were wise and true.

The Writing on the Wall

After Nebuchadnezzar's death, the next king of Babylon was Belshazzar. One day, this new king decided to give a great feast for a thousand of his lords. He used the gold and silver cups that his father, King Nebuchadnezzar, had brought from Jerusalem, at the feast. These had been used in the holy temple, but now King Belshazzar's guests drank wine from them. It was a very merry party and, as they drank, the guests praised the gods that they had made out of gold and silver, brass, iron, wood and stone.

Suddenly, Belshazzar started back in fear and astonishment, for he saw a hand writing words on the plaster wall, near to the place where a candlestick stood.

The king grew pale, and his knees knocked together with fright. 'Bring in the wizards and the wise men!' he cried.

When they were brought before him, he said, 'Whoever can read this writing, and tell me what it means, shall be dressed in scarlet with a gold chain round his neck, and he shall be the third ruler in the kingdom.'

All the wise men put their heads together, and tried very hard; but they could not read the writing, or understand its meaning.

Just then, the queen came into the banqueting hall, and greeted her husband.

'O king, live for ever! Do not let your thoughts trouble you. There is a man in your kingdom who has the spirit of the holy gods. In your father's time, he was the wisest man in the land – his name is Daniel, and he understands dreams and the meaning of visions. Why not call him?'

So Daniel was brought before King Belshazzar.

'Are you the Daniel who was brought a captive from Judah?' the king asked. 'I have heard of you, and how wise you are. None of my clever men can read that writing and tell me what it means; but, if you can do so, you shall have a scarlet robe and a gold chain, and I will make you the third ruler in my kingdom.'

'Give your rewards to someone else,' Daniel said, 'but I will read the writing and explain it. When King Nebuchadnezzar reigned, he had to learn the lesson that God is greater than any earthly king – and, in the end, he did. But you, Belshazzar, his son, have not learnt to be humble, and have set yourself up against the Lord of Heaven. You have used the vessels from his house to drink wine at your feast: you have praised idols who cannot see, or hear, or know; you have not glorified the God who gave you life – and it was he who sent the hand that wrote on the wall. This is what is written: 'MENE, MENE, TEKEL, UPHARSIN!'

Then Daniel went on to explain the meaning of the words. '*Mene* means that God has made an end of your kingdom; *Tekel*: you have been weighed in the scales and found to weigh too little! *Upharsin*: your kingdom is to be divided, and given to the Medes and the Persians.'

Because Daniel had told the king what the writing meant, Belshazzar insisted on giving him the red robe and the gold chain, and making him the third ruler of his kingdom. But, that night, King Belshazzar was slain, and a new king – Darius – ruled in his place.

The Lions' Den

King Darius gave Daniel a very important place in his kingdom, and all the other presidents and princes were jealous of him, and sought to do him harm; but Daniel was such a good ruler that they could not accuse him of doing anything wrong.

At last they said, 'We shall not find anything for which we can blame Daniel, unless it is something to do with the law of his God.'

They went to the king, and bowed to him.

'King Darius, live for ever!' they said. 'All the princes, presidents, counsellors and captains of your kingdom have decided to issue an order that any person who asks something of any god or man, except you, O king, during the next thirty days, shall be cast into a den of lions. Now, O king, draw up this decree and sign it, for then it will become a law of the Medes and Persians which can never be changed.'

So the king did as they asked.

When Daniel knew what Darius had done, he went into his own house and opened the window which faced in the direction of Jerusalem, his home. Here he prayed three times a day.

The men who had plotted against Daniel saw him doing this, and eagerly they went to tell the king.

'Daniel, who is one of the captives from Judah, is not obeying the king's decree,' they said. 'Three times a day, he prays to his God!'

The king was very sad when he heard this, because Daniel had helped him, and he did not want to have to put him in the lions' den. He tried very hard to think of a way of

sparing Daniel, but the counsellors and captains said, 'You cannot go back on your word; it has become a law, which can never be changed.'

So the king was forced to give the order that Daniel should be cast into the den of lions. But he said to Daniel, 'Your God will deliver you – for you serve him so faithfully.'

A big stone was brought, and the entrance to the lions' den was blocked up. The king sealed it with his signet ring, and then went home with a heavy heart. Darius did not want to eat or listen to music, and could not sleep, for all the time he was thinking about Daniel.

Daniel is Delivered

Very early next morning, the king got up and hurried to the lions' den. Darius did not think that Daniel could possibly be alive,

but nevertheless he called out very sadly,

'O Daniel, servant of the living God! Is your God, whom you serve faithfully, able to deliver you from the lions?'

'O king, live for ever!' Daniel's voice answered him. 'My God has sent his angel, and has shut the lions' mouths so that they have not hurt me: for I was innocent in his sight, and I have done no wrong before you, O king.'

The king was glad, and ordered his men to let Daniel out.

Daniel walked out of the den, quite unhurt, because he believed in God.

The king then punished the men who had spoken against Daniel, and he issued another decree: 'Let everyone in every dominion of my kingdom know that Daniel's God is the one living God, and his kingdom shall not be destroyed. He saves and rescues those in danger, and does wonderful things. He has delivered Daniel from the lions.'

A Brave Man

Daniel was a brave man,
Who did not cease to pray
Although the king's advisers
Had told him he should say
The king alone was worthy
To listen to the pleas
Of any of his subjects.
Yet Daniel on his knees
Addressed the God he worshipped,
Although he knew that then
He might be kept a prisoner
Within the lions' den.
He must have gone there bravely,
With heart still undismayed,
And when his jailers left him,
Again he must have prayed.
The lions did not touch him,
And he was not afraid.

Hosea 14, 8
The Faithful Fir Tree

God said, 'The fir is ever green,
Its leaves are never shed;
So I will be, and faithfully
Will be my people's head.
I will be constant, come what may;
My love will never change.
Look at this tree — remember me,
And do not think it strange.'

Joel and the Locusts

Joel told the people that, very soon,
their land
Would be attacked by locusts, with swarms
on every hand.
The locust is an insect which quickly
multiplies
And then, with all its fellows, the busy
creature flies,
And no green thing's protected from the
locust and its friends,
When on the trees and pastures the insect
once descends.
The house-beams, too, are eaten — it is
a sorry day
For any folk, when locusts swarm and
fly their way.

Amos and the Mountain

Amos was a prophet who lived in the country, looking after cattle. He saw country sights and heard the sounds of the fields and hills, so it was natural for him to look towards a mountain, and warn people of troubles to come.

Mount Carmel stood near the blue Mediterranean Sea, and there were beautiful woods on its slopes. There was always a heavy dew on Mount Carmel, so lovely flowers grew there then that would not grow anywhere else, and so did green trees. Honeysuckle and hollyhocks could be found there as well as almond and pear trees.

So when Amos told the people: 'The top of Carmel shall wither!' it made them very sad. No green trees on their mountain? No lovely flowers? It would not be the Carmel that they knew, and which meant so much in their parched country.

Amos, however, was really telling the people about the difficult times that were coming to their land.

Jonah and the Big Fish

There was a man named Jonah, who heard God telling him to go to a great city called Nineveh, where the people were doing many wrong things. When he arrived, Jonah must tell the people to repent of their wickedness and turn to a better way of life.

Jonah did not want to obey God, so he made up his mind that he would escape to Tarshish. So he went to Joppa, which was by the sea, and found a ship going to Tarshish.

Soon after the ship put to sea, a great wind began to blow and a mighty storm arose. It seemed as though the ship might be smashed to pieces, and the sailors were afraid. They all began to cry to their gods, and to throw everything they could overboard, to make the ship lighter.

Jonah was lying down, fast asleep, in the bottom of the ship, so the captain of the ship went below and woke him up.

'What do you mean by falling asleep?' he cried. 'Get up and call on your God, if you think that he can save us!'

'Let us draw lots and find out who is responsible for getting us into this trouble,' said the sailors. They believed that it was the fault of someone on board that they had run into the storm.

So the sailors drew lots, and it looked to them as though Jonah was the one to blame.

'Tell us why this trouble has come upon us,' they said to him. 'What is your work? Where do you come from? Who are you?'

'I am a Hebrew,' Jonah told them, 'and I fear the Lord, the God of Heaven, who has made the sea and the dry land.'

The sailors grew frightened.

'What have you done?' they asked. They knew that Jonah had tried to run away from God's orders, because he had told them about it. Now they thought that God had

sent the storm because Jonah had been disobedient.

'What shall we do to you to make the sea calm for us?' they asked him.

'Take me up and throw me in the sea,' Jonah said, 'for I am sure it is my fault that the tempest has risen about you!'

The men did not want to do this, and they tried very hard to row towards land, but they could not manage it. So, at last, they cried out, 'We beseech you, O Lord, we beseech you, let us not perish because of this man's life, and do not blame us for what we are doing, for you, O Lord, have done as it pleases you.'

Then they picked up Jonah and threw him into the sea. The storm ceased, and they thanked God for their deliverance.

As for Jonah, he was safe and sound, for a huge fish had swallowed him. He stayed inside the fish for three days and nights, and then the fish cast Jonah out on to dry land.

Jonah Obeys

Once again, Jonah knew that God was telling him to go to Nineveh, and this time he obeyed.

It was a very great city, and as he drew near it, Jonah cried, 'In forty days, Nineveh will be overthrown!'

The people of Nineveh listened to Jonah, and were sorry for the wrongs they had done. Even the king came down from his throne, to dress in sackcloth and put ashes on his head, to show that he repented.

So God forgave and saved them, for they were truly sorry.

But Jonah was annoyed at this and he grew angry. He had been ordered to go to Nineveh and tell the people what was in store for them, and had run away to Tarshish. Then he had thought better of it, and obeyed God – and now nothing was going to happen, after all. Jonah felt God was being too gentle with the people of Nineveh.

'You can take away my life,' he said to God. 'I would rather die than live.'

'Why are you so angry?' God asked him.

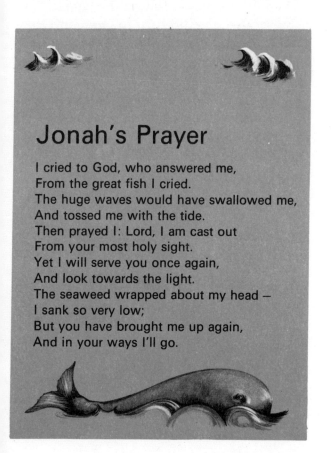

Jonah's Prayer

I cried to God, who answered me,
From the great fish I cried.
The huge waves would have swallowed me,
And tossed me with the tide.
Then prayed I: Lord, I am cast out
From your most holy sight.
Yet I will serve you once again,
And look towards the light.
The seaweed wrapped about my head –
I sank so very low;
But you have brought me up again,
And in your ways I'll go.

which has so many people living in it? There are children and innocent animals there who deserve help!'

And, in his heart, Jonah knew that God was right. He was showing love and mercy to the people whom he had made.

The Two Staves

Zechariah, another prophet, was commanded by God to be like a shepherd to the people and to feed his flock.

Zechariah agreed, and he took two staves, like those a shepherd would carry to guide his sheep. He called one of them Beauty and the other Union. Zechariah tried to help the 'sheep', but they would not listen to him, so he broke the staff that he had called Beauty in two, as a sign that the covenant with God was broken.

A few people – whom he called the poorest 'sheep' – did turn to God, and they gave Zechariah thirty pieces of silver, which he threw to a potter in the temple, according to God's wishes.

Then Zechariah cut the other staff, which he had called Union, into pieces, as a sign that the people of Israel and the people of Judah would not be united.

But Jonah went outside the city and made himself a little hut out of branches, to shade himself from the hot sun. Then he sat down in it, and watched Nineveh, to see what would happen.

It was still very hot, however, and God caused a tree to grow over Jonah; and he was very glad of its cool shade, but next day, the tree withered and died.

The sun beat down on Jonah again; it was more than he could stand, and he fainted in the heat. When he came to his senses, Jonah still wished he could die, for he was so miserable. He felt sorry, too, for the tree, which had withered in the heat.

'Why are you so sad about the tree?' God asked Jonah.

'Am I not right to be sorrowful?' Jonah replied.

'You have pity on the tree,' God replied, 'yet you did not work for it or help it to grow, and it grew up and died in a night. Should I not spare Nineveh, that great city,

Zechariah 8, 3–5
Zechariah's Vision

'Jerusalem,' said Zechariah, 'shall be our own once more.
"City of truth" shall be its name, and in it, as of yore,
Old men shall lean upon their sticks, and boys and girls shall play
Along the streets, so happily, all through the livelong day.'

144

The
New
Testament

The Angel comes to Mary

In a little town called Nazareth, in Galilee, there lived a young woman whose name was Mary. She was engaged to a man named Joseph, who was descended from King David.

One day Mary was sitting alone, when the angel Gabriel appeared to her.

'I greet you!' he said. 'You are greatly favoured. The Lord is with you; you are the happiest of women.'

Mary looked at him, puzzled and half afraid. What did he mean?

'Do not be afraid, Mary,' Gabriel said, seeing that she was puzzled. 'God has chosen you for a very special purpose. You are going to have a baby boy, and you must call him Jesus. He will be great. He will be called Son of the Most High. God will give him the throne of David, and he shall reign over the people of Jacob for ever.

'How can this be?' Mary asked. 'I am not yet married.'

'God's Holy Spirit will come upon you,' Gabriel replied. 'The power of the most high God will overshadow you. When this holy babe is born, he will be called the Son of God. Your cousin Elisabeth, too, though old, is also going to have a baby boy; nothing is impossible to God.'

Mary bowed her head in obedience before the angel.

'See, I am God's servant,' she answered. 'Let it happen to me as you have said.'

Then Gabriel left her, and Mary thought and wondered about the wonderful news he had brought.

Cousin Elisabeth

Mary's cousin Elisabeth was many years older than she. Elisabeth's husband was named Zacharias, and he was a priest; they had no children.

One day, Zacharias was taking part in a service, he was offering up incense to God, as a sign that the congregation were offering up their prayers.

Suddenly, he saw the angel Gabriel standing near the altar, and he started back.

'You have nothing to fear, Zacharias,' the angel said. 'God has heard your prayers. You and Elisabeth, your wife, are going to have a little son. You must call him John. You will be very happy about it, and so will many other people. He will be a great man in God's sight. From the very first, he will be filled with the Holy Spirit, and he will lead many of his own people back to God. He will go before them, as noble and as great as Elijah the prophet. He will bring fathers and children together, and show the disobedient how to obey. He will make the people ready to receive the Lord.'

Zacharias found it very hard to believe this wonderful news.

'How can I be sure that this will happen?' he asked the angel. 'I am an old man, and my wife is growing old, too.'

'I am Gabriel, who stands before God,' the angel told him. 'I have been sent especially to bring you this news. You will be dumb and unable to speak, until this thing happens, because you do not believe me – but it will indeed prove true.'

Zacharias was so wrapped up in what Gabriel was saying that he forgot all the people waiting for him to come out of the holy place. But, suddenly, Zacharias remembered where he was, and that he was in the middle of a service.

He went through to the outer court, and opened his mouth to speak to the people, but no words came. As the angel had foretold, Zacharias was dumb.

All the people looked at him in surprise; but they felt, by the look on his face, that he had seen a vision. When he beckoned and made signs to them, they realised that he could not speak, and they looked at one another, wondering what it all meant.

As soon as he was free, Zacharias hurried home. Doubtless, he wrote down all that had happened, and gave the words to Elisabeth as he could not speak to her.

Elisabeth was overjoyed, and began to prepare for the baby who was coming.

Mary's Visit

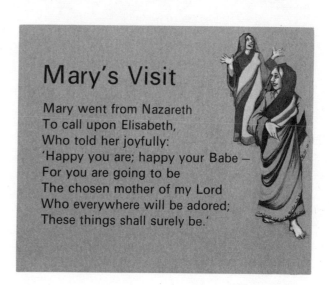

Mary went from Nazareth
To call upon Elisabeth,
Who told her joyfully:
'Happy you are; happy your Babe –
For you are going to be
The chosen mother of my Lord
Who everywhere will be adored;
These things shall surely be.'

Mary's Answer

When Mary went to visit her cousin, Elisabeth greeted her as the chosen mother of Jesus and rejoiced at the wonderful news.

Then Mary replied to her cousin, 'My soul praises the Lord, and my spirit was made glad in God my Saviour. He knows that I, his servant, am humble and lowly; yet everybody ever afterwards will call me specially blessed, for the mighty God has done great things for me. Holy is his name; his mercy rests on all who reverence his name, in generation after generation. He has shown his mighty strength. He has scattered all those who were proud and imagined themselves great. He has raised up the humble folk. He has given the hungry good things to eat, but rich men have been sent away with nothing. He has helped the house of Israel, his servants, as he promised Abraham and our forefathers. He said that he would look after us always.'

Mary stayed with her cousin Elisabeth for three months, and during that time they must often have talked with wonder of the babies who were coming to them – Jesus and John.

At the end of her visit Mary went back to her own home, in Nazareth.

Elisabeth's Baby

It all happened, just as the angel Gabriel said it would – Elisabeth had a baby boy. All her neighbours and cousins gathered round to admire the new baby, and of course she told them about the angel's visit, and the wonderful things that he had said to Zacharias.

When he was eight days old, the priest took the baby in his arms and said, 'He must be called Zacharias, after his father.'

'Oh no!' Elisabeth said quickly. 'He must be called John.'

'But you have no relatives called John,' the priests objected, for it was usual to call babies after their relations. They turned to the baby's father, and tried to find out from

him what he wanted his son to be called.

Zacharias still could not speak, so he sent for a writing tablet, and wrote: 'His name is John.'

They all looked at one another in astonishment. Then, at that moment, Zacharias found that he could speak once more, and joyfully he began to praise God for his wonderful gift.

The news about the baby called John spread to other villages throughout Judaea, and some people were half afraid, because it seemed such a strange story. But most of them said, 'What sort of man is this child going to be?' For they thought God must be with him.

What Zacharias Said

Zacharias was filled with joy and thankfulness at the birth of his son, John, and he said, 'Blessed is the Lord God of Israel, for he has visited and saved his people, and has raised up a mighty Deliverer from the family of his servant David. He spoke through the mouths of his holy prophets, ever since the world began, saying that, one day, we would indeed be saved from our enemies, and those who wish us ill. He promised our great ancestor, Abraham, and all our forefathers, that he would do this, so that when we are saved from our enemies, we might serve him without fear all our lives, walking in holy and right paths.

'You, my child, shall be called the prophet of the Highest, for you shall go before the Lord, to prepare his way. You shall teach the people that they may find forgiveness for their sins and be saved from them, through God's tender mercy. The Light from Heaven will shine on us, to brighten those who sit in dark and shadowy places, and guide us into the Way of Peace.'

John grew up to be wise and brave, ready to carry out God's wonderful plan for him.

Joseph and the Angel

Joseph, who was going to make Mary his wife, could not understand her story about the angel, Gabriel, who had told her that she was going to be the mother of baby Jesus. It worried him until, one night, Joseph himself saw an angel in a dream, and everything became clear.

'Do not be afraid, Joseph,' the angel said. 'Mary's baby is going to be given to her by the Holy Spirit of God himself. You will call him Jesus, and he will save people from sin.'

The great prophet Isaiah had written, long, long ago, that such a child would indeed be born; and when Joseph woke up, he understood, as Mary did, what a very special boy was to be born and that God was entrusting him to their care.

To Bethlehem

Nazareth was part of the kingdom of Herod the Great, a kingdom which belonged at that time to Augustus, Emperor of Rome, who made an order that everyone should go to the place where he had been born, in order that his name should be registered.

Joseph came from the little town of Bethlehem, which was David's city, because he belonged to the family whose ancestor David was. So he saddled his ass, and he and Mary left Nazareth together, to go to Bethlehem, which was near Jerusalem.

Mary was tired, and was longing to reach Bethlehem and rest; but many other people were travelling the same road, and when they reached the little town at last, all the inns were full. But then one kind innkeeper saw how weary Mary was, and told them, 'There is no room in the inn, but you can sleep in the stable, if you like.'

It was only a cave, but glad to find anywhere to rest, Joseph and Mary lay down on the straw, with their ass and the inkeeper's ox munching hay close by. It was at least warm, and they had a roof over their heads.

That night, in the humble stable, Mary's baby was born. She had no cradle for him, so she wrapped the boy in the clothes which she had made for him, and laid him in a manger from which the animals ate their food.

'His name is Jesus,' Mary said, 'for that is what the angel, Gabriel, told me to call him!'

150

The Shepherds

In the fields, the shepherds watching
Saw a brilliant light appear,
And an angel stood beside them,
Saying to them, 'Do not fear.
I have brought you joyful tidings:
On this day, in Bethlehem,
Lies a baby in a manger,
With his mother. Go to them,
For the child is Christ the Saviour,
Born in David's city there.'
Suddenly a host of angels
Descended on them through the air.
'Glory be to God,' they chanted.
'Peace on earth; goodwill to men.'
When they vanished all the shepherds
Ran to see this marvel then.
They came to Mary and her baby
In the draughty stable bare,
And the little group of shepherds
Fell on their knees and worshipped there.

Simeon

When he was still very tiny, Mary and
Joseph took Jesus to Jerusalem. Mary took
him into the temple, while Joseph brought
two doves in a basket, as their offering. They
were going to present their baby to God, as
parents of boys did in those days.

There was an old man in the temple
named Simeon. He was a good man, who
loved God, and he longed to see the
Messiah, the Holy One whom the prophets
had promised. Simeon knew that he would
see him, as God promised.

When Mary and Joseph entered with
Jesus, Simeon's heart leapt for joy; he knew
this was the child for whom he had been
waiting.

Simeon held out his arms, and gently
Mary laid Jesus in them. Then the old man
blessed God, and said, 'Lord, now I can go
in peace, because my eyes have seen your
salvation, which you have made plain to
everybody – a Light to lighten people who
are not of our race, and the Glory of your
people Israel.'

Mary and Joseph listened with awe to
what was being said about Jesus, and
Simeon gave them his blessing.

'This boy is going to be a sign from God
which people will not accept,' he told
Mary, 'and you will be very sad about it.
Many people in this land will be either on
his side or against him, and their secret
thoughts will be known.'

There was someone else in the temple
watching Mary and her child: Anna, a very
old woman who spent all her time there,
worshipping God, and praying.

She looked at Jesus, as he lay in his
mother's arms, and then she thanked God
for him. Anna could not forget him, and she
talked about him to everyone who hoped
the Saviour would soon come.

The Wise Men

As King Herod sat in his palace, at Jerusalem, three wise men arrived on camels
from eastern lands to see him.

'Where is he that is born King of the
Jews?' they asked. 'We have seen his star in
the east, and have come to worship him.'

King Herod was troubled by their words.
These men could read the future in the
stars, and if they had seen a new star which
they believed meant that the Jews had a
new king, then what would become of him
– King Herod?

He called a meeting of all the chief priests, lawyers and wise men in Jerusalem. 'Where did the prophets say that the Messiah would be born?' he asked them.

'At Bethlehem, in Judaea,' they told him. They fetched a scroll, and showed him where one of the old prophets had written: 'Bethlehem, in Judah, you are by no means least in the eyes of Judah's rulers, for from you shall come One who shall be the ruler of my people, Israel.'

Herod called the wise men from the east to meet him privately.

'What time did this star appear?' he asked them, and they told him.

'Go to Bethlehem, and inquire about the child,' King Herod ordered them. 'When you have found him, come back and tell me, so that I may go and worship him.'

Herod's plan was to learn what he could about the rival king who had been born; he did not really intend to pay him homage.

The three wise men mounted their camels and rode off, following the star. It led them on until they drew near to Bethlehem. When it hung over the place where Jesus lay, the star stopped.

'He is here,' said the wise men and they collected the presents which they had brought for the new-born king.

One by one, they filed in, to see Jesus.

They bowed low before him, and then laid their gifts at his feet. One had brought gold, one frankincense, which gave a sweet smell when it was burned, and one some costly perfume called myrrh.

The wise men were warned in a dream not to go back to King Herod, so when they left Bethlehem, they took another way home to the east.

The Flight into Egypt

Soon after the wise men had gone on their way, Joseph had a strange dream. An angel appeared to him, and said, 'Get up, Joseph, and take the young child and his mother, and go quickly to hide yourselves in Egypt. You must stay there until I tell you that it is safe to come back, for King Herod will seek your baby and try to take his life.'

So, while it was dark, and no one could see them, Joseph saddled his ass and tied their belongings together. Mary wrapped

up Jesus and carried him in her arms, and they left their own country behind, travelling the long, dusty road to Egypt.

There they stayed until the death of King Herod, when it was safe to return. It was well that they went, for Herod – when he knew that the wise men had disobeyed him and had not returned with news of the baby king – gave a command that all the babies in Bethlehem and nearby, of two years old or under, were to be slain. Thus he planned to rid himself of this new king, who might have taken his place.

The Return to Nazareth

After King Herod had died, Joseph, who was still in Egypt, had another dream. Again the angel came to him, and this time he said, 'Get up, and take the young child and his mother, and return to the land of Israel. He is no longer in danger, for the one who would have killed him is dead.'

So, once again, Joseph and Mary packed up everything that they had. Then, saddling the ass, they took little Jesus back home to their land.

Joseph then had another dream, and this time it seemed as though God was telling him to go to Nazareth. It was their own city, and this really meant that they were going home.

Joseph was a carpenter, and as he worked, the young Jesus must often have watched him, carefully smoothing and sawing the wood, to make chests and ploughs. Day by day the boy grew, and everyone who saw him realised that he was good and wise.

Jesus's Home

Jesus lived in a square white house,
And the stairs went up outside.
The roof was flat, and a place to sit,
Where the view of the hills was wide.
The animals lived in the lower room,
And when the family slept,
They spread their mats on a platform, raised.
In a wooden chest were kept
Their clothes, and perhaps a precious scroll.

The lamp was put up on a stand,
And basins, cooking pots and jars
Were always close at hand.
Mary went often to the well
With a jar upon her head,
She patched old garments, swept the floor,
And baked their daily bread

Jesus's School

They went to the synagogue every Sabbath,
To pray, and to give God praise;
But the little boys of Nazareth
Went there on other days.
It was their school, and there they learnt
The Law, as such boys must,
And sat in a circle on the ground
While their teacher, in the dust,
Wrote all he wanted them to know.

In the Temple

When Jesus was twelve years old, Joseph and Mary took him to Jerusalem, to keep the Feast of the Passover. Every year, Joseph and Mary had gone with other pilgrims from Nazareth to visit the great temple, and remember the time when their ancestors had been brought out of Egypt, across the Red Sea to the land God had promised them. Jesus was now old enough to go too, and it was a very special day for them all.

They joined the singing crowds that grew bigger as they neared the city, and stayed there several days, attending the services and walking through the temple courts, listening to the learned men who sat there.

When it was time to start for home, Mary and Joseph looked about for Jesus; but he was nowhere to be seen. After searching everywhere for him, they decided that he must be with a group of friends, and they started back without Jesus.

But when they looked for him among their friends and relations, no one had seen him. Mary and Joseph decided that they had better go back to Jerusalem.

For three days they searched anxiously, and then at last they found Jesus. He was sitting with the learned teachers, listening, and asking questions; others were looking on, amazed at the wise things he said, although he was such a young boy.

Mary and Joseph were astonished, too; but they had also been very worried.

'Son, why have you treated us like this?' Mary asked Jesus reproachfully. 'Your father and I have been looking everywhere for you, and we have been so worried.'

'Why did you look for me?' Jesus asked her. 'Did you not know that I must be in my Father's house?'

Mary and Joseph did not understand that he was talking about God, his heavenly Father.

The family returned to Nazareth, and Jesus grew up, obedient to his earthly parents, but becoming ever wiser, and more filled with loving-kindness, day by day.

John the Baptist

As Elisabeth's little son, John, grew up, he realised that God had special work for him.

He was to tell everybody that the Great Deliverer – the Christ – was coming, and that in order to be ready for him, they must be sorry for the wrong things they had done and confess their sins. They must be baptised in the River Jordan, as a sign that their past lives were finished, their sins forgiven, and that now they were going to live a better life. John told them the Kingdom of Heaven was coming.

Dressed in animals' skins, with a leather belt round his waist, John tramped about the desert, preaching. He lived on what food he could find – mostly locusts and honey. Many people thought that, with his shaggy hair and his eager words, he was like one of the old prophets. They came out to listen to John in crowds from Jerusalem, and all Judaea and heard all he had to say.

'I baptise you with water,' John told them, 'but someone is coming after me who will baptise you with God's Holy Spirit. I am not worthy even to stoop down and unfasten his shoes.'

'What shall we do, then?' someone asked.

'If you have two coats,' John said, 'give one away to someone who has none. Do the same with your food – share it with those who are hungry.'

'What about us?' asked the tax-gatherers.

'Take no more money from people than you are supposed to,' John told them.

'And what shall we do?' asked some soldiers.

'Do not behave violently to anyone, nor say that someone has done something wrong when he has not,' John said, 'and be content with the money paid to you.'

'When the Mighty One comes,' he told the people, 'he will be like a farmer who gathers all the good wheat into the barn, and burns up what is not worth keeping.'

Jesus is Baptised

One day, Jesus went to John, and asked him to baptise him.

John shook his head. 'I need to be baptised by you,' he said humbly. 'Why do you come to me?'

'Do as I ask,' Jesus told him quietly. So Jesus and John stepped into the River Jordan, and John dipped Jesus under the water. As he rose out of the water again, God's Holy Spirit came upon him, like a dove alighting, and a voice was heard, saying, 'You are my beloved Son, in whom I am well pleased.'

Jesus had waited a long time for this moment. For years he had been studying and thinking and praying. Now Jesus was ready to begin his work.

Jesus, the Carpenter's Son

Joseph worked in his carpenter's shop,
And Jesus, too, would be there,
Helping to hammer or chisel or saw,
Measuring wood with great care.

In all the tasks that Jesus could do,
He would always give of his best,
Working with patience, and not giving up,
Learning from Joseph with zest.

What did they make, at the carpenter's bench?
Tables, and boxes and chairs,
And no one in Nazareth ever produced
Workmanship better than theirs.

Jesus is Tempted

Jesus knew that, soon, he was going to begin the work which God had sent him into the world to carry out. He knew that he was God's Son, in a very special way, and that he had to tell the people what God was really like, and show them how to follow his way of life.

Now Jesus needed time to think and plan and pray, so he went away alone into the wilderness.

Jesus stayed there for forty days, and he became very hungry. He heard the voice of the Tempter whispering to him, 'If you are the Son of God, you can turn these stones into bread at a word.'

Jesus knew that he had not come to work magic. He remembered something that he had often read in the old scroll books, and

On the Hillside

When work was over, Jesus loved
To climb a nearby hill,
And think about his Father, God,
Whilst everything was still.

He saw the flowers which God had made,
And listened to the birds.
He may have said King David's psalms,
And thought about their words.

He prayed, alone among the hills,
And offered thankful praise
To One who claimed him as his Son,
And ordered all his days.

answered, 'It is written: "Man does not need only bread to keep him alive – he needs all God's laws and promises." '

Then Jesus climbed up on to a high hill, and saw all the countryside spread out before his eyes. He thought about the shining temple in Jerusalem, and all the other great cities, about which he had heard but had never seen.

'If you will worship me instead of God,' said the Tempter's voice, 'you could rule over all the kingdoms on earth. You could have great power, if you would follow my way.'

'Get behind me, Satan,' Jesus answered quickly. 'For it is written: "You shall love the Lord God, and him only shall you serve." '

Once more the Tempter tried: 'You could throw yourself off the topmost part of

the temple, and you would not be hurt,' he said. 'For it is written: "He shall give his angels charge of you, to keep you safe, whatever you do. They shall hold you, lest you stumble over a stone." '

Thus Satan, the Tempter, was able to speak of the scriptures, too. It would have been easy for Jesus to win people over to him by performing astonishing deeds, but Jesus knew that was not God's way. He remained steadfast.

'It is written: "You shall not tempt the Lord your God",' he replied.

Nothing could persuade Jesus to give way to the temptations of Satan. He came out of the wilderness, tired and hungry, but quite clear in his mind what God wanted him to do.

John's Answer

John told the people who crowded round him about Jesus.

'He is the One I was telling you about,' he cried. 'Moses gave us the law, but Jesus Christ brings us grace and truth. No man has ever seen God, but his Son has shown us what he is like.'

The priests in Jerusalem heard about John and his preaching, and some of them came to ask him who he was.

'I am not the Christ,' John said.

'Who are you, then?' they persisted. 'We must take back an answer to those who sent us. Who do you call yourself?'

John said, 'I am the voice of one who cries in the wilderness: "Make straight the way of the Lord", as Isaiah told us to do.'

'Then why do you baptise people,' they asked him, 'if you are neither the Christ, nor Elijah?'

'I baptise with water,' John told them, 'but there is someone coming after me, who will be so much greater than I am, that I am not worthy even to unfasten his shoes.'

John sees Jesus

The next day, as he preached, John saw Jesus walking towards him.

'See!' John cried to the crowd. 'Here comes the Lamb of God, who will take away all the sins of the world. This is he of whom I said that a Man would come after me who would be so much greater than I am. I have been baptising, and I baptised him. A Voice told me: "When you see God's Holy Spirit coming upon One you baptise, and remaining on him, you will know that he himself is going to baptise with the Spirit." Then I saw the Spirit come down from heaven, like a dove, and rest on him, when he came to me, and I tell you he is the Son of God.'

Nathanael

The very next day, when Jesus
Was walking in Galilee,
He saw a young man named Philip,
And said to him, 'Follow me!'
Philip first fetched his brother,
Nathanael, who could not see
That Jesus was the Messiah –
How could this strange thing be?

But Jesus, seeing him, knew him:
'I saw you under a tree,'
He said, and Nathanael marvelled.
'You know me already!' said he.
'You are God's Son.' Said Jesus,
'Still greater things you shall see.'

Jesus Calls Four Men

Simon and Andrew were brothers;
Their home by the Galilee lake.
They cast their nets in the water,
To see what a catch they could make.

One day, when the brothers were fishing,
Jesus walked there on the shore.
'Leave your nets, Simon and Andrew,
And you shall go fishing no more;
But come, follow me – I will make you,
In future, fishers of men.'
They looked at Jesus, obeyed him,
And they followed him, there and then.

Another pair of brothers,
Whose father was Zebedee,
Were mending nets, when Jesus
Called to them, 'Follow me!'
These two were also fishers;
Their names were James and John.
They, too, would have followed Jesus,
No matter where he had gone.

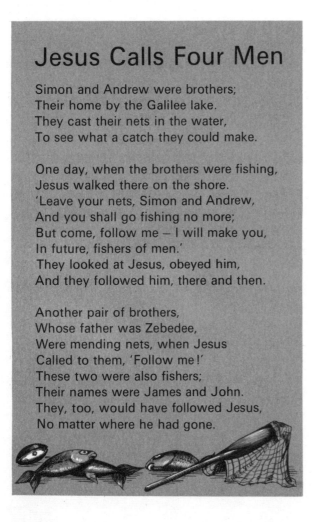

The Wedding Party

One day Jesus and his followers, who were called his disciples, were invited to a wedding in the little village of Cana. Mary, Jesus's mother, was a guest too.

Afterwards there was a party, with good things to eat and drink, but presently the guests had finished up all the wine.

'They have no more wine,' Mary whispered to Jesus.

'Can I do anything about it?' Jesus said gently. 'The time has not yet come when I can show everybody who I am.'

Nevertheless, Mary said to the servants who were waiting on the guests, 'Do whatever he tells you.'

There were six big water pots standing nearby.

'Fill the pots with water,' Jesus said, and the servants filled them to the brim. 'Now pour them out,' Jesus said, 'and take what you pour to the one in charge of the party.'

The servants did as they were told, and when they tilted a jar over a man's cup, wine flowed into it.

He tasted it, and enjoyed it very much. 'Usually, men set out their best wine first,' he called to the bridegroom, 'but you have kept the best wine to the end.'

He did not know what Jesus had done; but his disciples did, and they realised he was a very wonderful leader.

The Money-Changers

The feast of the Passover had come round once more, and Jesus and his friends went to keep it in the great temple in Jerusalem.

But the outer court was more like a busy market place. Men had set up stalls, to sell oxen, sheep and doves; they were calling out their wares, and people were bargaining with them.

Money-changers were also there, changing the coins that people had brought with them. The temple did not seem like the House of God, with so much wrangling and noise.

Jesus could not bear to see it. He drove all the sellers and their animals out of the temple court. Jesus overturned the tables of the money-changers, so that they began scrambling eagerly for the coins, as they rolled away.

'Take these things away!' he ordered the sellers of doves. 'Do not turn my Father's House into a market-place!'

'Seeing that you do these things,' the Jews said to Jesus, 'what sign will you give us?'

'Destroy this temple,' Jesus said, 'and in three days I will raise it up again.'

The Jews laughed scornfully. 'It took forty-six years to build this temple,' they said, 'and do you say that you can rebuild it in three days?'

But they did not understand that Jesus was speaking about himself. After he had died, he would rise again three days later. When this actually happened, the disciples remembered what Jesus had said in the temple.

159

The Woman by the Well

One day, Jesus and his friends were walking along a road which led from Jerusalem to Nazareth, and they had to pass through a small country called Samaria.

They were hungry and thirsty, and while the disciples hurried away to buy food in a village, Jesus rested on the edge of a well. It was the very well that Jacob had used, long, long ago.

Presently, a woman came towards Jesus, carrying a water-pot on her head; she was coming to get water from the well.

'Would you please give me a drink?' Jesus asked her.

The woman looked at him. 'How is it that you, who are a Jew, ask me, a Samaritan, to draw water for you?' she asked – for the Jews and the Samaritans were not friendly to one another.

'If you understood God's gift to the world,' Jesus said, 'and who it is who asked you for water, you would have asked him the same question, and he would have given you living water.'

The woman did not understand.

'Sir,' she said, 'you have nothing to draw the water with, and the well is deep. Where are you going to get this "living water"? Are you greater than our ancestor Jacob, who gave us this well and drank from it himself?'

'Anyone who drinks of this water will grow thirsty again,' Jesus told her. 'But whoever drinks the "water" that I can give will never thirst, for I am talking about a "well" that is within men's hearts, and I can give them the "water" of deep, eternal life.'

Still the woman did not really understand Jesus.

'Sir, give me this water,' she said, 'so that I do not get thirsty any more and shall no longer need to come to the well every day.

'I can see that you are a prophet. Our

ancestors worshipped God on this mountain, but the Jews say that he should be worshipped in Jerusalem. Tell me who is right?'

'The time will come,' Jesus said, 'when you shall worship your heavenly Father neither on this mountain, nor in Jerusalem. You do not know what you worship, but we do; the Saviour will come from the Jews. The hour is coming – indeed, it has already come – when true worshippers will worship the Father in spirit and in truth; those are the worshippers he seeks. God is Spirit, and those who worship him must worship him in spirit and in truth.'

'I know the Messiah – the Christ – is coming,' said the woman. 'When he comes, he will explain everything.'

'I am he,' Jesus told her.

The woman could not keep the great news to herself. She hurried back to the village and told a group of men what had been happening.

They went back to the well with her, and Jesus talked to them.

In the end, he went back with them to their village and stayed with them for two days. Many people listened to Jesus and believed what he said.

'This is indeed the Christ, the Saviour of the world,' they told one another.

The Nobleman's Son

Jesus went back to Cana, the village where he had gone to attend a wedding, and news that he was there reached a nobleman whose home was in Capernaum, by the Lake of Galilee.

His young son was ill, and not expected to get better. The nobleman was sure that Jesus could cure him, and so he made the journey to see Jesus and begged him to come and make his boy well again.

'Will you only believe my message if you

see wonderful things happening?' Jesus asked him.

'Sir, come, before my child dies,' the nobleman begged him, for he could think of nothing else.

'Go your way,' Jesus told him. 'Your son lives!'

The man believed that Jesus spoke the truth. He hurried home with joy in his heart, and before the man reached his own house, his servants came to meet him.

'Your son is going to live!' they called eagerly.

'At what time did he start to become better?' the nobleman asked.

'The fever left him yesterday, at the seventh hour,' they told him.

It was the exact time when Jesus had said, 'Your son lives!'

No wonder the nobleman and all his household believed in Jesus!

Jesus preaches in Nazareth

Jesus went to the little town of Nazareth where he had grown up, and on the Sabbath day he went to the synagogue, as he always did. During the service, Jesus stood up to read, and he was handed the scroll-book which held the words of the great prophet Isaiah.

'The Spirit of the Lord is upon me,' he read aloud, 'because he has set me apart to preach the gospel to the poor. He has sent me to heal broken hearts; to preach that prisoners will be set free, and blind people see again; to free those who are hurt by life; to preach that the Lord's special time has come.'

Jesus closed the scroll book and gave it back to the minister, and sat down. Everyone was watching him closely.

'Today these words are coming true,' Jesus said.

The people began to murmur to one another about his strange words. Could he mean that he was the Saviour – for whom the world had waited, ever since Isaiah had said that he would come one day? But they knew Jesus so well, he was the son of Joseph the carpenter; they had watched him grow up among them; he was one of themselves.

'Truly, I tell you, a prophet is never accepted in his own country,' Jesus said.

The congregation grew very angry, that Jesus should make such great claims for himself. They caught hold of him and pushed him out of the synagogue. Then they led Jesus through the streets of Nazareth, and up a hill behind the little town.

There they would have thrown him down, in their great anger, but quietly Jesus escaped from them and went his own way alone.

Jesus heals a Leper

There was a man who suffered from the illness called leprosy, and he heard that Jesus of Nazareth was going about the towns and villages, healing those who were ill.

He found out where Jesus was, and fell on his face before him.

'Lord, if you will, you can make me well,' he said.

'I will,' Jesus answered, and stretching out his hand, he touched the man.

Immediately the disease left the leper; he looked wonderingly at his hands, which had once been so badly marked with signs of his leprosy, and now were healthy.

'Do not tell anyone what I have done for you,' said Jesus, 'but go and show yourself to the priest, and make an offering of thankfulness to God for your healing.'

The man hurried off to do as he was told, but he simply could not keep the wonderful news to himself.

'Look – I am quite well, after having been a leper for years!' he told everyone, and they all looked at him and marvelled.

'Jesus of Nazareth healed me,' the man told them, and of course great crowds came to be healed and to listen to his teaching. They had never before heard a man who spoke as Jesus did.

The Man let down through the Roof

Once, when Jesus was in the city of Capernaum, on the lakeside, people crowded into the house where he was, and he spoke to them all.

They were so tightly packed together that there was no room for anyone else, and when four men arrived – carrying their sick friend on a bed – they could not get anywhere near Jesus.

But they would not give up. Carefully, they carried their friend on to the flat roof of the house, and began to move away some of the tiles to make an opening big enough for the bed to pass through. When they had done this, they gently let their sick friend's bed down through the roof until he lay before Jesus.

Jesus was touched by their faith, and he said to the sick man, 'Son, your sins are forgiven.'

Some learned men were sitting there, and they turned to one another indignantly. 'Why does this man say such shocking things?' they asked one another. 'Who can forgive sins except God?'

'Why do you ask yourself such questions?' Jesus said, turning to them. 'Is it any easier to say to a sick man: "Rise take up your bed and walk", than it is to tell him: "Your sins are forgiven"? But, in order that you may know that the Son of Man has power to forgive sins on earth –' at which Jesus turned to the man lying before him and said, 'I tell you – rise, take up your bed, and go home.'

Immediately the man stood up, cured. He picked up his bed and walked through the crowd to the door, praising God for this wonderful healing.

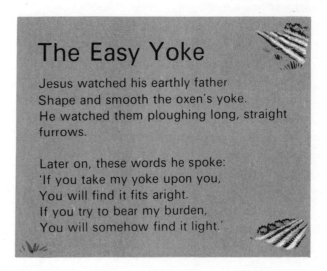

The Easy Yoke

Jesus watched his earthly father
Shape and smooth the oxen's yoke.
He watched them ploughing long, straight furrows.

Later on, these words he spoke:
'If you take my yoke upon you,
You will find it fits aright.
If you try to bear my burden,
You will somehow find it light.'

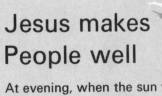

Jesus makes People well

At evening, when the sun was setting,
By the Lake of Galilee,
Many ill and crippled people
Heard a voice say, 'Come to me!'

Jesus laid his hand upon them,
And the blind could see again;
Lame men walked; the dumb were speaking;
Many sick folk lost their pain.

Jesus Calls Matthew

Jesus was walking near the lake, with a crowd following to see what he would do, when they came upon a man named Matthew, sitting in a little office, collecting taxes. Now tax-gatherers were not popular, for sometimes they charged too much, and kept the extra money for themselves.

As Jesus passed by, he looked at Matthew.

'Follow me!' he said. And just as the four fishermen had left their nets, so Matthew left his money-gathering, and followed Jesus.

Matthew arranged a feast at his house, and Jesus was there.

Two groups of Jews, known as the Scribes and Pharisees, did not approve at all. They were very strict about keeping the Jewish laws: 'How is it that your leader eats with people like that?' they asked the disciples scornfully.

Jesus heard the question. 'Those who are well do not need a doctor,' he said. 'The doctor attends to those who are ill. In the same way, I have not come to call the good people, but those who do wrong. I want to teach them to be sorry, and to live a better life.'

The Pool of Bethesda

In Jerusalem, there was a pool named Bethesda, the water of which people thought had power at certain times to cure sick people. Every now and then, as the pool rippled, they said that an angel was moving the water, and whoever stepped down into it first would be healed. All day long, people lay around the pool, watching the water, and hoping that they would be able to get into it before anyone else.

One man who lay there had been ill for thirty-eight years.

When Jesus saw him, and heard how long he had been ill, he went up to him. 'Do you want to be cured?' Jesus asked.

'Sir,' the man answered, 'I have no one to carry me into the pool, and someone else always gets there first.'

Jesus looked at him. 'Rise, pick up your bed, and walk,' he said.

At once the man did as Jesus told him. Then he went off joyfully, carrying his bed. Now it happened to be the Sabbath day, when the law said that Jews must not carry burdens or do any work.

'It is the Sabbath day!' some Jews said sternly. 'It is not lawful for you to carry your bed.'

'He who cured me told me to take up my bed and walk,' the man answered.

'Who was it?' asked the Jews; but the man did not know that it was Jesus.

Later, the man saw Jesus in the temple, and then he was able to tell the Jews who had healed him.

They were very angry, because Jesus had healed a man on the Sabbath, and told him to carry his bed.

In the Cornfields

Through the cornfields, Jesus walked
Upon a Sabbath day.
His followers picked ears of corn,
And threw the husks away.
They ate, for they were hungry,
But Pharisees, passing by,
Said, 'Doing that, you break the law!'
But Jesus made a swift reply:
'Because we pick corn on the Sabbath?
Long, long ago, it has been said
That David too was hungry,
And so he ate the temple bread.
Not lawful? I say the Sabbath
Was made for man; yet you cry
That man was made for the Sabbath —
The Lord of the Sabbath am I.'

The Man who could not Use his Hand

Once, when Jesus was sharing in a service at the synagogue on the Sabbath, there was a man there who had a hand which was quite useless.

'Perhaps Jesus will make his hand better,' the people thought. To see what Jesus would do, they asked him a question.

'Does the law allow healing on the Sabbath?' they asked slyly. They knew that it did not, and that if Jesus said 'Yes', they could accuse him of breaking the law.

Jesus, instead of answering their question, asked one of his own.

'Which of you,' he said, 'if you had a sheep which fell into a pit on the Sabbath, would not pull it out? How much better is a man than a sheep – so it is lawful to do good on the Sabbath.' He was sad, because they did not understand him.

Jesus turned to the man saying, 'Stretch

out your hand to me. Do not be afraid.'

Wonderingly, the man stretched out his hand, and found that it was as easy to use as the other, for Jesus had cured him.

The Pharisees were very angry about this, and they held a meeting to discuss how they could get rid of Jesus.

When he knew this, Jesus moved on to another place, and went on healing and preaching, always followed by crowds.

Jesus Calls his Disciples

Jesus often went away alone into the hills, to pray to his heavenly Father. The time came when he knew that he must choose a band of men who would be his faithful disciples, and carry on his work when he was no longer with them.

It was very important that the right men should be chosen, so Jesus went alone into the hills and there, in the silence and peace, he spent all night praying about his choice.

In the morning, he came back to his friends with his mind made up. He chose twelve men to bear the name of 'Apostles', telling them that they were set apart especially to be with him. Later he would send them out to spread the good news, and they would be able to heal those who were ill, or troubled in mind.

The twelve whom Jesus chose were: Simon, to whom Jesus gave the name Peter, and Andrew, his brother; James and John, the sons of Zebedee, to whom Jesus gave the nickname 'Sons of Thunder'; there were Philip and Matthew, Bartholomew and Thomas, Thaddeus, another James, another Simon, and Judas Iscariot.

The crowds that followed them were so great that, one day, Jesus told his disciples to bring a boat. He sat in it, and they pushed it out a little way on the lake, so that Jesus was able to speak from the boat to the many people on the shore.

The Sermon on the Mount

One day, Jesus and his friends climbed part of the way up a mountain, and great crowds came to hear what Jesus said.

He told them who the truly happy people were.

'Happy are the poor in spirit,' he said. 'The kingdom of heaven is theirs.

'Happy are those who are sad, for they shall be comforted.

'Happy are those who have a gentle spirit, for the earth is theirs.

'Happy are they who are hungry and thirsty for goodness, for they shall be filled.

'Happy are they who show mercy, for they shall have mercy shown to them.

'Happy are the pure-hearted, for they shall see God.

'Happy are the peace-makers; they shall be called the children of God.

'Happy are those who are ill-treated because they try to do good, for theirs is the kingdom of heaven.

'Happy are you when people say unkind things about you falsely, for my sake. Rejoice about it, for your reward in heaven will be great.

'You are like the light in the world. You cannot hide a city that is set on a hill. When men light a candle, they do not put it under a flour-measure, but on a candlestick, where it gives light to everyone in the house. Let your light so shine before men, that they may see the good life you lead, and give the glory to your heavenly Father.'

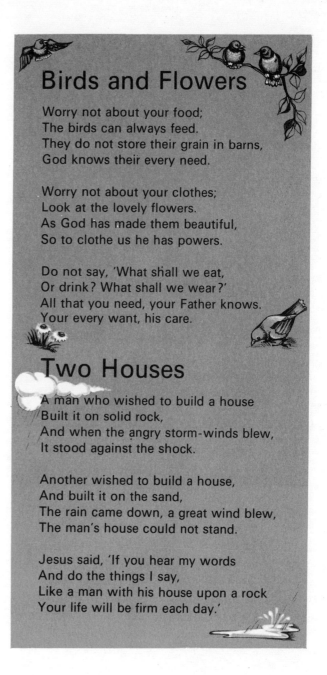

Birds and Flowers

Worry not about your food;
The birds can always feed.
They do not store their grain in barns,
God knows their every need.

Worry not about your clothes;
Look at the lovely flowers.
As God has made them beautiful,
So to clothe us he has powers.

Do not say, 'What shall we eat,
Or drink? What shall we wear?'
All that you need, your Father knows.
Your every want, his care.

Two Houses

A man who wished to build a house
Built it on solid rock,
And when the angry storm-winds blew,
It stood against the shock.

Another wished to build a house,
And built it on the sand,
The rain came down, a great wind blew,
The man's house could not stand.

Jesus said, 'If you hear my words
And do the things I say,
Like a man with his house upon a rock
Your life will be firm each day.'

The Widow's Son

Jesus and his followers went to a city called Nain; and on reaching the gate of the city, they had to wait for a funeral procession to pass by.

A widow had lost her only son, and she was very sad. When Jesus saw the weeping mother, he felt very sorry for her.

'Don't cry!' Jesus said gently, and he went up and touched the bed on which the

young man was lying; those who were carrying it stood still.

'Young man, I tell you to get up,' Jesus said.

Immediately, the widow's son sat up, alive and well, and began to talk.

Jesus had given him back to his mother, and she was overjoyed. Those who saw what had happened were amazed.

'A great prophet has risen up among us,' they said to one another. 'God has visited his people.'

The fame of Jesus spread far and wide, throughout the land.

The Precious Gift

One of the Pharisees asked Jesus to come and share a meal at his house. While they were eating, a woman slipped into the room; she had not always lived a good life, and everyone knew about her.

Now the woman had met Jesus, and was sorry for the life she had lived. She stood by him, crying, as he lay on a couch to eat – as the custom was – and her tears fell on his feet. Gently the woman wiped them away with her long hair, and then brought out the most precious thing she had – a box of sweet-smelling ointment that had cost a lot of money – and began smoothing the ointment on Jesus's feet.

The host, whose name was Simon, saw what was happening, and he thought to himself: 'If Jesus were really a prophet, he would have known, without being told, what sort of woman this is; she has done many wrong things.'

But Jesus knew exactly what the Pharisee was thinking. 'Simon!' he said, 'I want to tell you something.'

'Say on, master,' Simon replied.

Then Jesus told him a story: 'There was once a man to whom two other men owed money – one owed five hundred pence, and the other fifty. When they could not pay, he forgave them both. Now tell me, which of them will love him most?'

'I suppose, the one who was forgiven most,' Simon said.

'That is the right answer,' Jesus said, and he turned to the woman.

'Do you see this woman?' he asked Simon. 'When I came into your house, you brought no water to wash my feet, but she has washed them with her tears, and dried them with her hair, you gave me no kiss of welcome, but this woman has not ceased to kiss my feet, since I came in. You did not anoint my head with oil, but she has anointed my feet with costly ointment. So I tell you that her many sins are forgiven, because she has loved much. Someone who only loves a little is only forgiven a little.' Jesus looked at the woman. 'Your sins are forgiven,' he said gently.

The other guests began murmuring to one another: 'Who is this, who can forgive sins?' 'Your faith has saved you,' Jesus said quietly to the woman. 'Go in peace!'

The Story of the Sower

Said Jesus: 'A sower went out to sow,
And the farmer waited to see his corn grow.
Some seed by the path was bound to fall,
And the birds came down and ate it all.
Some more fell in among stones — the sun
Then rotted and withered every one.
Some seeds dropped between thorns, and they
Soon were choked and faded away.
But the seed that fell into good, rich soil
All came up, and the sower's toil
Brought forth much fruit. For the words I speak,
Good soil in the hearts of men I seek.'

Jesus's Stories of the Kingdom

The kingdom of heaven is like a pearl:
The most beautiful pearl on earth.
And a man will sell everything he has
To buy this pearl of great worth.

The kingdom of heaven is like a treasure
Hid in a field; and when a man
Discovers it, he sells his all:
That field he must buy, if he can.

The kingdom of heaven's like mustard seed;
At first it is only small,
But the seed grows until the birds can perch
In its branches, thick and tall.

The kingdom of heaven is like a net:
Men drag in their catch, and they
Sit down and pick out every good, fine fish,
But the bad they must throw away.

The Leaven in the Loaf

'I tell you,' said Jesus, 'the kingdom of heaven
Is like a woman who takes some leaven
(Or yeast), which will cause her bread to rise.
It is mixed with the flour and, before her eyes,
The loaves are formed.' He was telling men
That God's power works in their hearts, and then
His kingdom begins, and grows and stands —
Like a woman shaping the bread with her hands.

Jesus stills the Storm

After a long, hard day, Jesus and his disciples climbed into a little boat to cross the lake. Jesus was so tired that he lay down and fell fast asleep.

Soon a great storm arose. The little boat began to rock violently, as great waves dashed against and over it. The disciples were very frightened, and they woke Jesus.

'Lord, save us, or we shall drown!' they cried. 'Do you not care what happens to us?'

'Why are you frightened?' Jesus asked them. 'You are men with little faith.'

Then he stood up in the boat, and spoke to the wind and the waves. 'Peace – be still!' Jesus cried. The storm died down at once, and the lake grew calm.

The disciples looked at one another. 'What kind of man is this,' they asked, 'that even the winds and the sea obey him!'

Jairus's Daughter

Jairus was a very important man in the synagogue, but he was very sad because his twelve-year-old daughter was seriously ill, and not expected to get better.

When Jairus saw Jesus coming up from the lakeside, he fell at his feet.

'My little daughter is not expected to recover from an illness,' he said, 'so I pray you, come and lay your hands on her. Then she will be well again, and live.'

Jesus went with Jairus, and a crowd followed, to see what would happen. On the way, a woman came up to Jesus, believing that, if only she could touch his clothes, it would cure the illness which she had borne for a very long time.

Indeed the woman was made quite well again, and while Jesus was talking to her, one of Jairus's servants came hurrying up. 'Your daughter has died!' he said sadly.

Jesus sends out his Disciples

The day came when Jesus decided that he would send out his twelve disciples to work on their own.

'I want you to go out, two by two,' he told them. 'Take nothing for your journey, except a staff to help you along. Wear your sandals, and do not take an extra coat. Do not take food or money with you.'

Jesus told them that they would be able to heal people who were ill, and that they were to tell everyone about God's kingdom.

'Stay in someone's house as long as you are in their city,' he said, 'and if anyone makes you feel unwelcome, shake the dust of that place from your feet, and go on somewhere else.

'You may find yourselves in trouble for speaking out; but, if you are taken before the court, do not worry about what answers you will give, for your heavenly Father will give you the right words to say.

'Do not be afraid. Remember, in the market-place they sell two sparrows for a farthing; yet not one of those little birds falls to the ground without God knowing about it. Do not be afraid, I say – you are worth more than many sparrows.

'Whoever gives even a cup of cold water to a little one in your name, will be rewarded for it one day.'

The disciples said goodbye to their Master, and set out, two by two, healing and preaching wherever they went.

'Why do you trouble the Master any more?'

As soon as Jesus heard this news, he turned to Jairus. 'Do not be afraid,' he said. 'Only believe.'

Jesus went into Jairus's house, taking with him only Peter, James and John, apart from the girl's father and mother.

Inside, Jairus's friends and servants were all standing round, crying.

'Do not cry!' Jesus said. 'The little one is not dead; she is only asleep.'

They laughed, not believing him, but Jesus sent them all out of the room, then he went up to the bed where Jairus's daughter lay, and took her hand.

'Little girl,' he said, 'I tell you to rise.'

At once the child sat up and lived again.

Her father and mother were astonished and overcome with joy.

'Do not tell anyone what has happened,' Jesus said, 'and give your daughter something to eat.'

Feeding Five Thousand

When the disciples came back to Jesus, after preaching to people, they had a great deal to tell him, and were very tired.

'Let us go away by ourselves into the hills and rest awhile,' said Jesus.

They all got into a boat, and quietly slipped across the lake; but people saw Jesus and his disciples setting off, and ran along the shore after them. More and more people came, from different towns and villages, and when they all gathered round Jesus, there were about five thousand.

Jesus began to talk to them, and the time passed very quickly. Suddenly it was evening, and the disciples whispered to Jesus, 'Send the people off to find food and lodging, for this is a very lonely place.'

'You give them something to eat,' Jesus said.

'Shall we go and buy a lot of bread for them then?' asked one of his disciples.

'There is a boy here,' Andrew said, 'with five barley loaves, and two small fish – but what good would they be among so many people?'

'Tell everyone to sit down,' Jesus replied.

The people all sat in rows on the grass, wondering what was going to happen.

Jesus took the boy's five loaves, and thanked God for his gift of food. Then he told the disciples to share out the bread and the fish among everyone.

The disciples obeyed, and there was more than enough food for them all. Indeed, when everyone had eaten as much as he could, Jesus told the disciples to gather up the scraps that were left, and these filled twelve baskets.

'This is truly the prophet for whom the world was waiting,' people said.

A Deaf Man hears

Jesus and his disciples went back to the shores of the Lake of Galilee, and some people brought a man to him. This man was deaf, and he could not speak properly either.

'Please make him better, Master,' they begged Jesus.

Jesus led the deaf man from the crowd, so that they were by themselves. He put his fingers into the man's ears, and touched his tongue.

'Be opened!' he said.

Immediately, the man could hear all the sounds about him: the murmuring crowd nearby, the birds, and the water rippling on the shore. He looked into Jesus's face, and began to speak quite clearly.

Everyone was astonished. 'He has done all things well,' they said of Jesus. 'He makes the deaf hear, and the dumb speak!'

Not long afterwards, they brought a blind man to Jesus to be healed.

Again, Jesus led the man away from the crowds, and touched his eyes.

'What can you see?' he asked.

The man looked about him. 'I can see men – but not clearly. They look like trees walking!' he said.

Jesus touched his eyes again, and then the man could see properly.

Jesus walks on the Sea

After the crowd had been fed, Jesus told his disciples to get into the boat and go across the lake, while he sent the people home.

When he was alone at last, Jesus found a quiet spot in the hills where he could pray.

It was now dark, and suddenly a great storm arose on the lake. Jesus saw that his friends were in trouble, and struggling to row their boat – for the wind was against them, and the boat was in danger of being swamped by the high waves.

He began to walk towards them, on the water; and when the disciples saw him, they did not know it was Jesus, and cried out in fear.

'Do not be afraid – it is I!' Jesus called to them.

'Lord, if it is you, tell me to come to you on the water,' Peter called back.

'Come!' Jesus beckoned to him.

Peter took one step outside the boat; but when he saw how rough the water was, he grew frightened and began to sink.

'Lord, save me!' he cried.

Jesus stretched out his hand and held Peter up in the water.

'O you of little faith,' he said. 'Why did you doubt?'

As they climbed into the boat together, the storm died away.

'Truly, you are the Son of God,' the disciples said reverently to Jesus.

The Greek Woman's Daughter

One day, Jesus went on a journey, and a Greek woman came up to him.

'Have pity on me, Lord,' she said, 'for my daughter is in need of help.'

The disciples wanted Jesus to send the woman away, lest she should trouble Jesus.

'I have come to help the "lost sheep of Israel",' Jesus told her gently.

She begged him again: 'Lord, help me!'

173

'It is not right to take the bread that is meant for the children, and throw it to the dogs,' Jesus said. He meant her to understand that, if he had come to help the people of Israel, he could not be expected to help others as well. He said this to test the Greek woman's faith.

Quickly, the woman answered, 'Yes, Lord, but the dogs under the table can eat the children's crumbs!'

It was a good answer, and very much what Jesus wanted her to say.

'You have great faith,' Jesus told the mother. 'You have what you have asked for.'

The woman asked no more questions. She hurried home, and found that her daughter was quite well again – Jesus had made her better.

On the Mountain

A day came when Jesus told Peter, James and John that he wanted them to walk up a mountain path with him. The three disciples obeyed and followed Jesus.

When they had climbed quite a long way, Jesus knelt down to pray; and, as his disciples watched, it seemed as though he was surrounded with light: his face and his clothes were shining. Then Peter, James and John saw that two men were talking with Jesus, and somehow they knew that the men were Moses and Elijah.

Peter was quite overcome by this.

'Master, it is wonderful that we are here!' he cried. 'May we make three shelters out of branches – one for you, one for Moses, and one for Elijah?' Peter really did not know what to say; it was all so strange and unearthly, that he was half afraid.

While Peter was speaking, a cloud came down and hid the three figures from sight, and a Voice said, 'This is my beloved Son; listen to him!'

Little Children

The disciples asked Jesus a question.
'Who is the greatest of all
In the kingdom of heaven?' And Jesus,
As a little child answered his call,
Said, 'Unless you are like little children,
And humble yourselves, without pride,
You cannot get into the Kingdom –
The simple and meek go inside.'

The Lost Sheep

If a shepherd has a hundred sheep,
And one of them goes astray,
He will leave the ninety-nine
And search along every way
Until he finds that one.
And then his heart more gladness holds
Because one sheep is found,
Than over all his other flocks
Safely in their folds.

Birds and Foxes

A man wanted to follow Jesus,
And go where he would go,
But Jesus told him truly
That birds have nests they know,
And foxes have their hide-out
Where they can make their bed.
'The Son of Man,' said Jesus,
'Has no place to lay his head.'

Then the cloud rolled away, and Peter, James and John, saw that Jesus was alone now.

They began to come down the mountainside, and the disciples were awestruck; they did not know what to say.

'Do not talk about the vision you have seen,' Jesus told them, 'until the Son of man is risen again.' This was the three disciples' special secret, and they did not talk to anyone about the wonderful thing which they had seen.

174

The Good Samaritan

A lawyer once asked Jesus a question.

'Master!' he said, 'what must I do to gain eternal life?'

'What do you read in the law?' Jesus asked him, in reply.

The lawyer answered, 'You shall love the Lord your God with all your heart, and with all your soul, with all your strength, and with all your mind; and your neighbour as yourself.'

'That is the right answer,' Jesus told him. 'Do that, and you will live.'

'Who is my neighbour?' asked the lawyer.

By way of answer, Jesus told him a story: 'A certain man went down the lonely road from Jerusalem to Jericho, and a gang of thieves set on him. They tore off his clothes, and wounded him, and went off, leaving him half dead.

'Presently a priest came that way, and when he saw the poor man lying there, he passed by on the other side of the road.

'Soon afterwards another man, a Levite, came along. He, too, just looked at the one lying in the road, and went on.

'But then a man from Samaria came by. Although he was not even from the wounded man's country, he felt sorry for him, and stopped.

'The Samaritan bent over the wounded man, and did what he could to make him better. Then he lifted him on to his own ass, brought him to an inn, and looked after him.

'Next morning, the good Samaritan took out some of his own money and gave it to the inn-keeper: "Look after this man," he said, "and if you have to spend more than I have given you, I will pay the extra next time I come this way."

'Now,' Jesus asked the lawyer, 'which of those three do you think was a true neighbour to the man who fell among thieves?'

'The one who was kind to him,' the lawyer said.

'Then you go and behave in the same way,' Jesus told him.

The Man born Blind

Jesus saw a blind man, begging by the way.
He stopped and, on his eyelids, Jesus laid some clay.
'Now,' he told the blind man, 'go and find the pool
Called Siloam. Wash there, in water that is cool.'
The blind man went off quickly, and found that he could see.
Men said, 'Is this the beggar?' He answered, 'I am he!'
They went and asked his parents, 'Was he not born blind?'
'Jesus made me better,' the man said, 'he is kind.
How or why it happened, I truly do not know.
Once blind, I now can see you: it simply happened so.'

The Good Shepherd

'I am the Good Shepherd,' Jesus said, 'I know
All my sheep; and their Shepherd they know also.
I will walk before them, and they know my voice,
The life that I will give them will make their hearts rejoice.
I am like the doorway to the sheep's own fold,
Where they rest in safety, sheltered from the cold.
Other sheep still wander; soon I must begin
Seeking till I find them, and bring them safely in.
I am the Good Shepherd – a faithful watch I keep;
I will lay my life down, for my own beloved sheep.'

Martha and Mary

As Jesus and his friends were walking along the road, not far from Jerusalem, they came to a village called Bethany.

Jesus went into a house where two sisters lived. The eldest, whose name was Martha, began bustling about, getting a good meal for him. The younger, Mary, sat near Jesus, and listened to his teaching.

Martha did not think this was fair; there was a great deal to be done, and Mary was not doing her share.

Hot and flustered from her cooking, Martha went to Jesus. 'Lord,' she said, 'do you not care that my sister has left me all the work to do? Please tell her to come and help me.'

'Martha, Martha!' Jesus said gently. 'You are so worried about such a lot of little details, but there is only one thing that really matters. Mary has chosen wisely; we must not take away what she has chosen.'

Learning to Pray

Jesus taught his disciples how to pray.

'Supposing someone on a journey stopped at your house to see you,' he said, 'and you had no food to give him. Even if it was midnight, would you not go and knock on another friend's door, and ask him to lend you three loaves?

'And supposing he called out: "Do not bother me! My family and I are in bed, and I have locked the door for the night."

'If you then went on asking, he would at last get up and give you the bread, because you had shown yourself to be very much in earnest and had not given up asking.

'So I say to you about prayer: ask, and it shall be given you; seek, and you shall find; knock, and the door shall be opened.

'If your son asked you for bread, would he be given a stone? If he asked for fish, would you give him a serpent? If you know how to give good gifts to your children, how much more ready will your heavenly Father be to give his Holy Spirit to those who ask him for it.'

Happy are the Meek

Jesus was invited to a party, at which he noticed how everyone scrambled and pushed to get the best places.

'When you are invited to a wedding,' he said, 'do not sit down in the best place, in case someone more important than you has been invited. Your host might come up to you and say: "Let this man sit here", and you would feel ashamed.

'But when you are invited, go and sit in the most humble place, so that when your host sees you, he may say: "Friend, move up higher", and everyone will respect you. For whoever thinks much of himself shall be of little worth; and he who is humble shall be raised up.'

The Man who built New Barns

There was a man who had much grain;
His barns were far too small.
He said, 'I'll pull the old ones down;
New barns will hold it all.'

He did not know, so Jesus said,
He would not live to see
The new barns stored with all his grain.
He'd build them needlessly.

He could not use the worldly wealth,
Which carefully he stored.
Far better if his treasures were
In heaven, said our Lord.

Heavenly Treasure

Sell all you have; give to the poor
Your silver and your gold,
And do not lock your treasures up
In bags that will grow old.

Store up treasure where rust cannot corrupt,
Or moths spoil and destroy.
In heaven let your treasure be
In that you'll find true joy.

Where your treasure is, there shall your heart be.

The Great Supper

This is a story that Jesus told:

A man decided to give a supper party. He invited all his friends, and when the evening came, everyone worked very hard, getting out the food and making everything ready.

At the proper time, the man told his servant to go and fetch his friends, telling them that the party table was now ready.

But not one of the guests who had been invited really wanted to come, and they all began to make excuses.

'I have bought some land,' said one, 'and I must go and look at it. Please make my apologies to your master.'

'I have bought new oxen,' said another, 'and I must try them out with the plough. Please make my excuses.'

'I have just got married,' said a third, 'so I cannot come.'

Then the servant went back and told his master what had happened. The man looked at the great supper he had prepared, and he felt very angry with his friends who had let him down.

'Go out quickly into the streets and lanes of the city,' he told his servant, 'and bring in the beggars – the poor, the crippled, the blind.'

So the servant did as his master told him. 'There is still room for more,' he said, when the guests were brought in.

'Then go out again, into the main streets and the little lanes,' said his master, 'and order them to come; my house must be filled. I tell you, none of those who were invited shall taste any of my supper.'

The lost Piece of Silver

'Supposing,' said Jesus, 'a woman
Had ten silver pieces, and then
She lost one – she'd soon take a candle,
And sweep till she found it again.
She would call to her friends: "I'm so happy!
My coin was there, on the ground."
Thus the angels rejoice,' explained Jesus,
'When a sinner who is sorry is found.'

178

The Son who came Home

Here is another story that Jesus told:

There was a man who had two sons. The younger son said to his father, 'Give me my share of the money that is to come to me.'

The father did as he was asked, and the boy took his share and went off to a far-away country. There he spent the money on enjoying himself.

When the younger son had spent all his money, there was a famine in the land, and he grew very hungry.

The boy began to work for a citizen of the country in which he was living, and had to look after and feed the pigs. He was so hungry that he would gladly have eaten the pigs' food.

Then the younger son began to think of what he had done in leaving home. 'My father's servants have more than enough bread to eat,' he thought, 'and I perish with hunger. I will go back home, and I will say to my father: "Father, I have done wrong in the sight of heaven, and in your sight, and am not fit to be called your son: make me one of your hired servants." '

So he set out for his own home. When he was still quite a long way away, his father saw him coming and, with his heart filled with love, ran to meet his son, and fell on his neck and kissed him.

'Father,' the boy said humbly, 'I have done wrong in the sight of heaven, and in your sight, and I am not fit to be called your son.'

His father forgave him at once. 'Bring out the best robe,' he said to his servants, 'and put it on him; bring out the calf that has been fattened, and kill it, and let us eat and be glad – for it was as though my son was dead, and he is alive again. He was lost, and now he is found.'

They all began to share in a happy feast, and to rejoice. But the elder son was working in the field when his brother came home,

and later, as he neared the house, he heard the sounds of music and dancing.

He called one of the servants. 'What is happening?' he asked.

'Your brother has come back,' the servant said, 'and your father has killed the fatted calf, to make a feast, because he is so glad that his son is safely home again.'

The elder son was jealous and angry, and he would not go into the party.

When the father knew that his son was outside, he begged him to come in.

'I have served you all these years,' the elder son said reproachfully, 'and I have never done anything wrong nor disobeyed you. Yet you have never given me special food, that I might have a party with my friends. But, when he comes back, having frittered away all the money given to him, you kill the fatted calf in his honour!'

'Son, you are with me all the time,' his father said gently, 'and everything I have is yours. It was right that we should be gay and rejoice, for your brother was as if dead, and now he is alive again. He was lost, and now he is found.'

The Ten Lepers

In a certain village, there were ten men who suffered leprosy. They were not allowed to mix with the other villagers, but when the lepers heard that Jesus was coming, they stood a long way off and called, 'Jesus, Master, help us!'

When Jesus saw them, he said, 'Go and show yourselves to the priests!' Then as the men went, they found that they were indeed quite well again.

Nine of them hurried off, thinking only how wonderful it was; but one of the men turned back and fell at Jesus's feet. He was a Samaritan.

'Thank you, Master,' he said gratefully, 'and glory be to God!'

'Where are the other nine?' Jesus asked. 'Did I not heal ten men, and only one has come back to say "Thank you" – and he is a stranger in the land.'

He turned to the Samaritan: 'Go your way,' he said kindly. 'Your faith has cured you.'

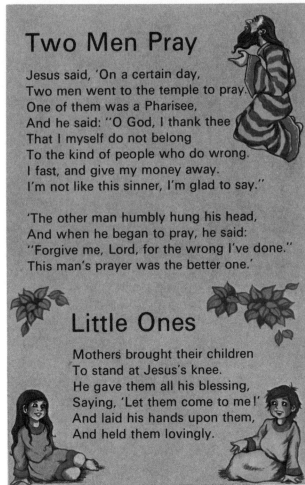

Two Men Pray

Jesus said, 'On a certain day,
Two men went to the temple to pray.
One of them was a Pharisee,
And he said: "O God, I thank thee
That I myself do not belong
To the kind of people who do wrong.
I fast, and give my money away.
I'm not like this sinner, I'm glad to say."

'The other man humbly hung his head,
And when he began to pray, he said:
"Forgive me, Lord, for the wrong I've done."
This man's prayer was the better one.'

Little Ones

Mothers brought their children
To stand at Jesus's knee.
He gave them all his blessing,
Saying, 'Let them come to me!'
And laid his hands upon them,
And held them lovingly.

The Young Ruler

A young ruler felt that he would like to know more about the kind of life that Jesus talked about, so he went to him to ask a question.

'Good Master,' he said, 'what good deed shall I do, in order to earn this "eternal life" about which you talk?'

'Why do you call me "good"?' Jesus asked. 'Only God is good! But if you want to live the kind of life I tell you about, keep the commandments.'

'Which commandments must I keep?' asked the young ruler.

'You shall not steal; honour your father and mother; love your neighbour as yourself . . .' So Jesus reminded the young man of these and the other commandments.

'I have kept all these since I was a boy,' the ruler said. 'What else must I do?'

'If you want to be perfect,' Jesus said, 'go and sell what you have, and give the money to the poor, and you shall have treasure in heaven. So follow me.'

The young ruler was sad when he heard this, for he was rich, and he felt he could not give away all that he had.

Sorrowfully, the young ruler went away; he was not ready to follow Jesus and obey him.

As he walked off, Jesus looked at his disciples.

'How hard it is for a rich man to enter into God's kingdom!' he said. 'Why it is easier for a camel to go through the eye of a needle!'

'Well, we have left everything to follow you,' Peter replied.

'There is no one who has left their home and family for my sake, and the sake of my good news,' Jesus told him, 'who will not be more than repaid, and later win everlasting life.'

The Workers in the Vineyard

'Many people who are important now will be unimportant one day,' Jesus said. 'And many who are thought little of will come to everyone's notice.'

Then he told a story: A man who owned a vineyard went out early one morning, to find men who would come and work in it. He found some labourers, and when they had agreed about wages, he sent them to work in his vineyard.

Some time later, the man went back to the market-place, and saw a group of men standing about doing nothing.

'Go and work in my vineyard,' he said, 'and I will pay you a fair wage.'

The man went back twice more, and said the same thing to two more groups of men.

Near the end of the day, he found yet another group.

'Why have you been standing here all day doing nothing?' he asked.

'Because nobody hired us,' they said.

'Go into my vineyard,' he said, 'and you shall receive fair wages.'

When evening came, the man said to his steward, 'Call all the workers and pay them, starting with those who came last.'

The men were given their wages, and when those who had worked longer went to receive theirs, they thought that they would be paid more; but everyone was given exactly the same.

'It is not fair,' they said. 'Those men only worked for an hour, and we have toiled in the hot sun all day – yet you have paid us the same wage.'

'Friend,' said the owner of the vineyard, 'I have been fair to you. You agreed to work for a certain wage, and that sum I have paid to you. Can I not reward the others equally, if I choose to do so? Sometimes the last shall be first, and the first last.'

A Place in the Kingdom

James and John, two of Jesus's disciples, asked him to do something very special for them. 'We want you to do for us whatever we ask,' they said.

'What is that?' Jesus asked.

'In your kingdom,' said James and John, 'let us sit on either side of you – one on your right, and one on your left.'

'You do not know what you are asking,' Jesus told them seriously. 'Can you go through the trials with which I am faced?'

'We can!' they said.

'You shall indeed do so,' Jesus said. 'But, as for sitting on my right hand and on my left – that is not for me to arrange.'

When the disciples heard this, they were cross with James and John for asking such a question.

But Jesus reminded them: 'Whoever wants to be great among you, shall serve the rest; whoever wants to be the most important must be the humblest of all. Even the Son of Man did not come to be waited on, but to serve others, and to die for them.'

The Man in the Tree

Jesus was passing through Jericho, and because his fame had spread, everyone wanted to see him, and they all ran into the streets.

There was one man named Zacchaeus, who was very small and could not see over the heads of the crowd. So he decided to climb a tree, and look down on Jesus!

Quick as a flash, Zacchaeus chose a tree and climbed into its branches. He had a splendid view. When Jesus reached the spot, he looked up and saw Zacchaeus peeping between the leaves.

'Hurry up and come down, Zacchaeus!' he called. 'Today I would like to stay at your house.'

Zacchaeus scrambled down, delighted that Jesus knew who he was, and wanted to come home with him. As he was rich, Zacchaeus knew that he could prepare a splendid meal for his guest. But he had also done many wrong things in his life, and other people in Jericho knew this.

'Jesus has gone to be the guest of a wrong-doer,' they said, disapprovingly.

Zacchaeus, however, made Jesus a promise that he would live a better life in future.

'I will give half my goods to the poor,' he promised, 'and if I have taken anything from a man when I should not have done so, I will give it back to him four times over.'

'Today, salvation is come to this house,' said Jesus. 'For the Son of Man is come to seek and to save that which is lost.'

Ten Pieces of Silver

'A certain nobleman travelled to a far country,' said Jesus, 'and before he left home, he called his ten servants, and gave each of them some money to use in whatever way they thought would be best.

'When the nobleman arrived home, he sent for his servants, to find out what use they had made of his money.

'Lord,' said the first, 'I have managed to make your money ten times as much.'

'Well done, my good servant,' said the master. 'Because you have proved yourself faithful over little things, I will make you ruler over ten cities.'

The second said, 'Lord, I have increased your money five times.' His master was pleased, and gave him charge of five cities.

The third brought back his money, just as he had received it.

'Lord,' he said, 'here is your money. I wrapped it up and hid it. I am afraid of you, because you are a stern man; you take up what you did not lay down, and you reap what you did not sow.'

'You are a bad servant,' his master told him. 'Why did you not put my money in the bank, where more would have been added to it?' He turned to the others. 'Take away his money,' he said, 'and give it to the man who has made ten times as much.'

Then Jesus added: 'I tell you that to every one who has, shall be given more; and from him who has not, shall be taken away even the little that he has.'

The Two Sons

Said Jesus, 'A man had a vineyard
And he said to his elder son:
"Go and work in my vineyard,
And labour till day is done."

'"No, I will not go, father,"
The boy was quick to say;
But afterwards he was sorry,
And he went and worked all day.

'The younger son was bidden,
And he said: "I hear you call!
I will work in the vineyard."
But he never went there at all.

'Which of the two,' asked Jesus,
'Obeyed his father best?
The first? Yes — those who are sorry
Count more than all the rest.'

Lazarus Lives

Jesus's friends, Martha and Mary, had a brother named Lazarus.

One day, Lazarus fell very ill, and the sisters sent a message to Jesus, asking him to come to their home at Bethany. 'Jesus will make our brother well again,' they told one another, and they longed for the Master to come.

Jesus received the message: 'Lord, he whom you love is ill.'

'This illness will not mean that Lazarus will die,' he said. 'But God's glory will be shown through his Son, because of it.'

Jesus loved Martha, Mary and Lazarus, but he did not feel able to go to them for three days.

Then he said, 'Let us go to Judaea again.'

'But Master, it is not safe,' the disciples protested. 'The Jews want to hurt you! Do you think it wise to go there again?'

Jesus knew that it was right to go, and he told his friends so.

'Our friend Lazarus is asleep,' he said, 'and I am going to wake him.'

'Lord, if he is sleeping, that is a good thing,' the disciples answered.

'I mean that Lazarus is dead,' Jesus said. 'I am glad, for your sakes, that I was not there, for in the end you may believe. Come, let us go to him.'

'Let us go, too, even if we have to die with him,' said Thomas to the other disciples.

They set out for the village of Bethany, where the sisters were being comforted by their friends.

When they heard that Jesus was coming, Martha hurried out to meet him, but Mary stayed indoors.

'Lord, if you had been here, my brother would not have died,' Martha said. 'But I know that, even now, God will grant whatever you ask.'

'Your brother will rise again,' Jesus said gently.

'I believe he will rise again in the end,' Martha said.

'Whoever believes in me,' said Jesus, 'though he were dead, yet he shall live; and whoever lives and believes in me shall never die. Do you believe that?'

'Yes, Lord,' Martha said. 'I believe that you are the Christ, the Son of God, who was promised to the world.'

Then she hurried back, and whispered to Mary, 'The Master is here, and wants to see you.'

Mary got up quickly, and her friends, thinking she was going to Lazarus's grave, went out after her. Mary hurried to Jesus and fell at his feet, saying sadly, 'Lord, if you had been here, my brother would not have died.'

When Jesus saw her tears, and that her friends were also crying, he felt sad. Then he said, 'Where have you laid Lazarus?'

'Come and see,' they said; and Jesus, too, wept.

'See how he loved him!' whispered Mary's friends.

'Could not this man have saved Lazarus?' asked one.

Jesus went to the grave where Lazarus lay; it was a cave with a big stone rolled across the entrance to seal up the tomb.

'Take away the stone!' Jesus commanded.

'But he has been dead four days . . .' Martha hesitated.

'Did I not tell you that you should see the glory of God?' Jesus asked her.

The friends put their shoulders against the stone and moved it away, and Jesus began to pray.

'Father, I thank you that you have heard me. I know that you always hear me, but I said what I did because of the people standing around – that they might believe that you have sent me.' Then he cried: 'Lazarus, come!'

At once Lazarus walked out of the cave, alive and well. Joyfully, his sisters led him home again. Many of the people who saw this then believed at last that Jesus must be the Son of God.

The Man who sent his Son

Here is another of the stories told by Jesus:

A man planted a vineyard, and put a hedge around it. He made a place where the juice could be squeezed from the grapes, and he built a tower. It was a very fine vineyard indeed.

Then the man let it to some farmers, while he himself took a long journey to a distant country. When the time came round for the fruit to ripen, he sent one of his servants to the farmers, to ask them to let him have some of the grapes.

The farmers set upon the poor servant, beat him, and sent him away empty-handed. Soon, the owner of the vineyard sent another servant; but the farmers threw stones at him, and he returned hurt.

The owner did not give up, however; he kept on sending different servants, although the farmers always treated them very badly.

Now the man had one son, whom he loved very much: 'They will not hurt my son,' he said. 'They will respect him.'

But when the farmers saw the young man coming, they said to one another, 'This is the man's heir; if we kill him, we shall have the vineyard for ourselves.'

So they set upon the son, and killed him. What would the owner of the vineyard do then? He would turn the wicked farmers out, and give his lovely vineyard to others!

Mary anoints Jesus

It was the time of the Passover feast, and crowds were going up to Jerusalem.

'Do you think Jesus will come to the feast?' people asked, as they stood about in the temple courts. The chief priests and the Pharisees had given orders that, if any man knew where Jesus was, they were to tell the priests, so that they might take him prisoner.

Six days before the feast, Jesus went to Bethany, to visit his friends – Martha, Mary and Lazarus. They got supper ready for him, and Martha served, while Lazarus sat at table with Jesus.

Presently, Mary came in, bringing a very precious box of sweet-smelling ointment. She broke the box and anointed Jesus's head.

The disciples were angry to see this.

'What a waste!' they said, and Judas added: 'Could this ointment not have been sold and the money given to the poor?'

'Let her alone,' said Jesus. 'Do not trouble her, for Mary has done something good. The poor you have with you always, and you can help them whenever you will; but you will not always have me. I tell you, she will always be remembered for this.'

Jesus rides into Jerusalem

The following day, Jesus called two of his disciples to him.

'Go into the next village,' he said, 'and

you will see an ass tied up, with her colt. Untie them, and bring them to me. If anyone asks you what you are doing, say: "The Lord needs them", and they will let you have them.'

The disciples did as Jesus told them, and everything turned out exactly as he had said it would.

They brought the animals to Jesus, and threw their coats over the back of the young ass, whereupon Jesus mounted the animal and rode slowly towards Jerusalem.

Many, many years before, one of the old prophets had said that the long-awaited king would come riding on an ass; so when the people saw Jesus, they spread their clothes in his path, and cut down branches of the palm trees, and threw them in front of him.

'Hosanna to the Son of David!' they cried. 'Hurrah! Blessed is the King who comes in the name of the Lord!'

The little children shouted with the rest, and waved their palm branches happily, as Jesus went by.

The Penny

The Pharisees always tried to trick Jesus into saying or doing something they thought was wrong so that they could accuse him. One day, they sent some men to him.

'Master,' they said pretending to believe him, 'we know you say and teach what is true, and that you will accept nobody's teaching except God's. Tell us, therefore, is it lawful to pay taxes to Caesar?'

Jesus knew that they were trying to trick him.

'Why do you ask me such a question?' he asked. 'Show me a penny!'

One of them brought out a penny and held it in his hand.

'Whose head is on it?' Jesus asked.

'Caesar's!' replied the man.

'Well then,' Jesus said, 'give to Caesar the things that belong to him, and give to God those things which belong to God.'

So because they could not find fault with the answer that Jesus had given them, the men said nothing.

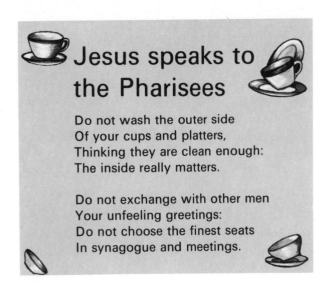

Jesus speaks to the Pharisees

Do not wash the outer side
Of your cups and platters,
Thinking they are clean enough:
The inside really matters.

Do not exchange with other men
Your unfeeling greetings:
Do not choose the finest seats
In synagogue and meetings.

The Widow's Gift

Near the entrance to the temple, there stood a special container into which people put their gifts of money.

One day, Jesus sat near the treasury, as it was called, and watched as many rich people came in and cast their coins into the container; they could afford to give a good deal of money.

Presently, a poor widow came by; she put in two tiny coins which, together, were only worth a farthing.

Jesus beckoned to his friends. 'I tell you,' he said, 'this poor woman has given the best gift of all. The rich people gave part of their wealth, but she gave everything that she had.'

The Wise Bridesmaids

Jesus told a story about some bridesmaids.

'There was going to be a wedding,' he said, 'and the bride had chosen ten of her friends to be bridesmaids. They decided to go and meet the bridegroom and, as it was evening, they took lamps with them.

'Five of the bridesmaids were wise, and took oil with them for their lamps; but five of them were foolish, and did not.

'The bridegroom was late and the bridesmaids got tired of waiting; and they all fell asleep.

'At midnight, someone called: "Look, here is the bridegroom coming!"

'The bridesmaids got up quickly, and trimmed their lamps.

'"Oh dear!" cried the foolish ones. "Our lamps have gone out. Give us some of your oil!" they begged the others.

'"We cannot do that," replied the wise bridesmaids, "because there might not be enough for us all. Go and buy some for yourselves from the oil merchant."

'The girls hurried off; but, whilst they were gone, the bridegroom arrived. The wise bridesmaids went in with him to the wedding, and the door was shut.

'Presently, the bridesmaids who had gone to buy oil hurried back.

'"Lord, Lord, open the door!" they cried.

'"I do not know who you are," called back the bridegroom, and the foolish bridesmaids missed the wedding.

'Always watch and be ready,' Jesus told the people who were listening. 'For you do not know when the Son of Man is coming.'

The Man with the Water Jar

It was time to get ready for the feast of the Passover.

'Where shall we prepare the feast for you, Master?' Jesus's disciples asked him.

'Go into the city,' Jesus told Peter and John. 'There you will meet a man carrying a pitcher of water. Follow him, and when he goes into a house, go too, saying to the man whose home it is: "The Master says, where is the guest-room in which I shall eat the Passover with my disciples?" And he will show you a big upper room; there make a Passover meal for us all.'

Peter and John did as Jesus said. It would be easy to find the man, for women usually carried water jars.

Soon a man carrying a pitcher came along, and the two disciples followed him. When he went into a house, Peter and John followed, and gave the owner of the house Jesus's message.

The man took them to a large room upstairs where there was a table, and Peter and John began to get the special meal ready, for they knew they had found the right place.

The Last Supper

That evening, Jesus and his twelve disciples sat down to supper.

As they were eating, Jesus said, 'One of you is going to betray me.'

The disciples were dismayed. 'Lord, is it I? Is it I?' several of them asked.

John, whom Jesus loved specially, was sitting next to him, and Peter signed to John that he should ask Jesus who it was.

'Lord, who is it?' John asked.

'I will dip bread in the dish and give it to the one who will betray me,' Jesus said.

He took a piece of bread and dipped it in the dish, as was the custom in those days, and he gave it to Judas Iscariot.

Judas had indeed been to the chief priests, and promised to betray Jesus for thirty pieces of silver.

'What you are going to do, do quickly,' Jesus said to Judas, who got up at once and left.

When he had gone, Jesus began to talk to his friends.

'I shall only be with you for a little while now,' he said. 'You will look for me, but you will not be able to go where I am going; so I am going to give you a new commandment: "Love one another. As I have loved you, so you must love each other."'

'Lord, why cannot I follow you where you are going?' Peter pleaded. 'I will give my life for you.'

'Will you, Peter?' Jesus looked at him. 'I tell you that you will deny me three times before the cock crows!'

Jesus washes his Disciples' Feet

When supper was over, Jesus got up, laid aside his outer garment, and took a towel and a basin of water. Then he knelt before one of his disciples, and began to wash his feet and dry them with the towel; in a hot and dusty country, it was the servant's place to wash a guest's feet, when he entered a house.

Jesus came to Peter, and knelt before him, and Peter felt that it was quite wrong for his Master to do this.

'Lord, do you wash my feet?' he protested.

'What I am doing, you do not understand now,' Jesus answered, 'but later, you will.'

'You shall never wash my feet,' Peter protested again.

'If I do not,' Jesus said, 'you are not really sharing my way of life.'

'Then, Lord, wash not only my feet, but my hands and my head, too!' Peter cried.

'If you have already washed, there is no need to do more than wash your dusty feet,' Jesus replied.

After he had put on his outer garment and sat down again, Jesus said, 'Do you understand what I have just done? You call me "Master", and "Lord", and you are right, for that is what I am. If I, your Lord and Master, have washed your feet, you ought also to wash one another's – I have set you an example, and you should do to others as I have done to you.'

In the Garden

After the Passover supper was ended, Jesus and his disciples went out, and walked through the dark streets of Jerusalem until they came to a garden named Gethsemane, just outside the city.

'Sit here while I pray,' Jesus said.

He took Peter, James and John with him, and the others stayed behind. These three were very close to Jesus, and he let them see that he was very sad and troubled at heart.

'Stop here, and watch with me,' Jesus said at last, and he moved a little way away and began to pray.

He prayed that, if God were willing, God should prevent his suffering. But nevertheless, he prayed, let God's will be done, and not his own.

When he went back to Peter, James and John, he found that they had all fallen asleep.

'Could you not watch with me, just for an hour?' he asked them.

Three times he went and prayed; and, each time, the disciples fell asleep.

'Sleep on now and take your rest,' Jesus said at last, 'for the time has come when I am going to be betrayed to my enemies.'

Judas betrays Jesus

Soon, there came the sound of footsteps drawing nearer, and the light of torches shone through the trees. It was Judas, with a crowd of priests and others, carrying swords and sticks. Judas had told them that they would know who Jesus was, because he would go up to his Master and kiss him.

He went up to Jesus in the garden: 'Hail, Master!' Judas said, and kissed him.

Then the crowd knew that Jesus was the man they were looking for, and they caught hold of him, to make him their prisoner.

Peter could not stand by and see them treating his Master in such a way. He had a sword, and slashed out at the high priest's servant, cutting off his ear.

'Put up your sword, Peter,' Jesus said. 'I am ready to do my Father's will.'

Jesus stretched out his hand, and healed the wounded man.

'Have you come out with swords and sticks to take me?' he then asked. 'I was with you every day in the temple, teaching: you could have taken me at any time.'

Then all the disciples deserted their Master; they were so frightened that they just ran away, and Jesus was left with the men who had come to take him prisoner.

191

Peter denies Jesus

The captain and officers of the Jews bound Jesus, and took him to the house of Caiaphas the high priest. They had taken him first to Annas, who was father-in-law to Caiaphas, and it was Annas who had told them to take their prisoner to the high priest. When they arrived there, many important men were waiting at his house.

Peter, like the other disciples, had run away; but he could not bear to leave his Master in such distress, so he followed the crowd, although a long way off.

When they reached the high priest's palace, Peter went in to the servants' hall, and sat and warmed himself by the fire.

One of the servants looked at him curiously.

'Are you not one of this man's disciples?' she asked.

Immediately Peter was frightened, so he said he was not one of the twelve. Then, as he went out to the porch, he heard a cock crow.

Later another maid saw Peter. 'This is one of them,' she said to the others, pointing at him.

'I am not,' Peter swore.

Presently, the people who were standing around Peter, turned to him again.

'Surely you come from Galilee?' they said. 'You talk as though you do – and the prisoner comes from Galilee.'

'I do not know what you are talking about,' Peter declared fiercely. 'I do not know this man!'

Again a cock crowed – and Peter remembered. Jesus had said to him: 'Before the cock crows twice, you will deny me three times.' And he had done so – his loyal promises to stand by Jesus had all been broken.

At that moment, Jesus was led past Peter, and he turned and looked at him. Peter went out and wept bitterly.

Jesus before Pilate

In the morning, Jesus was taken to the judgement hall, to appear before Pontius Pilate, the Roman governor.

Pilate looked at the prisoner standing quietly before him.

'Are you the King of the Jews?' he asked Jesus.

'You say that I am,' Jesus answered.

The Jews had brought Jesus to Pilate, saying that he had said he was their king, not Caesar, and that they should not pay tribute money to the Emperor.

'Your own people, and the chief priests, have delivered you to me,' Pilate said. 'What have you done?'

'My kingdom does not belong to this world,' Jesus replied. 'If it did, my servants would fight to save me; I came into the world to bring people the truth.'

'What is truth?' Pilate asked.

Jesus made no answer, nor would he

reply to the charges that the chief priests brought against him.

At last Pilate went out and told the Jews: 'I find no fault in him at all.'

Jesus before King Herod

Pilate heard that Jesus came from Galilee.

'Then he comes under the rule of King Herod,' Pilate said, glad that he could pass on this prisoner to some other judge.

King Herod was in Jerusalem at that time, and was pleased when he heard Jesus was being brought before him. Herod had heard a great deal about this teacher from Nazareth, and now he would see him for himself.

'Perhaps he will do a miracle in front of me,' he thought.

But Jesus did nothing of the kind; and to all Herod's questions, he answered nothing, although the chief priests accused him of many things that he had not done.

At last Herod gave up his questioning, and handed Jesus over to his soldiers. They mocked him and dressed him in a gorgeous robe, because Jesus was supposed to have said he was a king; then they sent him back to Pilate.

King Herod and Pontius Pilate, the Roman governor, had always been enemies, but that day they became friends.

Jesus or Barabbas?

At the feast of the Passover, it was the custom for the governor to let one prisoner go free, and the people were allowed to choose whom it should be. One of the prisoners at this time was a well-known robber, whose name was Barabbas.

Pilate went out to ask the crowd which of the two prisoners should be set free.

'Whom shall I release?' he cried. 'Barabbas or Jesus, the King of the Jews?'

'Not this man!' they all shouted, 'but Barabbas!'

While Pilate was sitting on the throne

from where he would have to give judgement, he received a message from his wife about Jesus: 'Have nothing to do with this man; who is in the right,' she said. 'I have had a strange dream about him.'

The chief priests were talking to the crowd, urging them to ask for Barabbas.

Again Pilate went to the people. 'What do you want me to do with the man whom you call King of the Jews?' he asked them.

'Crucify him! Crucify him!' they cried.

This meant that the crowd wanted Pilate to sentence Jesus to death.

'Why, what evil has he done?' Pilate protested. 'I have found no reason why he should die – I will have him beaten, and then let him go.'

They only cried the louder: 'Crucify him! Crucify him!'

Pilate, feeling that there was no more he could do to save Jesus, called for a bowl of water and washed his hands, as a sign that he was not guilty of Jesus's death.

'I am innocent, as far as this just man is concerned,' he said. 'You must see to it.' Then Pilate freed Barabbas.

The Soldiers mock Jesus

Jesus was taken away and beaten. Then the soldiers jeered at him: they dressed him in a scarlet robe, placed a crown of thorns on his head, and gave him a reed to hold, like a sceptre, then they knelt before him, saying mockingly: 'Hail, King of the Jews!'

Although they struck him and spat on him, Jesus suffered it all without a word.

Presently, Pilate led Jesus – still dressed in his kingly robe and crown of thorns – out to see the crowd.

'Behold the man!' he cried.

But the chief priests and the crowd were unmoved by the sight of Jesus standing there.

'Crucify him! Crucify him!' they cried again. 'We have a law, and by our law he ought to die, because he made himself out to be the Son of God.'

Pilate was very troubled; he went back with Jesus to the judgement hall.

'Where do you come from?' he asked, urging Jesus to answer. But Jesus did not reply to Pilate.

'Will you not speak to me?' Pilate cried. 'Do you realise that I have the power to have you crucified, or to release you?'

Then Jesus spoke. 'You could have no such power at all,' he said, 'unless it had been granted to you from above. The man who handed me over to you is the more guilty.'

Pilate then tried hard to free Jesus, but the Jews cried out against him: 'If you let this man go, you are no friend to Caesar. Anyone who makes himself a king is an enemy to Caesar.'

Thus all Pilate's efforts were in vain, for always the people shouted: 'Away with him. Crucify him! We have no king but Caesar!'

So Pilate allowed them to take Jesus to be crucified. The soldiers dressed Jesus in his own clothes, and led him away.

The Road to Calvary

Jesus set out with a guard of soldiers and a great crowd following behind.

Two other prisoners who were to die with Jesus, were in the procession. They carried their own crosses, but Jesus was weakened by his toil and he staggered and fell under the weight.

The soldiers chose a man from the crowd, whose name was Simon of Cyrene, to carry the cross for him, and Simon walked behind Jesus, following him on his way to a hill called Calvary.

When the procession reached the hill, the soldiers would have given Jesus something to drink which would have numbed his pain, but he refused it.

They crucified him, fastening him to the cross, and set it up on the hill between the other two prisoners, who were thieves.

Over Jesus's head they fastened a notice which read: 'Jesus of Nazareth, the King of the Jews.' Pilate had written this, and the chief priests had wanted him to put: 'He said: "I am the King of the Jews"' – but Pilate would not alter it.

Then, as was the custom, the soldiers divided Jesus's clothes among themselves, and cast lots to find out who should have his tunic. Then they sat down and watched Jesus on his cross.

On the Cross

Many of Jesus's enemies stood at the foot of the cross and mocked him.

'You who say you can destroy the temple and build it again in three days – if you are the Son of God, save yourself. Come down from the cross!'

'He saved other people, but he cannot save himself!' they told one another scornfully. 'If he really is the King of Israel, let him come down from the cross now, and we will believe him. He trusted in God; now let God deliver him.'

Mary, Jesus's mother, stood nearby, with her sister and Mary Magdalene, whom Jesus had cured. John, Jesus's dearly-loved disciple, was also there.

Jesus looked down and saw them. 'Here is your son,' he said to his mother. And to John he said, 'Here is your mother.'

When he was gone, Jesus wanted these two whom he loved so much to comfort one another.

That very day, John took Mary to his own home, and looked after her all his life.

Presently, one of the thieves turned on Jesus. 'If you really are the Messiah, save yourself and us,' he cried.

But the other thief scolded him. 'Do you not fear God? We have done wrong, and now we are getting what we deserve. But this man has done nothing wrong.' He turned his head towards Jesus. 'Lord,

remember me when you come into your kingdom,' he said.

'Truly, I tell you,' Jesus said, 'today you shall be with me in paradise.'

Jesus Dies

The sun went in, and a strange darkness fell over the land which lasted for three hours.

Suddenly Jesus cried out: 'My God, my God, why have you forsaken me?'

Then he said faintly, 'I am thirsty.'

Someone dipped a sponge in vinegar and put it on the end of a reed, so that it could be held up to Jesus's mouth.

Jesus spoke again. 'Father, into your hands I commend my spirit,' he cried.

He only spoke once more. 'It is finished,' he said, and then he died.

Just at that time there was an earthquake,

when rocks moved and split, and the curtain in the temple before the Holy of Holies was ripped in two.

A Roman centurion, a soldier in charge of a hundred men, looked up at the still figure of Jesus on the cross.

'Truly this man was the Son of God,' he said reverently.

The women who had believed in Jesus stood together a little way off, watching.

They saw the soldiers pierce Jesus's side with a spear, and presently he was taken down from the cross.

That evening, a rich man named Joseph of Arimathea, who was a follower of Jesus, went to Pilate, and asked that the body of Jesus might lie in a tomb which he had in his garden.

Pilate agreed, so Joseph brought fine linen to wrap around his body, and he was placed in the tomb, which was hewn out of a rock. Then a big stone was rolled across the entrance.

The women followed, and watched, before going home to prepare sweet-smelling spices and ointment. When the Sabbath was over, they would come back and anoint the body of the Master whom they had loved so much.

The Tomb is Sealed

Next day, the chief priests and the Pharisees went to see Pilate.

'Sir,' they said, 'we remember what that deceiver said – whilst he was still alive – that, after three days, he would rise again. Will you not set a guard on this man's tomb, lest his disciples come in the night and take his body away? For if they did, they could say he had risen, and that would be a worse deception.'

'You have watchmen of your own,' Pilate said. 'Go your way, and make the watch as sure as you can.'

The priests and the Pharisees went off to the garden tomb where Jesus lay. They sealed the big stone in front of the entrance so that it could not be moved, and they set men to watch it.

'His disciples cannot take him away now!' they said triumphantly.

Jesus Lives

Very early the following morning, before it was light, Mary Magdalene got up and made her way to the garden tomb.

As she drew near, she saw to her amazement that the great stone had been rolled away from the entrance. She could see into the tomb in the dim light of dawn, and she saw that the body of Jesus was no longer there.

Quickly she turned and ran back to Peter and John.

'They have taken the Lord out of his tomb,' she told them breathlessly, 'and I do not know where they have laid him!'

Peter and John did not hesitate; they both ran as hard as they could to the tomb, and John got there first.

Stooping, he looked into the cave, where the body of Jesus had been laid in a niche carved out of the wall. He could see the linen clothes which Jesus had been wearing lying there; but John did not go in.

When Peter reached the cave, he went inside and saw the clothes, together with a cloth that had been about his head, lying by itself. John followed him.

They marvelled, and believed that Jesus must indeed be alive. John and Peter came out and went home, but Mary stayed behind, weeping.

Presently, Mary stooped down and looked into the burying place; and there she saw two angels in white.

'Woman, why are you crying?' the angels asked Mary.

'Because they have taken away my Lord,' Mary answered, 'and I do not know where they have laid him.'

Just then she turned, and saw a figure in the misty, dim half-light.

'Woman, why are you crying?' asked the stranger. 'Who are you looking for?'

Mary thought that the man must be a gardener. 'Sir,' she said, 'if you have taken him away, tell me where you have laid Jesus, and I will go there for him.'

But the man was not a gardener – he was Jesus himself, alive again, as he had promised to be.

'Mary!' he said, and then she knew him.

'Master!' she breathed, and put her hand out to make sure that Jesus was indeed there; but he drew back.

'Do not touch me,' he said. 'I have not yet ascended to my Father! But go to my followers, and tell them that I shall ascend to my Father, who is also yours – to my God, who is yours, too.'

Mary did as Jesus told her, and went back to the sorrowing disciples with her joyful news.

On the Way to Emmaus

That same day, two friends of Jesus were walking from Jerusalem to a nearby village called Emmaus.

As they walked, the friends talked together about everything that had happened during the last week. Then Jesus himself drew near and walked beside them along

the road, but they did not recognise him.

'What are you talking about?' Jesus asked them. 'And why are you so sad?'

One of the two, whose name was Cleopas, looked at him in surprise.

'Are you a stranger in Jerusalem,' he asked, 'that you do not know all the things that have been happening in the past few days?'

'What things?' Jesus asked.

'Things concerning Jesus of Nazareth,' they told him. 'He was a prophet, who said and did wonderful things, but the chief priests and our rulers had him sentenced to death. We trusted that he was the one who would come to set Israel free. All this was three days ago. However, some of our company went to his tomb early this morning, and found that his body was not there; but angels were in Jesus's tomb who said he was alive, but they did not see him.'

'O, you are slow to understand,' Jesus said. 'Did not the prophets tell us that the deliverer would suffer, before he entered into his glory?'

And as they walked, he reminded them of what Moses and the prophets had said, and explained the scriptures which foretold his coming.

They reached Emmaus at last, and Jesus would have gone on, but they invited him to their home.

So Jesus went into the house with them, and presently they sat down to share a meal.

Jesus picked up bread, blessed and broke it; then he gave it to them. As he did so, Jesus's friends recognised him at last.

He went from their sight then, but they said to one another, 'Did not our hearts burn, while he talked to us along the road?'

Late as it was, they got up and walked all the way back to Jerusalem, their tiredness forgotten because of their joy. They went straight to the house where Jesus's friends were gathered, and poured out their story: 'The Lord is risen indeed!' they said.

Jesus appears to his Friends

While they were talking among themselves, Jesus himself appeared to his disciples.

'Peace be unto you,' he greeted them; but the disciples were afraid when they saw him.

'Why are you frightened?' Jesus asked. 'Look at my hands and feet; touch me, and see that it is really I myself. You can see that I have flesh and bone, so I cannot be a spirit.'

He showed them his hands and his feet, with the marks of the nails through them.

Although they were filled with joy, it was still hard for the disciples to realise that Jesus, their Lord, was indeed alive and with them again.

While they were still hesitating, Jesus said, 'Have you any food?'

They gave him a piece of boiled fish and some honeycomb, and he ate before them. Jesus was indeed alive.

Thomas Believes

One of the disciples, Thomas, was not there when Jesus came; but directly he returned, all the others told him excitedly: 'We have seen the Lord!'

But Thomas could not take their word for it. 'Unless I see the print of the nails in his hands,' he said, 'and put my finger into them – and also thrust my hand into his side – I will not believe.'

Eight days later, when Thomas and the other disciples were together, and the door was shut, Jesus suddenly came among his friends again.

'Peace be unto you,' he greeted them.

Then Jesus turned to Thomas. 'Stretch out your finger,' he said, 'and feel my hands; thrust your hand into my side. Do not be faithless, but believe.'

'My Lord, and my God,' Thomas replied reverently.

'Thomas,' Jesus said, 'because you have seen me, you have believed. Happy are they who have not seen me, and yet have believed.'

By the Lake of Galilee

Peter, Thomas, and several of the other disciples, were together on the shore of the Lake of Galilee.

'I am going fishing!' Peter said suddenly.

'We will come with you,' said the others.

They climbed into the boat and fished all night, but caught nothing. In the early morning, Jesus stood on the shore, but the disciples did not recognise him.

'Children, have you any food?' he called.

'No!' they shouted back.

'Cast your net on the right side, and you will find plenty,' Jesus said.

The disciples threw out their net as he told them, and it was immediately full of fish; it was so heavy that they could hardly drag it into the boat.

'It is the Lord,' John said to Peter.

Peter pulled on his coat, and jumped into the water, to wade towards Jesus as quickly as he could; the others followed in the little boat.

As soon as they landed on the shore, the disciples saw that Jesus had already made

a good fire and laid some fish on it to cook.

'Bring the fish you have caught,' he said.

Peter went back and dragged the net ashore. Later, when they counted them, the disciples found that they had caught a hundred and fifty-three fish; but despite the weight their net had not broken.

'Come and eat,' Jesus said.

None of the disciples dared ask him who he was, but they all recognised Jesus.

'Do You Love Me?'

When the meal was finished, Jesus turned to Peter, whose other name was Simon.

'Simon, son of Jonas!' he said. 'Do you love me more than the rest?'

'Yes, Lord,' Peter replied. 'You know I do.'

'Feed my lambs,' Jesus said. Then he asked a second time: 'Simon, son of Jonas, do you love me?'

'Yes, Lord, you know that I love you,' Peter said again.

'Feed my sheep,' Jesus told him. And he asked a third time: 'Simon, son of Jonas, do you love me?'

Peter was sad because Jesus asked him the question three times.

'Lord,' he said, 'you know everything: you know that I love you.'

'Feed my sheep,' Jesus said again. 'Truly, I tell you that, when you were young, you tied your own belt and went where you chose; but, when you are old, you will stretch out your hands and someone else shall bind you, and take you where you would not choose to go.'

Jesus was telling Peter of the way in which he would die.

'Follow me!' he said.

Peter looked at John. 'Lord,' he asked, 'what will happen to this man?'

'Even if I wished him to stay till I come again, what has it to do with you?' Jesus said. 'You must follow me!'

Jesus goes to his Father

Jesus came again to his disciples when they were all gathered on a mountain in Galilee, where he had told them to go.

'All power is mine,' Jesus told them. 'Go and teach all people, baptising them in the name of the Father, and of the Son and of the Holy Spirit. Teach them to live as I have taught you. I am with you always, even to the end of the world.'

Jesus moved among his friends for forty days, showing them that he was alive again, and teaching them about God's Kingdom.

'You must stay in Jerusalem,' he told them, 'because you must wait for my Father's gift. John baptised with water, but you will be baptised with the Holy Spirit very soon.'

'Lord, is this the time when you will set up the kingdom of Israel?' they asked.

'It is not for you to know dates or times,' Jesus said. 'Those are in my Father's

hands; but, when the Holy Spirit comes upon you, you will receive power, and will be my witnesses in Jerusalem, in Judaea and Samaria, and all over the world.'

They were gathered on a hill called Olivet; then as they watched, Jesus was lifted up, and a cloud hid him from his friends.

As the disciples were gazing after him, two men in white stood before them.

'Men of Galilee,' they said, 'why are you looking up at the sky? This same Jesus, whom you have seen taken up to heaven, will one day come back in the same way.'

Then the disciples returned to Jerusalem, to pray and bless God in the temple.

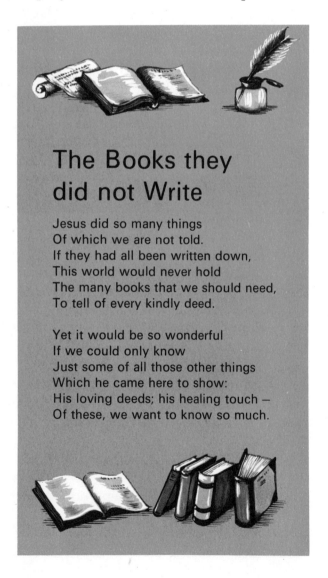

The Books they did not Write

Jesus did so many things
Of which we are not told.
If they had all been written down,
This world would never hold
The many books that we should need,
To tell of every kindly deed.

Yet it would be so wonderful
If we could only know
Just some of all those other things
Which he came here to show:
His loving deeds; his healing touch —
Of these, we want to know so much.

The New Disciple

The disciples went back to Jerusalem, their minds full of that last meeting with their risen Master.

They were lodging in an upstairs room in the city, and made their way to it. There was quite a large gathering there, among whom were Mary, the mother of Jesus, and his brothers. They spent much time in praying together, and in talking about Jesus and all the wonderful things that he had said and done.

One day, when there were about one hundred and twenty people gathered together, Peter stood up and addressed them.

'My friends,' he said, 'the time has come when we should find a man to take the place of Judas, who betrayed our Master and is gone from us. One of those who has been with us all the time that the Lord Jesus was among us must join our company of eleven, to bear witness that he is risen.'

Two names were suggested – Joseph Justus, and Matthias. Which should the disciples choose? They must pray about it, and ask God to help them choose aright.

'O Lord,' they prayed, 'you can read the hearts of all men. Show us which of these two men you have chosen to take the place of Judas.'

Then the disciples drew lots, and Matthias was chosen. He joined the eleven other disciples whom Jesus had set apart, so that they were a company of twelve again.

The Gift of the Holy Spirit

It was the Jewish feast of Pentecost, and the followers of Jesus had gathered together in one place.

Suddenly, it was as though a great wind swept through the room, and tongues of flame seemed to be resting on them all. This

was a sign that the gift which Jesus had promised his disciples was being given to them all; God's Holy Spirit was filling them with power, and they found that they could speak in languages unknown to them before.

The people of Jerusalem heard the noise, and drew near to find out what was happening. Many of them were foreigners and were amazed to hear the disciples.

'Why!' they exclaimed. 'These men have all come from Galilee – so how is it that we can each hear our own language spoken? They are talking about the great things which God has done, and we all know what they are saying, because they speak as though they were from Egypt, Rome, Crete, Arabia, and many other places. What does it mean?'

'They have had too much wine!' some said scornfully.

But Peter stood up, with the other eleven apostles gathered round him.

'Fellow Jews and citizens of Jerusalem,' he cried, 'listen to me! We are not drunk – it is still early in the morning! Remember the prophet's words: "God says: In the last days, I will pour out my Spirit on everyone. Your sons and daughters shall speak like prophets; your young men shall see visions; your old men shall dream dreams."

'I speak to you of Jesus of Nazareth, whom God chose, and who, as you know, did wonderful things with God's help, when he was among you. You sent him to his death, but God raised him to life again, and death had no power over him. Let everyone in Israel believe that God has made Jesus, whom you crucified, our Lord and Deliverer.'

When they heard this, the people were deeply moved.

'What should we do?' they asked.

'Repent,' said Peter, 'and be baptised in the name of Jesus, and you, too, will receive the gift of the Holy Spirit. God's promise is made to you, to your children, and to those who are a long way off – it is for everyone who is called by him.'

Three thousand people were baptised that day. They came to hear the apostles' teaching; they shared their lives, and broke bread and prayed together. They shared everything, and sold what they could, using the money for the good of them all. Many wonderful things happened, and new believers were added to their numbers every day.

The First Followers

'We will follow Jesus,' Peter heard men say.
'Come with us,' he told them. 'Study day by day
Everything he told us – all we have to do.'
All their own possessions – all their money, too –
They shared among the brethren, and every one was fed.
They prayed and met together, daily breaking bread.
Others came to join them, and shared their lives as well,
Listening to the good news which Peter had to tell.

At the Beautiful Gate

One afternoon, Peter and John walked to the temple. Very often they saw cripples begging for money, and on this day, as they came to the temple entrance which was known as the 'Beautiful Gate', Peter and John saw a man who could not walk, lying beside it. He had always been a cripple, and every day his friends carried him to this place, so that he might beg from the people going into the temple.

When he saw Peter and John, the cripple asked them for money.

'Look at us,' Peter said, and the man did as he was told, expecting them to give him a coin or two.

'I have no gold or silver,' Peter said, 'but I will give you what I have. In the name of Jesus Christ of Nazareth – walk!'

Peter held out his hand, and took that of the crippled beggar. The man sprang to his feet, and found that he could walk – in fact, he could even leap for joy! So leaping and praising God, the man went into the temple with Peter and John, to give thanks for his marvellous cure.

Everyone knew him, and they stared to see him moving about like everybody else. He stood in the temple court, clinging to Peter and John, telling them how grateful he was, and a crowd gathered round.

'Men of Israel, why do you look so

you ordinary men done this thing?' they asked.

'Rulers of the people,' Peter said, 'if you are asking us about a crippled man, and how he was cured, this is our answer: it was in the name of Jesus Christ of Nazareth, whom you crucified and whom God raised from the dead, that this man was cured, and now stands before you all.'

Peter went on talking about the Lord Jesus, and Caiaphas and the others were astonished that such an ordinary man could speak with such power. Then he recognised Peter and John, and realised that they had been friends and followers of Jesus.

It was plain for all to see that the crippled man was healed, and there was really nothing that the high priest and the council could say in answer to Peter.

'Take the prisoners away, while we discuss the matter,' they said.

Peter and John were led outside, and the council consulted one another.

'What can we do with these men?' they said. 'Everyone in Jerusalem knows that they have worked a miracle, and we cannot pretend that they have not done so; but let us warn them that they must never again address anyone in the name of Jesus of Nazareth.'

Then the council had the prisoners brought back. 'You must not speak in public, or teach in the name of Jesus,' they said.

But Peter and John would not agree to this. 'Would it be right for us to obey you, rather than God?' they said. 'We cannot promise to do what you ask.'

The council warned them again, and let them go – it might be unwise to punish these men, when all Jerusalem was singing their praises.

How glad Peter and John were to return to their friends, and how happy the others were to see them! They all praised God for his goodness.

astonished?' Peter asked. 'Why do you look at us, amazed, as though we cured this man by ourselves?'

Peter and John went on to talk to them about Jesus; and, while they were doing so, the chief priests came out angrily to break up the crowd. They did not approve of Peter and John telling people that Jesus had risen, and was alive for evermore.

So Peter and John were arrested and put in prison. Yet they were happy, for still more people had learnt to believe in Jesus, because of what had happened that day.

'By What Power?'

The following day, Peter and John were brought before Annas, the high priest, Caiaphas, and other Jewish leaders.

'By what power, or in whose name, have

Barnabas

Barnabas from Cyprus came
With money in his hand;
He was quite a wealthy man.
And he had sold his land,
His house, and his possessions
And given all he had
To help his fellow Christians;
So then their hearts were glad.

Healing the Sick

'Peter can make people better!'
In Jerusalem, that was the cry.
They brought out the sick that his shadow
Might fall on them, as he passed by.
They flocked in from town, and from village,
And Peter laid hands on them all.
He was never too tired or too busy
To answer a troubled man's call.

Before the Council

As the apostles' fame spread, the priests grew jealous; once more they arrested and imprisoned them.

But during the night, an angel opened the prison doors and led them out. 'Go to the temple,' he said, 'and continue to preach the good news to everyone.'

So, very early the next morning, the apostles went into the temple and began to preach to all who would listen.

When the high priest and members of the council arrived, they sent for the prisoners. The guards came back and said, 'We found the prison locked everywhere, and the warders on duty; the prisoners had vanished.'

The high priest looked at the other men with him. They were all very puzzled.

Just then, a messenger arrived. 'The men you put in prison have escaped,' he said. 'They are preaching in the temple!'

The guards went off and fetched Peter and the others, and brought them before the council.

'We told you to stop preaching,' the high priest said sternly, 'and you have disobeyed. You have spread your teaching through Jerusalem, and you are saying that we put your leader to death.'

'We must obey God, rather than men,' Peter replied bravely. 'We are witnesses to the fact that God raised Jesus to new life, after you had put him to death. He is our deliverer, who can forgive Israel's sins. We are witnesses to it, and so is the Holy Spirit, God's gift to those who are obedient to him.'

Members of the council became angry at these words, and some wanted the apostles put to death. But one member, a Pharisee named Gamaliel, stood up; he was a teacher, and everyone thought very well of him.

'I suggest that the prisoners be sent outside while we talk,' he said.

When the council was alone, Gamaliel said, 'Men of Israel, take care, for this is not the first time that something like this has happened. A man named Theudas claimed to be a leader, and four hundred people followed him; but when he was killed, he was soon forgotten. The same thing happened over another man – Judas the Galilean, who tried to start a revolution. Leave these men alone – if their ideas are man-made, they will soon die out; but if

they are really from God, nothing can stop them.'

The council members listened to Gamaliel; then they had the prisoners brought back, ordered them to be beaten, and told them again to stop talking about Jesus; after which they were set free.

The apostles went away, happy that they had suffered for the sake of Jesus. Bravely they went on spreading their good news in the temple and in the homes of the people.

Stephen is Chosen

Some of those who followed the apostles' teaching were Jews, and some were Greeks. One day they began to disagree. The Greeks said that when food was distributed, some Greek widows did not get their share.

The twelve apostles called everybody together.

'We are busy spreading the good news,' they said. 'We cannot spare time to arrange how the food is shared out, so choose seven wise, good men, and let them look after all this while we continue to pray and speak.'

Everyone thought that this was a good idea, and they chose seven men, one of whom was named Stephen. They brought the seven to the apostles, who blessed them and prayed for them.

Stephen soon showed that he could do much more than share out food to the needy; he spoke with great power, and could himself work miracles.

Some members of the synagogue argued with him, but Stephen spoke more powerfully than them all. Then they found men who accused Stephen of speaking against God, and stirred up the people until, at last, he was brought before the council.

False witnesses spoke against Stephen. 'This man is always speaking against our law and our temple,' they said. 'We have heard him say that Jesus of Nazareth will

change the law of Moses, and pull down the temple.'

Everyone looked at Stephen, and his face was alight with goodness, as though he were an angel.

'Is this true?' the high priest asked.

Stephen made a wonderful speech, in which he reminded the council of the way in which God had led the people of Israel all through the years. He talked about Abraham and Isaac, Joseph and Moses, and the Israelites' return to the Promised Land. He talked of Joshua and David, and of Solomon who built the temple.

'Was there a prophet who did not suffer for what he said?' Stephen demanded. 'They slew those who said that the Deliverer was coming, and now that he has actually come, you have killed him, too. You were given the Law, but you did not keep it.'

This made his judges angry; but Stephen, filled with God's Holy Spirit, gazed up to heaven, and saw God's glory, and Jesus, his Lord.

'Look,' he said, 'the sky is parting, and I can see the Son of Man at God's right hand!'

No Jew was allowed to say such things, or even to listen to them. They put their hands over their ears and rushed at Stephen, shouting furiously.

Stephen was hustled out of Jerusalem, with the mob hurling stones at him. The witnesses laid their coats at the feet of a young man named Saul, so that they could be more free to fling their stones.

Suddenly, Stephen called out: 'Lord Jesus, receive my spirit!' As he sank to his knees, he said, 'Lord, do not hold this sin against them' – and then he died.

Following Jesus

It was not easy then to follow Jesus –
His friends were often scattered far and wide.
Some were imprisoned, and often they were beaten;
Others were mocked at; some, like Stephen, died.
Yet they gave thanks and went on preaching bravely,
Sure that the Lord was standing at their side.

Simon Believes

The apostles travelled from town to town and village to village, carrying their message about Jesus. Philip went to a town in Samaria, to preach to the people there.

Crowds gathered round to listen, and because Philip was able to cure those who were ill or crippled, everyone was very glad that he had come.

Another man had been there first, and once the Samaritans had listened to him eagerly; his name was Simon, and he had been able to perform clever tricks that made everyone think he was God's messenger.

But when Philip began to speak, they knew that he was the true follower of God, and they turned to him instead. Simon himself came to be baptised, for he knew that Philip's good news was true.

The apostles who had stayed behind in Jerusalem were very pleased to hear what was happening in Samaria. Peter and John joined Philip, and laid hands on the new believers, praying that they might receive the gift of God's Holy Spirit.

Simon watched them, and wished that

he could do this, too. He went to the apostles and offered to pay them, if they would teach him how to share the power they had, which made it possible for people to receive the Holy Spirit when Peter or John laid their hands on them.

'You cannot buy God's gift,' Peter told him. 'You must be sorry that you thought you could, and pray to be forgiven.'

'Pray for me,' Simon begged.

Peter and John stayed on for a while, sharing their good news with the Samaritans, and then they set out for Jerusalem, stopping to speak to the people in the villages through which they passed.

Philip in the Chariot

Now Philip knew that it was time for him to move on: an angelic voice told him to set out and travel south until he came to a road that led from Jerusalem to Gaza, which was in the desert.

Philip obeyed; and, as he went on his way, he met a man from Ethiopia – an important person, in charge of his queen's treasures. The man had been to Jerusalem to worship God, and now he was sitting in his chariot, reading the scroll-book which held the words of the prophet Isaiah.

Within himself, Philip knew that he was meant to go up and talk to the Ethiopian, so he ran across to the chariot.

'Do you understand what you are reading?' Philip asked.

The Ethiopian shook his head. 'How can I, unless someone explains it to me?' he asked. 'Come and sit beside me.'

These were some of the words he was reading: 'He was led like a sheep to be killed; like a lamb who is dumb before the man who shears him, he said nothing.'

'Who is the prophet speaking about?' the Ethiopian asked Philip. 'Is he talking of himself, or of another man?'

Philip told the Ethiopian about Jesus, who had come, and been put to death, but not reproached those who had injured him.

Presently, as the chariot journeyed on, they saw some water by the roadside.

'See,' said the Ethiopian, 'there is water! Why should I not be baptised?'

He stopped the chariot, and they both stepped into the water together. Philip baptised the Ethiopian, and he went on his way, feeling very happy.

On the Road to Damascus

Saul, the man who had watched Stephen being stoned, had done everything he could to make life hard for the followers of Jesus. He went into their homes, and had many of them seized and put in prison unjustly.

One day he went to the high priest. 'Give me letters to the synagogues in Damascus,' he said, 'that will give me the right to arrest anyone, man or woman, who is a follower of Jesus, and to bring them to Jerusalem.'

Taking the letters with him, Saul set out for Damascus, a city in the north. He was near the end of his journey, when a bright light suddenly shone round him, and he fell to the ground.

Then he heard a voice saying, 'Saul, Saul, why are you making me suffer?'

'Who are you, Lord?' Saul asked, afraid.

'I am Jesus,' the voice answered. 'It is I whom you are hurting.'

Saul began to tremble.

'Lord, what must I do?' he asked.

'Arise and go into the city,' the voice told him. 'There you will learn what you must do.'

The men who were with Saul stood round him, speechless and amazed; they heard the voice, but they saw no one.

Saul stood up, but he could see nothing. His companions took his hand, and led him to the city. For three days he was blind, and he would not eat or drink.

Ananias goes to Saul

In Damascus there lived a man whose name was Ananias, who believed in Jesus.

He heard the Lord calling him: 'Ananias!'

'I am here, Lord,' he said.

'Get up and go to Straight Street,' the voice told him. 'In the house of Judas, you must ask for a man from Tarsus whose name is Saul. He will be praying; he has seen, in a vision, a man named Ananias arriving to give him back his sight.'

'Lord,' Ananias answered, 'many people have told me about him. He has done great harm to your followers in Jerusalem, and now he has the power to take prisoner all those who call on you here.'

But the Lord answered, 'Go – for I have chosen him to speak of me to the Gentiles, and to kings, and to the children of Israel. I will show him what he will have to bear, for my sake.'

So Ananias set off for Straight Street. He found the house of the man named Judas, and the blind Saul was there.

'Brother Saul,' Ananias said, laying his hands on him, 'the Lord Jesus, whom you saw on your way here, has sent me, so that you may see once more, and be filled with the Holy Spirit.'

At once Saul found that he was no longer blind. He asked to be baptised, and then he was ready for whatever he might have to do.

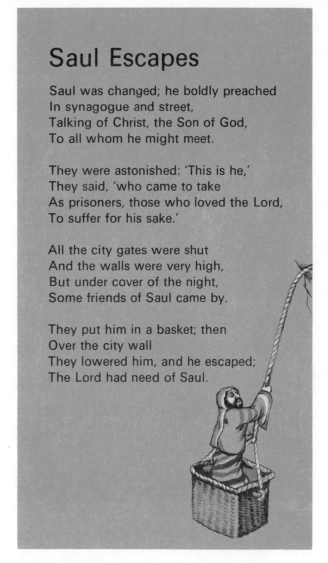

Saul Escapes

Saul was changed; he boldly preached
In synagogue and street,
Talking of Christ, the Son of God,
To all whom he might meet.

They were astonished: 'This is he,'
They said, 'who came to take
As prisoners, those who loved the Lord,
To suffer for his sake.'

All the city gates were shut
And the walls were very high,
But under cover of the night,
Some friends of Saul came by.

They put him in a basket; then
Over the city wall
They lowered him, and he escaped;
The Lord had need of Saul.

Saul joins the Apostles

Saul made his way to Jerusalem. He hoped to join the followers of Jesus, but he had tried to harm them for so long that they were afraid to welcome him. 'He cannot really be a follower of the Lord Jesus,' they told one another.

But one man, Barnabas, believed in Saul, and became his friend. He himself took Saul to the apostles and told them all that had happened: how Saul had seen a vision of Jesus on the road to Damascus, and how Jesus had spoken to him, and how Saul had then begun to preach bravely about Christ to the people of Damascus.

Then the apostles knew that Saul was now one of themselves, and so he began to preach with them.

A group of Greeks who heard Saul speak were angry, because of his teaching, and would have killed him if they could.

'We must send Saul away, to keep him safe,' the apostles said, and they sent him to Tarsus.

After that, the enemies of the church were quiet for a while, and the good news spread through Judaea, Galilee and Samaria. Many people believed all that they heard about the Lord Jesus.

Peter heals People

Now Peter went to a place called Lydda, where there was a little company of believers. A man named Aeneas lived in Lydda, and he had been ill in bed for eight long years.

Peter went to see him, and stood by his side. 'Aeneas,' he said, 'Jesus Christ makes you well. Get up, and make your bed!'

At once Aeneas rose from where he had been lying for so long; he was quite well again. Everyone who knew him was astonished, and many people believed in the Lord Jesus, because of what had happened to Aeneas.

In the nearby town of Joppa, there had lived a good woman named Dorcas, who had become a follower of Christ; she had spent her life doing good and kind things for other people. But Dorcas became ill and died, and her friends were very sad. When they heard that Peter was in Lydda, they sent two men to beg him to come to them.

Peter went at once with the messengers, and they took him to the room where Dorcas lay. All her friends were crying, and some of them showed Peter the coats and other clothes which Dorcas had made so beautifully, while she was alive.

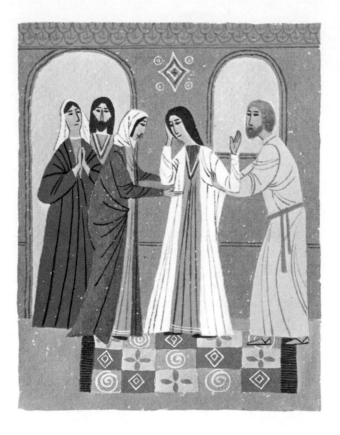

Peter told them all to go out of the room; then he knelt and prayed.

After that, he said, 'Dorcas, get up!'

Dorcas opened her eyes and sat up.

Peter gave Dorcas his hand and helped her up. Then he called all her friends back into the room.

'Here is Dorcas, alive again!' he said.

The news spread through Joppa, and many people believed in the Lord Jesus because of the way in which Peter had given Dorcas back to them.

Cornelius

Not very far away, in Caesarea, there lived a Roman soldier named Cornelius. He had charge of a hundred men, and thus was called a centurion.

Cornelius was a good man, who, with his family, worshipped God. He prayed often, and was kind to the poor.

One afternoon, Cornelius had a vision of an angel who spoke to him.

'Cornelius!' the angel said.

Cornelius was startled. 'What is it, Lord?' he asked.

'God has heard your prayers,' said the angel, 'and he knows of your gifts to the poor. Now send men to Joppa, to fetch Simon Peter, who is lodging with Simon the tanner; he lives at the edge of the area. He will tell you what you must do.'

The angel vanished, and Cornelius sent for two of his servants and a faithful soldier, and told them what had happened. They agreed to go to Joppa to fetch Peter.

Next day, as the three men drew near to Joppa, Peter was on the flat roof of Simon's house, praying. He was very hungry, and presently asked for something to eat.

While food was being got ready, Peter, too, had a vision. He saw the sky open, and a big sheet, knotted at its four corners, was let down to earth; in the sheet were all kinds of animals and birds.

A voice said: 'Get up, Peter, and eat.'

Some of the animals were known as 'unclean', which meant that the law laid down that they must not be used as food.

'No, Lord!' Peter said. 'I have never eaten anything that is common or unclean.'

'What God has made clean,' said the voice, 'you must not call unclean.'

This happened three times, and then the sheet disappeared.

While Peter was wondering what his vision meant, the three men from Caesarea arrived. They knocked at the gate, and asked if this was the house of Simon the tanner, and if Simon Peter lodged there.

'Three men are looking for you,' the heavenly voice told Peter. 'Go with them, and do not be afraid, for I am sending you.'

Peter and Cornelius

Peter went down to meet the men who had come to fetch him.

'I am the man you are looking for,' he told them. 'Why have you come?'

'Cornelius the centurion was told by an angel of God to send for you,' the men said. 'He is a good man, much respected by all the Jews; he serves your God.'

Peter took them indoors and arranged for them to stay the night, and next day they all set out for Caesarea.

Cornelius was waiting for them, and as Peter entered the house, Cornelius stepped forward to greet him, and bowed low to the ground in reverence.

Peter held out his hand. 'Stand up!' he said. 'I am an ordinary man, like any other.'

They began to talk, as they moved into the house, and Peter caught sight of Cornelius's friends who were waiting to meet him.

'You know,' he told them, 'that it is against the law for a Jew to mix with people of another nation – but God has shown me that nobody is common or unclean. That was why I came, as soon as you sent word. What do you want of me?'

'Four days ago,' Cornelius told him, 'I was fasting until this very hour; and then as I prayed, a man in shining clothes stood before me and told me that my prayers were heard, and that I was to send for you. It is good that you have come; now we are all gathered here to listen to what you have to tell us about God.'

'I see that God does not choose one man rather than another,' Peter said. 'He accepts all who do good and worship him, whichever nation they belong to.' Then Peter went on to tell the company about Jesus, and his life on earth, and how he rose and is alive for evermore.

The people, both Jews and Gentiles, listened eagerly, and the Holy Spirit filled them all, no matter which race they belonged to.

Many were baptised, and Peter promised to stay with them for several days.

Peter Explains

Waiting in Jerusalem, the friends of Peter heard
That to the Gentiles and the Jews he preached God's holy word.
When Peter met them, they exclaimed: 'To do this is not right.'
But Peter said, 'I know all men are equal in God's sight.
'He showed me, in a vision, all kinds of food are clean,
'And God loves every nation – that's what my dream must mean.'

The Christians

To Antioch, Christ's followers came,
And many there believed.
Saul and Barnabas went too,
To those who had received
The Word of God in Antioch;
And it was there they earned
A new name – 'Christians' – men were called
Who from their Saviour learned.

Peter in Prison

King Herod was angered by the way in which the good news about Jesus Christ was spreading, and he had James, John's brother, put to death.

When he saw that the Jews were glad about this, he set out to capture Peter, and had him thrown into prison. Herod ordered his soldiers to keep Peter there for the present, because it was the Passover time; after the feast was over, he meant to bring Peter out and show him to the people. Meanwhile, all Peter's friends prayed for him.

On the night that Herod would have sent for Peter, the prisoner was asleep, bound in chains between two soldiers, with guards at the door. Suddenly, a light shone in the prison, and an angel appeared.

'Get up quickly,' the angel told Peter, helping him to rise; and the chains fell from Peter's hands.

'Put on your sandals and fasten your belt,' said the angel, and Peter obeyed.

'Now throw your cloak around you, and follow me,' the angel commanded, and again Peter did as he was told.

The angel walked out of the prison, and Peter followed. They went past the first guard, and then past the second, and they came to an iron gate leading into the city, which opened without being touched.

They went out and walked down the street, and then the angel vanished.

Peter began to collect his thoughts. 'Now I know for certain,' he said to himself, 'that the Lord sent his angel and has saved me from Herod.'

Presently, Peter came to the house where John Mark, a young follower of Jesus, lived with his mother Mary. Many of Peter's friends were gathered there, praying for him.

Peter knocked on the door, and a little maid named Rhoda came to open it.

When she heard Peter's voice, Rhoda was so excited that she left him standing there, and rushed back to the others.

'Peter's standing outside!' Rhoda said breathlessly.

They simply couldn't believe her. 'You are mad,' someone said.

But Rhoda kept on telling them that it truly was Peter at the door.

'It must be his angel,' they said unbelievingly.

Peter went on knocking, and at last they opened the door, and saw that he was indeed standing there.

They were astonished, and all began to talk at once, but Peter asked them to stop, and he told them his story.

'Go now and tell James, and my other friends, what has happened,' Peter said, when he had told them everything.

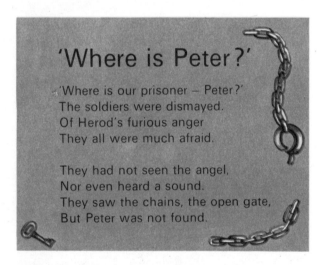

'Where is Peter?'

'Where is our prisoner – Peter?'
The soldiers were dismayed.
Of Herod's furious anger
They all were much afraid.

They had not seen the angel,
Nor even heard a sound.
They saw the chains, the open gate,
But Peter was not found.

'They are Gods!'

Saul became known by a new name when he became a Christian – he was called Paul.

One day, the Christians felt that God wanted Paul and Barnabas to go on a journey across the sea, preaching to the people in far-away places.

They gave the apostles their blessing, and prayed for them, and Paul and Barnabas sailed away to the island of Cyprus, where they gave their good news to the people. Presently they came back to the mainland, and Paul spoke boldly, in the synagogue at Antioch, to all the Jews.

A week later, almost everyone in the city came to hear the apostles; but the Jews were angry that they were preaching to the Gentiles as well as to themselves and they had Paul and Barnabas driven out of their city.

They travelled on, and presently came to Lystra. There the apostles saw a crippled man, who had never been able to walk.

He listened very hard to what Paul was saying, and Paul noticed him among the crowd. He looked into his eyes, and felt that this poor cripple's faith was strong.

'Stand upright on your feet!' he commanded.

At once the man jumped up and walked about, for the first time in his life, and everyone was astonished.

'These men must be gods come down to

216

the people to turn against the apostles. The crowd grew angry; picking up stones, they threw them at Paul until he fell to the ground. Thinking him dead, the people dragged Paul out of the city.

His friends gathered round him anxiously, and presently Paul recovered; he got up and went back into the city. Next day, he and Barnabas left Lystra, and went on.

The Second Journey

One day, Paul felt that the time had come to make another journey.

'Let us go again,' he said to Barnabas, 'and visit our brothers in every city where we have preached the word of the Lord, and see how they are getting on.'

Barnabas agreed, but he wanted to take the young Christian, John Mark with them. Paul did not wish to do this, and so they parted company. Barnabas took Mark, and sailed away to Cyprus, while Paul chose another companion – whose name was Silas – and these two went back to Lystra.

In Lystra, Paul met a young Christian

us in the shape of men,' they said. They gave the names of two of their gods to the apostles: Barnabas they called 'Jupiter', and to Paul they gave the name of 'Mercury'.

Then the priest of Jupiter brought oxen and fine garlands, and was ready to offer sacrifice to his 'god'.

Paul and Barnabas were very worried by this. They hurried among the crowds, saying urgently, 'Sirs, why are you doing this? We are ordinary men, with feelings like yours, and we preach that you should turn from these worthless things to the living God who made heaven and earth, the sea and all things.

'In times past, people were allowed to go their own way, but you have signs of God's loving care: he gives rain from heaven, and fruitful harvests that bring you both food and gladness.'

Thus, Paul and Barnabas tried to stop the people offering sacrifices to them.

Then some Jews arrived who persuaded

called Timothy. His mother was Jewish, and his father a Greek, and everyone spoke very well of him.

Paul felt that Timothy should join them on their journey, as they went from place to place, encouraging the new Christians and the churches that were springing up.

One night Paul had a vision. He saw a man from Macedonia, a land across the sea.

'Come over to Macedonia and help us,' the man was saying.

Paul knew that he must go, and at once he and his friends made their plans. They crossed the sea, and made their way to Philippi, which was the most important city in that part of Macedonia.

Paul at Philippi

One Sabbath day, Paul and the others who were with him walked to the bank of the river, and sat down. It was a place where people used to gather to pray, and as a little group of women was there, the Christians began to talk to them.

One of the listeners named Lydia knew that she wanted to become a Christian, so she and her family were baptised, and she begged Paul to stay in her house.

While they were on their way to pray together, a young girl met them. She had a gift for telling the future, and her masters made her do this for money.

She ran after Paul, Silas and the others, calling out: 'These men are servants of the Most High God, and they can show us how we may be saved!'

The girl did this several times; and at last Paul, feeling sad that her mind was troubled, spoke to the girl. She then grew calm, but had lost the strange gift of foretelling what was going to happen.

Her masters were angry about this, for now she would not earn money for them. They seized Paul and Silas, and brought them before the magistrates.

'These men are Jews,' they said, 'and they are teaching us Roman customs which are against the law.'

The crowd murmured angrily, and the magistrate ordered that Paul and Silas should be beaten, and put into prison.

The jailer put Paul and Silas in the inner prison. Then, to make quite sure that they did not escape, he fastened their feet in the stocks, which meant that the prisoners were held fast between two wooden bars.

'Now they cannot possibly get away!' the jailer told himself.

The Earthquake

At midnight, Paul and Silas sang praises to God in their cell, and prayed, and the other prisoners could hear them. Suddenly, the prison walls began to rock in an earthquake; the doors flew open, and the prisoners' chains fell off.

The keeper of the prison woke up and seeing the doors open, he imagined that his prisoners had escaped, and was so frightened that he drew his sword to kill himself. Then, at that moment, Paul cried loudly: 'Do not harm yourself – we are all here!'

So the keeper of the prison called for a light and went into Paul's cell. He fell down before Paul and Silas, trembling; then he brought them out himself.

'Sirs, what must I do to be saved?' he asked humbly.

'Believe in the Lord Jesus Christ,' the apostles told him, 'and you will be saved – you and your household.'

They talked to the keeper and his family about Jesus, and he was baptised together with his household. Then the keeper washed Paul's back, and that of Silas, for they hurt from the beatings both men had been given. After that, he took them to his own house for a meal. He felt so happy, because of the good news, which the prisoners had shared with him.

When daylight came, the magistrates sent orders that Paul and Silas were to be allowed to leave. 'Go in peace,' the prison-keeper told them gladly.

But Paul was proud. 'They have beaten us in public – though we are Romans – and have not given a fair trial,' he said. 'Now let them come themselves and fetch us out!'

When the magistrates heard that the prisoners were Roman citizens, they were afraid that they might get into trouble, so they went humbly to Paul and Silas, and begged them to go. Then the two apostles left the prison and went to Lydia's house, where they met all their friends again.

Jesus is Our King

'They've turned the whole world upside down!'
About the Christians this was spoken;
But still they preached and met to pray,
And still their daily bread was broken
Because of Jesus, who had said:
'Remember me, and take this bread.'
The people Caesar's praise would sing,
But Christians said, 'Our Lord is King.'

The Unknown God

The day came when Paul journeyed to Greece, and arrived in the important city of Athens. There, he stood on Mars Hill, and preached to all who would listen.

'Men of Athens!' he said, 'as I passed by, I found an altar which had these words on it: "To the Unknown God". Now I have come to tell you about him. The God who made everything in the world, seeing that he is Lord of heaven and earth, does not live in temples made by men – he is always near each of us. As we are his children, we ought not think of him as made of gold or silver or stone carved by men.'

He went on to talk about Jesus, who had arisen after he had been put to death. Some who listened mocked at Paul, but others said, 'You must tell us more about this later!' Some did believe his words and followed him.

Presently, Paul moved on to the city of Corinth, and there he stayed with Priscilla and Aquila, who made tents; Paul was a tent-maker, too, so he felt very much at home with them.

Every Sabbath day, he talked of Jesus to the Jews, in their synagogue, and he reasoned with the Greeks as well.

Then Paul sailed to Syria, and Priscilla and Aquila left Corinth and went with him.

Apollos and his Followers

There was a Jew whose name was Apollos. He knew all about the teachings of John the Baptist, and he talked of them in the synagogue at Ephesus.

When Paul's friends Aquila and Priscilla visited this city, they heard Apollos preach, and decided that they must tell him about the words and works of Jesus, of which he had not yet heard.

Apollos was eager to visit another district, to spread the good news, and the Christians gave him leave to go, making sure he would be welcomed where he went.

While Apollos was away, Paul himself arrived at Ephesus, and there he met several people whose lives had been changed by hearing about Jesus Christ.

'Did you receive the Holy Spirit when you became Christians?' Paul asked them.

'No,' they said, puzzled. 'We have never heard about the Holy Spirit.'

'How were you baptised?' Paul asked.

'With John's baptism,' they answered.

Then Paul told them what Apollos had not known before Aquila and Priscilla talked to him. 'John's baptism was a sign to people that their sins were forgiven,' he explained, 'but he told of one greater than himself who was coming – and that was Jesus.'

About twelve men said that they would like Paul to baptise them in the name of Jesus. Paul laid his hands on them, in Jesus's name, and they received the power of the Holy Spirit.

'Great is Diana!'

There was a silversmith, whose name was Demetrius; many others worked for him, making silver settings for statues of Diana, the goddess of the Ephesians.

When Demetrius saw how Paul was turning people to the true God, he grew worried, and called together all his workers and other tradesmen like himself.

'Friends,' he said, 'you know that we live on the money earned by our work. Now this man Paul is going round everywhere, telling people that there are no gods made by man's hands. Before long, we shall not only be unable to make a living, but even the temple of our great goddess, Diana, will be neglected!' When the craftsmen heard this, they were very angry. 'Great is Diana of the Ephesians!' they shouted.

The whole town was in an uproar. Having captured some of Paul's friends, the crowd dragged them into the open-air theatre.

Some people in the crowd were shouting one thing, and some another, and most of them wondered what the trouble was.

One man, Alexander, tried to make himself heard. He raised his hand, trying to quieten the mob; but when they knew he was a Jew, they would not listen.

'Great is Diana of the Ephesians! Great is Diana of the Ephesians!' The shouting went on for two hours.

Presently, the town clerk spoke reasonably to the people, and they calmed down. At last he was able to send them home.

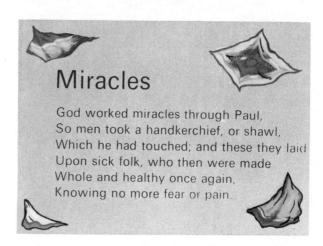

Miracles

God worked miracles through Paul,
So men took a handkerchief, or shawl,
Which he had touched; and these they laid
Upon sick folk, who then were made
Whole and healthy once again,
Knowing no more fear or pain.

The Young Man at the Window

Paul and his friends moved on from place to place. When they were in Troas, the Christians gathered together on the first day of the week to break bread, and Paul addressed them all. Paul had so much to say that he went on talking until midnight.

All the lamps were lit in the upper room where the meeting was being held, and it was very hot. One young man, whose name was Eutychus, sat on the sill at the open window. As Paul went on preaching, he grew sleepy, and his head began to nod. Soon he fell fast asleep.

In his sleep, Eutychus toppled through the open window. When his friends realised what had happened they ran down the stairs and into the street, where they found that Eutychus was dead.

At once, Paul went out to him, and kneeling beside Eutychus, took him in his arms. 'Do not worry,' he said to his friends.

'As you can see Eutychus is still alive.'

The young man recovered, and the Christians went back to the upper room and broke bread together. Paul went on talking till dawn, when he had to leave them.

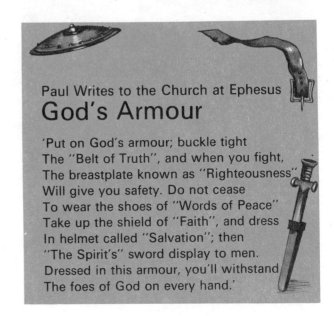

Paul Writes to the Church at Ephesus
God's Armour

'Put on God's armour; buckle tight
The "Belt of Truth", and when you fight,
The breastplate known as "Righteousness"
Will give you safety. Do not cease
To wear the shoes of "Words of Peace"
Take up the shield of "Faith", and dress
In helmet called "Salvation"; then
"The Spirit's" sword display to men.
Dressed in this armour, you'll withstand
The foes of God on every hand.'

Paul leaves the Ephesians

Paul was in Miletus, and called all the chief members of the church in nearby Ephesus to him, for he had something important to say to them.

'You know that I have served the Lord while I have been among you,' he said, 'and how I have taught you, going from house to house. Now I am going to Jerusalem, not knowing what will happen to me when I get there. But nothing troubles me, so long as I finish my task with joy. You, in Ephesus, will not see me again; and, after I am gone, certain people will try to turn you away from all that I have taught you – so watch and remember that for three years I warned you about this. Support those who are weak, and remember the words of the Lord Jesus. He said: "It is more blessed to give than to receive."'

When he had said this, Paul kneeled down and prayed with them all. They were so sorry to see him go that many people were crying. Then they went with him to his ship.

Paul and his friends journeyed from place to place, and when they came at last to Caesarea – which was not very far from Jerusalem – they stayed in Philip's house; whilst he was there, a prophet named Agabus came to see Paul.

Agabus took Paul's belt from him, and tied his own hands and feet with it. Then he said, 'The Holy Spirit tells me that so shall the Jews in Jerusalem bind the man who owns this belt, and shall deliver him into the hands of the Gentiles.'

When Paul's friends heard this, they begged him not to go to Jerusalem, but Paul answered, 'Why are you so upset? You are breaking my heart! I am not only ready to be bound in Jerusalem, but to die, for the Lord Jesus's sake.'

When his friends saw that there was no hope of making Paul change his mind, they stopped trying to persuade him.

Paul in Jerusalem

Bravely, Paul went on to Jerusalem, where his own friends were very glad to see him.

Paul was in the temple, when certain Jews began to stir up the crowds to turn against him.

'Men of Israel, help!' they cried, catching hold of Paul. 'This is the man who teaches harmful things about our people, the law, and this place. Also he has brought Greeks into the temple, and that, as you know, is not allowed.'

All the people started shouting angrily: they seized Paul and hustled him out of the temple, and the doors were shut. They would have killed him, but news of the uproar reached the captain of the Roman guard, and he hurried down with a band of soldiers. When the crowd saw them, they stopped beating Paul. The captain came up, ordered him to be bound with chains, and then asked who Paul was, and what he had done.

Some cried one thing, and some another.

The captain could not make out what it was all about, so he ordered his men to take Paul into the castle.

When they had struggled through the crowds and reached the castle stairs, the soldiers had to carry Paul up them, because angry people were pressing in on every side.

The crowd followed, pushing and struggling, crying: 'Away with him! Away with him!'

As he was led into the castle, Paul said to the captain, 'May I speak to you?'

'Can you speak Greek?' asked the captain. 'Are you not that Egyptian who has been causing a lot of trouble?'

'I am a Jew of Tarsus,' Paul told him, 'a citizen of no mean city. Will you let me speak to the people?'

When the captain had given permission, Paul stood on the stairs and held up his hand for silence.

The crowd at once grew quiet, waiting curiously to see what would happen next.

Much to their surprise, Paul began to speak to them in Hebrew, their own language. 'I am a Jew,' he said, 'born in Tarsus, but I grew up in this city, taught by Gamaliel.'

He went on to tell them how unkind he had been to the followers of Jesus, and how one day, he had seen a vision of the Lord which had changed his life. But when he told them that he had been commanded by God to take the good news to Gentiles, they grew angry again.

'Away with such a fellow!' they shouted. 'He ought not to be allowed to live!'

They made such an uproar that the captain told the soldiers to take Paul into the castle. There he ordered that he should be beaten; but, as they were binding him, Paul said to a soldier who stood by, 'Is it lawful for you to beat a man who is a Roman citizen, without a proper trial?'

The soldier hurried to the chief captain. 'Be careful!' he warned him. 'This man is a Roman.'

Then the captain went to Paul. 'Tell me,' he said, 'are you a Roman?'

'I am,' Paul replied.

'I won my freedom as a Roman citizen by paying for it,' said the captain.

'But I was born free,' Paul answered.

After that they left Paul alone for the time being, because they knew care would be necessary in dealing with a prisoner who was a Roman citizen.

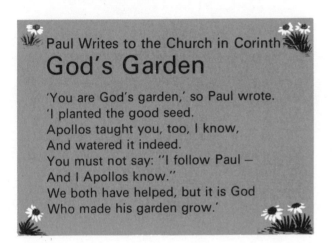

Paul Writes to the Church in Corinth
God's Garden

'You are God's garden,' so Paul wrote.
'I planted the good seed.
Apollos taught you, too, I know,
And watered it indeed.
You must not say: "I follow Paul –
And I Apollos know."
We both have helped, but it is God
Who made his garden grow.'

Paul is sent to Felix

Next morning, the captain ordered that Paul should be brought before the chief priests and council of the Jews.

Paul spoke to them, saying that he himself was a Pharisee. The chief priests began to argue and bicker among themselves; in the end, the Roman captain became so afraid for Paul's safety that he ordered his soldiers to take him back to the castle.

That night, Paul had a vision – the Lord stood beside him.

'Be of good cheer, Paul,' he said. 'As you have borne witness to me in Jerusalem, so you must do in Rome.'

The following morning, a group of Jews made a vow, saying that they would neither eat nor drink until they had killed Paul. Then forty of them went to the chief priests and elders to tell them about it.

'Have this man brought before you tomorrow,' they said, 'and we will be ready to do what we have vowed.'

But Paul's nephew heard about this scheme, and he went to the castle to warn Paul, who sent his nephew to the chief captain. When the Roman officer heard what the young man had to say, he ordered two of his men to take a large band of soldiers – some of them horsemen, and others with spears. They were to go to Caesarea by night, with Paul on horseback, and there to take their prisoner to Felix, the governor. The captain also wrote a letter for them to take, explaining who Paul was.

The soldiers duly left Paul with the governor, and when Felix heard that Paul came from Tarsus, he said, 'I will hear what you have to say when your accusers arrive.'

He gave orders that Paul was to await his trial in King Herod's judgement hall.

Paul before Felix

Five days later, Ananias the high priest, arrived in Caesarea. He brought with him a clever speaker called Tertullus, and they both spoke against Paul to the governor.

'We have always been very happy under your rule,' Tertullus said, flattering Felix. 'We have found this man to be a trouble-maker, and a leader of the sect known as the Nazarenes. If you question him yourself, you will find this is so.'

Felix then made a sign to Paul that he might speak, and Paul explained that he had done nothing wrong.

'When the chief captain arrives from Jerusalem,' Felix said, 'I shall learn more of what happened.'

He put Paul in the charge of a centurion, but allowed his friends to come to see him.

After a few days, Felix sent for Paul again, and the governor and his Jewish wife, Drusilla, listened while Paul talked to them.

At last Felix said, 'That will do for now – I will hear you again later.' He found some of Paul's words troubled him, and knew that it would not be easy to become a Christian. Secretly, Felix hoped that Paul might offer him money to let him go, but of course Paul did no such thing.

After two years, a new governor took the place of Felix. His name was Porcius Festus, and he still kept Paul a prisoner, because he wanted to please the Jews.

'I Appeal to Caesar!'

Soon after Festus became governor, he went up to Jerusalem. When he arrived, the high priest told him about Paul.

'Send for him to be brought here,' the high priest begged, secretly planning to have Paul waylaid and killed.

But Festus would not agree to this. 'No,' he said, 'we will keep him in Caesarea. Those of you who want to speak against this man shall come there with me.'

When Festus returned to Caesarea, he had Paul brought before him, and the Jews who had come from Jerusalem with Festus began to accuse him of many things.

'I have never done anything that is against your laws,' Paul answered, 'nor against the temple, nor against Caesar.'

'Will you go to Jerusalem, where I will be your judge?' Festus asked him. He said this because he wanted to please the Jews.

'I stand at Caesar's judgement seat,' Paul answered. 'I have done no wrong to the Jews, as you know. If I have done anything worthy of death, I am not afraid to die. I appeal to Caesar!'

Festus talked with his council for a while, and then he said to Paul, 'So you have appealed to Caesar? Then to Caesar you shall go.'

King Agrippa

A few days later, King Agrippa and his queen, Berenice, arrived in Caesarea, and Festus told the king about Paul.

'I would like to hear this man myself,' King Agrippa said.

'Tomorrow,' Festus answered, 'you shall hear him.'

Next day, King Agrippa and Queen Berenice arrived. The chief captains and the important men of the city were there, too. Paul stood up before them all.

'King Agrippa, and all men present,' Festus said, 'you see this man, whom the Jews say should not be allowed to live. I cannot find him guilty, and now he wants to appeal to Augustus Caesar, and I am ready to send him to Caesar. I do not really know what to say about him, and so I have had him brought before you, O King Agrippa. Perhaps when you have examined him, I shall know what to write.'

'You may speak for yourself,' the king said to Paul, standing quietly before him.

Once again, Paul told his story; but when he said that Jesus was restored to life again, Festus said angrily, 'You are beside yourself! All your learning has made you mad!'

'I am not mad, most noble Festus,' Paul said gravely. 'I speak the truth. The king knows about these things. King Agrippa, do you believe the prophets? I know you do.'

'You almost persuade me to become a Christian,' the king said humbly.

'I wish that not only you, but all who are listening to me today, were not "almost" but "altogether" like me,' Paul answered.

The king, the queen and Festus, and a few other important men, turned aside to talk the matter over.

'This man has done nothing that deserves either death or chains,' they agreed.

'If he had not appealed to Caesar, he could have been set free,' Agrippa said to Festus.

Now Paul would have to go to Rome, to be taken before the Emperor.

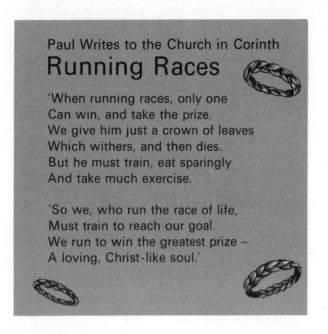

Paul Writes to the Church in Corinth
Running Races

'When running races, only one
Can win, and take the prize.
We give him just a crown of leaves
Which withers, and then dies.
But he must train, eat sparingly
And take much exercise.

'So we, who run the race of life,
Must train to reach our goal.
We run to win the greatest prize —
A loving, Christ-like soul.'

The Storm

Paul and some of his friends were put on board a ship with other prisoners, to make the journey to Rome. The sea was rough, and they ran into storms.

'Sirs,' Paul said at last, 'I think our

voyage will prove a dangerous one; much damage will be done to the ship, and our lives are in danger.'

The sailors, however, listened to their captain, rather than to Paul; instead of sheltering for the winter months in a safe harbour, they sailed on.

When the south wind blew softly, they thought they had done the right thing, but presently another storm began to rage.

They were close to an island, and afraid of quicksands. The tempest tossed the boat about on the huge waves, and the sailors threw what they could overboard to lighten it. For days they were lost; they could not see the sun by day, nor the stars at night, and many gave up hope.

Then Paul stood up and encouraged them: 'You should have taken my advice,' he said, 'and put into harbour. Then you would not have lost so much. But I tell you to be of good cheer, for it is only the ship that will suffer. No lives will be lost. Last night, God's angel spoke to me, "Fear not, Paul," he said. "You must be brought before Caesar, and God will protect all who sail with you." I believe God, and that it will all turn out as the angel said — but we are going to be shipwrecked on a certain island!'

The Shipwreck

After they had been at sea for two weeks, the sailors thought that they were nearing land.

The water began to get shallower, and they were afraid of running their ship on to the rocks. It was night, so they let down their anchors, and waited for daylight.

Some of the sailors were about to escape in a small boat, by pretending that they were going to let down still more anchors, but Paul saw what was happening.

'Unless these men stay with the ship,' he

said, 'you cannot be safe.' So the soldiers cut the ropes of the little boat.

None of them had eaten for the last fourteen days, and Paul begged them to take some food.

'You are going to be taken care of,' he promised them, and ate some food himself, giving thanks to God before them all. Then they followed his example, and felt much more cheerful.

When they had all eaten as much as they wanted, the rest of the cargo was thrown into the sea, to lighten the ship.

When daylight came, they could see land, but did not know where they were. The crew took up the anchors, hoisted the sail, and tried to enter a creek, in order to reach the shore; but the prow of the ship stuck fast, and the stern broke up, battered by huge waves.

'We had better kill the prisoners,' the soldiers said, 'lest any of them swim away and escape.'

But their officer wanted to keep Paul, and would not agree. He ordered that those who could swim should jump into the sea, and

that the rest should try to reach land by using broken boards as rafts.

In the end, all on board reached the shore safely. They had landed on the island we call Malta.

Paul Writes to the Church in Corinth
Eyes and Ears

'Suppose one day the foot should say:
"Because I'm not a hand,
I am not part of a whole man."
Or ears should understand
That, since they are not eyes, they have
No role that they can play.
If all the body were an eye,
How could it hear, I say.
If all the body were an ear,
How could it ever smell?
God made each part to do its work,
And he made all things well.
So some are Jews and some are Greeks,
Some slaves, and some are free,
But God made all to play their part,
And together to agree.'

they decided that Paul must be a god.

The most important man there was named Publius, and he received the ship-wrecked men kindly, taking Paul and his friends to stay with him for three days.

Publius's father was ill, so Paul laid his hands on him and healed him. When the islanders heard about this, many sick folk were brought to Paul, and he made them better. He and his friends were loaded with gifts and praised and thanked by everybody.

After three months, they left Malta in a ship which had spent the winter there; so at last they landed in Italy and made their way to Rome. There were Christians in the city who, when they heard of Paul's coming, set out to meet them.

In Rome

The prisoners were handed over to the captain of the guard in Rome, and Paul was kept by himself, with one soldier to look after him.

After three days, Paul was allowed to call the Jews in Rome together, and he told them his story.

'We never received any letters about you,' they told him, 'and none of the brethren who came to Rome ever spoke against you. But we want you to tell us about the Christians, because we know that they are spoken against everywhere.'

They arranged to come again, and for a whole day Paul talked to them about the prophets, and Jesus, who had made their words come true. Some who listened to Paul believed him, and some did not.

'You must know,' Paul told the Jews, 'that the good news is for the Gentiles, and they will hear it.' And the Jews went away, arguing among themselves.

Paul stayed for two years in a house which he rented in Rome, preaching about the Lord Jesus to all who came to him.

In Malta

The islanders of Malta ran down to the beach to see these strangers who had been shipwrecked on their coast.

It was raining and cold, and the islanders lit a fire, and did what they could to help and comfort the men from the ship.

Paul helped, too. He gathered a bundle of sticks and threw them on the fire, but as he did so, a snake wriggled out and fastened on to his hand.

The ignorant islanders, seeing this, said to one another: 'This man is probably a murderer; though he has escaped from the sea, he is not meant to live!' They wanted to see what would happen but Paul shook his arm, and the snake fell into the fire.

The islanders were quite sure that Paul's arm would swell and that he would fall down dead; but, when nothing happened,

The Servant who ran away

Paul wrote many letters to his friends, to cheer and encourage them. One of those he wrote, whilst a prisoner in Rome, was to his friend Philemon, who had worked with him, and who welcomed other Christians to meetings he held in his own home.

Philemon had once had a servant named Onesimus. He had been lazy, and, when scolded for it, had run away.

Now Onesimus was in Rome with Paul, and had changed. He was like a son to Paul – loving and helpful – and Paul felt that Philemon should take him back, not as his master, but like a brother.

If Onesimus has wronged Philemon in any way, or owed him money, Paul offered to put it right, or to pay his debts himself.

Then he sent Onesimus back to Philemon with the letter. It was hard to part with him, but Onesimus was a Christian, and Paul knew that Philemon would find his runaway servant very helpful.

John's Vision

There was a follower of Jesus whose name was John. Because he was a Christian, he had been sent to live alone on a little island named Patmos. There, thought his enemies, he would not be able to spread the gospel of Jesus; but John wrote down all that he wanted to say.

'One day,' he wrote, 'I heard a loud voice behind me: it was like the sound of a trumpet. "Write down the messages you are given, and send them to the seven churches of Asia," the voice said.

'I turned round, and saw seven golden lamps. In the middle of them stood a man in a long robe with a golden belt. His eyes shone and his voice was like the sound of a waterfall. In his right hand were seven stars. It seemed as though from his mouth came a sharp sword, and his face shone like the mid-day sun.

'When I saw him, I fell at his feet; I could not move. He laid his right hand on me, and said, "Do not be afraid. I was dead, but now I am alive for evermore, and I hold

the keys of death. Write down what you have seen. The seven stars in my hand stand for the angels of the seven churches, and the seven lamps are the seven churches themselves." '

Then John knew that he was seeing a vision of the Risen Christ.

He was given messages from the Lord to the churches in Asia, and he wrote seven letters.

The church at Ephesus was not as faithful as it once had been, but John was given a promise for them: 'To him who wins through, I will give fruit from the tree of life, which grows in the midst of the paradise of God.'

The church in Smyrna was told to be faithful, even though its members were made to suffer, and they were given a great promise, too. If they were indeed faithful, they would win a crown of life.

The church in Pergamos was warned about some of the wrong things that the people had believed. They too were promised a reward, if they overcame these mistakes.

The church in Thyatira was also told about their good deeds and their bad ones, and their reward for taking the right path would be that they would become leaders and rulers; they would also be given the morning star.

The church in Sardis was reminded that its members must be watchful and strong. Then the church in Philadelphia, which had kept God's word, would be made a pillar in the temple of God, and from then on would never leave it.

The church in Laodicea had lost its keenness. To them, the Lord said, 'See, I stand at the door and knock! If any man hears my voice, and opens the door, I will come in and eat with him, and he with me.'

To those who won through even as he had, the Lord promised a seat beside his own throne.

John sees Heaven

John had a vision in which he looked right into heaven itself.

'Come,' said the voice which had sounded like a trumpet, 'I will show you what is going to happen.'

Then John found that he was actually in heaven. He saw a great throne, with a rainbow round it, bright as an emerald. In front of the throne were seven brightly burning torches, and what seemed like a sea of glass.

There were twenty-four other thrones set in a circle, and on each one sat an Elder dressed in white, each with a gold crown on his head.

Four creatures, one like a lion, one like an ox, one like a man and one like an eagle, were singing: 'Holy, holy holy is God, the Lord of everyone!'

While the creatures gave thanks and praise to him who sat upon the throne, the Elders fell down and worshipped, laying

their crowns before the great throne and crying: 'You are worthy, O Lord our God, to receive glory and honour and power, because you made all things!'

Then John noticed a scroll in the right hand of the one who sat on the throne. It had writing on it, and was sealed with seven seals.

An angel called out: 'Who is worthy to break the seals and open the scroll?'

There seemed no one who was able to open the scroll and John felt tears come into his eyes. It mattered so much that someone should be found who was worthy to break the seals.

One of the Elders seated round the throne spoke to him. 'Do not weep,' he said. 'The Lion of the tribe of Judah, of the house of David, is worthy to break the seven seals and open the scroll.'

Then John saw, standing in the centre of them all, a Lamb – and he knew it was Jesus, whom John the Baptist had called the Lamb of God.

The Seals are Broken

As John watched, the Lamb took the scroll from the right hand of him who sat on the great throne; and, as he did so, the twenty-four Elders and the four creatures fell down before him.

The Elders each had a harp, and a golden bowl full of sweet-smelling incense, which John knew represented the prayers of the good people on earth.

They began to sing a song that had never been sung before: 'You are worthy to take the scroll and break the seals around it, for you were slain, and won for God by your blood men of every tribe and country, and have made them into a royal company to serve God on earth.'

Then John heard thousands upon thousands of angels singing: 'Worthy is the Lamb who was slain to receive power, riches and wisdom, strength, honour, glory and blessing!'

John heard everyone on earth, as well as in heaven, echoing their cry, and the four beasts said: 'Amen!' And the Elders fell down in worship.

John saw many other strange and wonderful things, and then he was told about the people dressed in white, standing round the throne.

'These are they who came through great trouble,' he learned, 'and have washed their robes and made them white in the blood of the Lamb. That is why they stand before the throne of God, and serve him day and night in his temple.

'He that sits on the throne shall dwell among them. They shall hunger no more; neither shall they grow thirsty any more; nor shall the sun give them heat – for the Lamb himself shall feed them. He will lead them to living fountains; and God shall wipe away all tears from their eyes.'

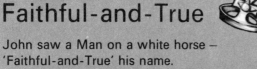

Faithful-and-True

John saw a Man on a white horse –
'Faithful-and-True' his name.
He wore a gold crown on his head;
His eyes shone bright as flame.
His other name was: 'God's Own Word',
And from his mouth there came a sword.
He had a third name: 'King of Kings
And Lord of Lords' was he.
He led a heavenly army on,
And ruled victoriously.

The Holy City

John's last vision was of a new heaven, and a new earth.

He heard a heavenly voice proclaiming: 'The holy place of God is with men, and he will dwell with them. They shall be his people. God shall wipe away all tears from their eyes; there shall be no more death, nor sadness, nor crying, and there shall be no more pain. All the old things will disappear for ever.'

The One who sat on the throne said, 'See, I make all things new!'

Then John was taken away to a high mountain; and from there he watched a great city, a new Jerusalem, coming to earth from heaven.

The light that shone on it was clear as crystal, and there were twelve gates into the city. The wall was made of jasper, and its foundations were decorated with precious stones. The city itself was pure gold.

There was no temple in the city, for the Lord God himself was there to be worshipped. The city did not need the sun or the moon, for the light of God's glory made it bright. The gates would never need to be shut, for there would be no night there, and those whose names were written in the Lamb's book of life would live in the city.

Then John saw a pure crystal river – the water of life – which seemed to flow from the throne of God itself. Beside the river grew the tree of life, with twelve different fruits, and the leaves had a special healing power.

'Happy are they who keep God's laws,' John was told, 'for they shall have a right to draw near to the tree of life, and to dwell in the Holy City.'

Index